T0362732

ACADEMIC CULTURE

Fourth edition

ACADEMIC CULTURE

A Student's Guide to
Studying at University

Jean Brick
Maria Herke
Deanna Wong

© Jean Brick, Maria Herke and Deanna Wong, under exclusive licence to
Macmillan Education Limited 2006, 2011, 2016, 2020

All rights reserved. No reproduction, copy or transmission of this
publication may be made without written permission.

No portion of this publication may be reproduced, copied or transmitted
save with written permission or in accordance with the provisions of the
Copyright, Designs and Patents Act 1988, or under the terms of any
licence permitting limited copying issued by the Copyright Licensing
Agency, Saffron House, 6–10 Kirby Street, London EC1N 8TS.

Any person who does any unauthorized act in relation to this publication
may be liable to criminal prosecution and civil claims for damages.

The authors have asserted their rights to be identified as the authors of
this work in accordance with the Copyright, Designs and Patents Act
1988.

This edition published 2020 by
RED GLOBE PRESS

Previous editions published under the imprint PALGRAVE

Red Globe Press in the UK is an imprint of Macmillan Education Limited,
registered in England, company number 01755588, of 4 Crinan Street,
London, N1 9XW.

Red Globe Press® is a registered trademark in the United States, the
United Kingdom, Europe and other countries.

ISBN 978-1-352-01033-6 paperback

This book is printed on paper suitable for recycling and made from fully
managed and sustained forest sources. Logging, pulping and
manufacturing processes are expected to conform to the environmental
regulations of the country of origin.

A catalogue record for this book is available from the British Library.

A catalog record for this book is available from the Library of Congress.

CONTENTS

PART 5   WRITING ACADEMIC TEXTS   215

ABOUT THE AUTHORS

Jean Brick

Jean Brick has been involved in the field of teaching and researching academic communication for over 25 years. She has worked in Australia, China, Indonesia, Thailand, Kiribati, Tonga, Sri Lanka and the Maldives with undergraduate and postgraduate students from both English-speaking and non-English speaking backgrounds. Her research interests centre on academic communication, especially in the sciences, and the use of figurative language in history. She is the author of several books, including *China: A Handbook in Intercultural Communication* (2nd edition, 2004).

Maria Herke

Maria Herke works as a senior lecturer and researcher in the Department of Linguistics at Macquarie University, Sydney. Her main research focus is communication strategies across a variety of professional contexts, including academic communication. Maria has presented her research at international conferences and has published numerous papers and a book. She teaches linguistics and academic writing to undergraduate, postgraduate and PhD students.

Deanna Wong

Deanna Wong has lectured in linguistics and academic communications at Macquarie University, Sydney. She is particularly interested in how features of written and spoken communications are transformed to suit online communication. Her research and publications examine feedback in online communication and face-to-face interaction using corpus linguistic methodologies.

ACKNOWLEDGMENTS

The authors wish to thank our enthusiastic students who continue to make useful suggestions, assisting us to refine this book to better suit their changing needs.

MARIA HERKE

INTRODUCTION

What this book is about

This book is about academic culture; that is, the attitudes, values and ways of behaving that are shared by people who teach, research or study in universities. It is grounded in the belief that current approaches to teaching English for Academic Purposes (EAP), and generic and learning skills, focus on the *how* rather than the *why*. This means that they spend a great deal of time in developing student skills without exploring why these particular skills are necessary. All too often, the result of this approach is the rote application of formula. One obvious example of this is the approach to plagiarism: students are presented with a number of arcane rules about how sources should be identified, together with dire warnings about the likely consequences of failure to do so appropriately. Little time is spent exploring why identifying sources is important. As a result, many students, both native speakers and non-native speakers of English, find it difficult to decide whether or not they should identify the source of a particular piece of information.

Through discussing some of the underlying attitudes and values that mould acceptable academic behaviour, this book attempts to provide students with the means to understand what lecturers expect of them. It also aims to provide them with understandings that will allow them to interpret the feedback they receive from lecturers. Equipped with these understandings, students are in a position to improve their academic performance.

Who this book is for

This book is aimed primarily at students who are entering university for the first time. While many of these will be international students and students of non-English-speaking backgrounds, it is of equal interest to students from English-speaking backgrounds who are starting their university studies. Postgraduate students who are returning to study after a period outside the academic environment are also likely to find the information useful.

Academics, language teachers and teachers concerned with the development of generic skills will find this book useful, as will individual students working in self-study mode.

What you will get out of this book

This book provides:

- an understanding of the attitudes and expectations shared by academics and researchers at universities in English-speaking countries

- an understanding of how these attitudes and expectations influence expectations about how students should behave
- an understanding of the importance of developing and expressing an individual voice and relating appropriately to the voices of others
- an increased ability to express a clear and appropriately authoritative voice
- an increased understanding of plagiarism, including why it is regarded so seriously, and how to avoid it
- an understanding of the demands of different types of written texts, including essays, reports, research reports and electronic texts
- an understanding of the way language is used in a range of popular and pedagogic texts that students are expected to read but not write, including textbooks and opinion pieces in newspapers
- an increased ability to structure logical, coherent texts
- an increased ability to take part effectively in tutorials, seminars and group work.

How to use this book

This book can be used in a variety of ways.

Firstly, it can be used as a textbook in courses in English for Academic Purposes. It especially lends itself to content-based approaches in these areas as it is structured as a tertiary textbook. This means that it shares many of the features of the textbooks that students use in first-year university subjects. Students have the opportunity to develop their academic English and generic skills while at the same time familiarising themselves with the type of teaching that they are likely to encounter in their early years of tertiary study.

Secondly, the book can be used in conjunction with other texts in EAP and generic skills courses. Some students will find it useful for individual study and reference.

Overview

In this fourth edition of the book, four new chapters have been added and chapters have been reorganised. The book is now divided into five major sections.

Chapters 1, 2, 3, and 4 explore some of the key features of studying at university and academic culture that are shared by disciplines across the university campus. These include academic values and the role of argument and discussion in developing academic knowledge and its characteristic features (Chapter 1); details about university staff, how to address them and course structure (Chapter 2); the expectation regarding the roles of students and lecturers (Chapter 3); and expectations about how students present and develop their own understanding, including the nature of independent learning (Chapter 4).

Chapters 5, 6, 7, and 8, deal with developing the skills and attitudes needed to research an issue and prepare for writing. Chapters 5 and 6 develop effective listening and academic reading and Chapters 9 and 10 explore tutorial and seminar presentations and the vexed issue of group work.

Chapters 9, 10 and 11 support students to become critical, and adept at selecting at academic sources. Chapter 6 compares opinions, positions and bias, Chapter 10 examines critical analysis and problem solving and Chapter 11 explores how to approach academic knowledge critically.

Chapters 12–16 explore the ways in which academic writers express their own voice and refer to the voices of others. Chapter 12 introduces the concept of voice, while Chapter 13 explores how students express their own voice and relate to the voices of their sources. This leads to a discussion of the concept of plagiarism in Chapter 14 Chapter 15 examines the ways in which voices are used in different types of text, focusing on textbooks and professional magazines. Chapter 16 expands the consideration of voice by exploring how the use of pronouns, hedges, boosters and attitude markers contribute to presenting an authoritative academic identity.

Finally, Chapters 17–25 bring together much of the argument in the preceding chapters. Chapter 17 seeks to establish a context for writing in the university, comparing the types of text that students are most likely to read and write and examining the importance of planning. Chapter 18 focuses on ways of making writing flow through the use of topic sentences at the discourse level and cohesive devices at the level of the paragraph. Finally the major text types that students are expected to produce during the course of their studies are examined. Chapter 19 examines essays, Chapter 20 reports, Chapter 20 research reports and Chapter 22 lab reports. Chapter 23 examines how to write electronic texts, including discussion forum posts, blogs, and e-portfolios, Chapter 24 reflective texts and finally, Chapter 25 looks at the different texts that might be required in exam writing.

Academic sources

This book draws heavily on the research of some of the major figures in applied linguistics, in particular that of Michael Halliday, John Swales, Ken Hyland, Paula Boddington, John Clanchy, Sue Hood, Nicky Solomon and Anne Burns. Footnotes indicate the specific chapters that draw on the work of each of these researchers.

Part 1
INTRODUCTION TO UNIVERSITY STUDY

WHAT IS ACADEMIC CULTURE?

LEARNING OBJECTIVES

When you have finished this chapter, you will be able to:

- explain some of the common meanings of 'culture'
- explain what is meant by 'academic culture'
- describe the main features of academic culture
- explain why students need to understand what academic culture involves.

WORD LIST

Do you know the meaning of these words in the context of academic culture? You can check their meaning in the glossary at the back of the book.

- [ ] academic
- [ ] academic culture
- [ ] article
- [ ] concept
- [ ] culture
- [ ] description
- [ ] discipline
- [ ] information technology
- [ ] lecturer
- [ ] rational argument
- [ ] research report
- [ ] researcher
- [ ] scholar
- [ ] text
- [ ] verifiable

What is culture?

When we talk about culture, we usually think about countries – we talk about Australian culture, Chinese culture, Lebanese culture, and so on. This book, however, is about academic culture; that is, the culture of universities. It focuses on the culture of universities in

English-speaking countries, especially in Australia. But before we talk about what academic culture is, what do we mean by 'culture'?

How do we know that someone is Australian or Italian? Chinese or Indonesian? Lebanese or Iranian? Usually we look at how they behave. We might notice things like:

- the type of food they eat
- the clothes they wear
- what they call each other
- how they greet each other
- how they show that they are being polite.

For example, most Australians call people by their first name, and greet each other by saying things like 'How are you?' or 'How're you going?' They say 'please' and 'thank you' to be polite. Most Chinese, however, use titles when they talk to someone older than themselves, or someone who has a higher status. They often greet people by asking 'Where are you going?' and may show politeness by remaining silent. They are not likely to use 'please' and 'thank you' with family members or friends or when buying things in shops. So from this simple example, we can see that a person's cultural background affects how they behave.

However, culture does not only refer to how someone behaves. People who share a culture also share many *attitudes* and *values*. Most Australians, for example, believe that people should all be treated in the same way, no matter how old they are, or what their job is. This is why they call almost everybody by their first name. In contrast, Chinese culture places importance on hierarchy. This means that Chinese people are likely to show respect to older people, or to people with higher status, and one of the ways they do this is by using titles and the whole of a person's name when they talk to such people.

What is academic culture?

Just as we can talk about Australian culture or Chinese culture, we can talk about the culture of universities. This is usually called 'academic culture'. Academic culture refers to the attitudes, values and ways of behaving that are shared by people who work or study in universities; for example, lecturers, researchers and students. In this book, we will identify what these academic attitudes and values are and how they affect the ways that students and lecturers are expected to behave.

Why is academic culture important?

As a new university student, you probably expect to learn new knowledge and to develop new skills. But this is not all that you have to learn. You also have to understand the attitudes and values of academic culture, because your lecturers will expect you to behave in ways that demonstrate these attitudes and values.

All students have to become familiar with this new culture, no matter where they come from. Academic culture is unfamiliar to many students who have been educated in Australia, just as it may be unfamiliar to students from China, India, Indonesia and other countries.

WHAT ARE ENGLISH-SPEAKING UNIVERSITIES?

This book is about academic culture in English-speaking universities, but what are English-speaking universities? In countries as diverse as India, Germany, Japan and Oman, English is used as the language of instruction in at least some universities. However, while universities in many countries teach in English, they do not necessarily share the same academic culture. In describing academic culture in English-speaking universities, this book is referring to the common culture of universities in Australia, Canada, Ireland, New Zealand, the United Kingdom and the United States of America. While this does not imply that universities in these countries are all the same, it does suggest that they share a number of attitudes and values. These attitudes and values are expressed most clearly in the types of academic behaviour that are expected from scholars and students alike. This book attempts to describe some of these behaviours, and to explore some of the attitudes and values that underpin them.

Do all disciplines share the same culture?

Is the culture of a discipline like economics the same as a discipline such as information technology (IT)? The answer is both 'yes' and 'no'! Some attitudes, values and behaviours are shared by all disciplines – from astronomy to zoology. Others relate to specific disciplines. For example, all disciplines expect you to be independent and critical learners, and they generally agree on what 'independent' means. (You will find more about being an independent learner in Chapter 4.) However, disciplines have different ideas about what being 'critical' involves. For example, in the natural sciences (physics, chemistry, biology and so on) and in the applied sciences – such as engineering and information technology – critical thinking often involves problem solving. This means that you have to decide what theories and concepts are most appropriate to solve a problem, and then use them to solve it. On the other hand, in the social sciences – such as economics, business studies, psychology, sociology and so on – you are more likely to compare and contrast different theories and concepts, and to evaluate their usefulness and applicability in specific situations.

Different disciplines ask different types of questions, and they may also vary in the methods that they use to answer those questions. The methods used to investigate questions in physics are different, for example, from those used to answer questions in business studies or IT.

Another area of difference between disciplines lies in the types of texts that you have to write. History students, for example, often have to write argumentative essays, while psychology students are more likely to write research reports. Students of biology and physics may have to work in groups to produce posters, while students in business studies – also working in groups – may produce reports.

In this book, we will mainly focus on the aspects of academic culture that are common to all disciplines.

THINK ABOUT THIS

- Do you think that physics and business studies share similar expectations about academic culture?
- What do you think might be similar or different?

What is academic communication?

Just as universities share a similar academic culture, they also share certain expectations regarding appropriate ways to communicate. For example, the language that you use in writing to your parents about what you have been doing on a holiday will be different from the language that you use in writing to a business associate about business-related matters. You should have no problems identifying which is which in the following example emails.

Hey Jean, Shouldve written this days ago, but I guess its better late than never. Amazing trip so far. Brugge was awesome and Berlin was amazing because of its history. Ive taken lots of pics to show you when I get home. See you soon

Love Hugh

Hi Stephen

I hope this email finds you well. I'm writing to enquire about progress on the marketing campaign. Are the brochures ready yet? Could you let me know their expected date of delivery?

Thanks.

Best regards,

Colin

Of course, the first was written to a family member and the second to a business associate, but how did you know? Did you notice the informal tone of the first, which uses contractions (*should've* instead of *should have*) to make the email sound like speech, colloquial language (*awesome*), non-standard capitalisation and punctuation (*I* is not capitalised, apostrophes are omitted from abbreviations, such as *its* rather than *it's* and *Ive* instead of *I've*). The language is vague – *see you soon*, rather than a specific time. And the salutation (*Hey Jean*) is not on a separate line.

The second email, in contrast, is more formal. It opens with a general pleasantry then tells the reader what the mail is about. The language is not colloquial; it is polite, everyday language, and the grammar and punctuation are standard – *I* is capitalised and apostrophes are included, the writer using *I'm* rather than *Im*. Finally, both the salutation and the sign-off are on separate lines.

The difference between the two emails illustrates an important point: The topic or purpose of a piece of writing and its audience – that is, the person or people it is aimed at – determines the language that is used. Something else also needs to be considered; that is, the medium by which the message is being transmitted. Email? Twitter? Blog post? Phone, which means that the message is spoken rather than written? Word-processed text? When you use any of these, the language you use changes. Think about how the language you use changed on Twitter, with its limited number of characters, rather than email.

THINK ABOUT THIS

Imagine you are away on a skiing holiday.

- How will you communicate with your very elderly grandmother? What will you tell her about your holiday and what language will you use?
- How will you communicate with your friends back home? What will you tell them and what language will you use?
- Just before the end of your holiday, you break your leg in a skiing accident and will be three weeks late in returning to work. How will you communicate with your boss? What language will you use?

The language we use is determined by the purpose of the message, its audience and the medium it uses, and this is especially so in university. So, not only do you need to understand something about the culture of universities, you also need to understand beliefs about the appropriate ways of using language according to the purpose, audience and medium of our communication because your tutors and lecturers will expect you to use appropriate language.

What are academic attitudes and values?

In this section, we will identify some of the most important attitudes and values of academic culture by looking at an important debate in economics (see the example). It does not matter if you are or are not studying economics – the attitudes and values that are illustrated are common to most disciplines.

> **e.g. EXAMPLE**
>
> Macroeconomics is the section of economics that asks questions such as:
>
> - How can a country avoid unemployment?
> - How can a country avoid inflation?
> - Should governments try to regulate the economy?
>
> There are two different approaches to answering these questions. Some economists believe in the free market. They think that if governments do not interfere in the economy, the free market will solve problems such as unemployment and inflation. Other economists believe that governments need to take active steps to reduce problems like unemployment and inflation. They do not believe that the free market alone is effective.

What can we learn from this example? The most important lesson is that there is usually more than one way to approach a problem. The economy is very complex, so different economists develop different answers to questions.

The same situation exists in other disciplines. For example, there are several different ways of explaining how children learn their native language. If you study management, you will find that there are many theories about how to motivate people, and students in the health sciences may argue about how to assist older patients most effectively or ways to cope with depressed patients.

Understanding that there is more than one way to approach a problem illustrates one of the central ideas of academic culture: that knowledge develops through debate and argument. Scholars compare and contrast different approaches to a problem, trying to see which describes the real world best, or which is most useful. As you study different subjects, you will notice how scholars in each subject refer to their own ideas and to the ideas of other scholars, agreeing with some and disagreeing with others. Each scholar presents ideas that he or she thinks best explain the real world and criticises ideas that he or she does not agree with. As students, you are expected to learn how to take part in this continuing debate.

Now let's go back to the two different approaches in macroeconomics that were described in the example on the previous page. One approach is to leave everything to the operation of the free market; the other involves government interference. At different times, each of these approaches has been popular. In the 1920s, for example, most economists believed that governments should not interfere in the economy. However, as a result of the Great Depression of the 1930s, when millions of people were unemployed, the idea that governments needed to take action to create jobs became widely accepted. This approach was called *Keynesian* after John Maynard Keynes, the economist who developed the theory. It remained the dominant approach until the 1970s, when the idea that government regulation affected growth in a negative way became influential. This idea led to the approach that is usually called *monetarist*. One of the most important monetarists is Milton Friedman. Since the Global Financial Crisis of 2008, Keynesian ideas are once again becoming popular.

The fact that one position is dominant does not mean that other positions do not exist. Economists are always developing ideas and theories that do not agree with the dominant ones. Even when Keynes' ideas were at their most influential, many economists continued to advance alternative views. Similarly, the influence of monetarist positions in the 1970s and 1980s did not mean that Keynesian approaches were abandoned by all economists.

Another point to note is that academics build on the work of other scholars. They do not develop their ideas in isolation. Friedman is a good example of this. While he agrees with the early twentieth-century economists, his ideas are not the same as theirs. His theories represent a major development of their position. More significantly, he developed his theories in debate with Keynes' ideas.

THINK ABOUT THIS

Think about your own experience in education.

- Does this description of academic communication fit with your own previous experience of education in high school or in your own country?
- Does it match your expectations regarding university study?
- In what ways is it similar?
- In what ways is it different?

What are the features of an academic argument?

Now that we understand that knowledge develops through discussion and argument, we need to identify some of the features of academic argument. Let's start by looking at Texts 1 and 2. Both are about deforestation, but they are written in very different styles.

TEXT 1: DEFORESTATION

The causes of deforestation are very complex. A competitive global economy drives the need for money in economically challenged tropical countries. At the national level, governments sell logging concessions to raise money for projects, to pay international debt, or to develop industry. For example, Brazil had an international debt of $159 billion in 1995, on which it must make payments each year. The logging companies seek to harvest the forest and make profit from the sales of pulp and valuable hardwoods such as mahogany.

Urquhart G., Chomentowski, W., Skole, D., & Barber, C. (n.d.).Tropical deforestation fact sheet. Page 1. Earth Observatory, NASA, http://earthobservatory.nasa.gov/Library/Deforestation

TEXT 2: LOGGING

The pace of logging in Tasmania is far, far higher than I have seen anywhere in Australia or elsewhere. Everywhere you travel in Tasmania, you will see logging trucks. Lots of them. Even in Hobart. I sat down at the Hobart Town Hall, and only had to wait a few minutes before I saw two logging trucks drive past, and I saw many more just wandering around town. For someone who enjoys wilderness areas, it is somewhat sickening to know that most of these trucks are carrying the remains of trees that are several hundred years old.

Unfortunately, apart from the logging trucks, the Tasmanian Government has become adept at hiding the logging from the public. Many areas have been logged so that a strip of trees is left around public roads, making it appear that there has been no logging. Locked gates abound in areas like this, access is possible, but difficult to obtain, so the general public are kept out.

The hardwood from these ancient trees is not even being used for fine furniture or the like, it is being chipped to make paper in Japan.

Hunter, E. (2004). Environmental Destruction in Tasmania.
Hiking Tasmania. www.ozhiker.com/tasmania/wilderness.html

Logical, rational argument

The purpose of the Text 1 is to explain why deforestation takes place, so its tone is logical, rational and impersonal. It is logical because it outlines a chain of cause and effect – first in general terms and then using the specific case of Brazil. The reader can follow the chain of reasoning and check that each step is clearly related to the previous one. The argument is outlined for you in Figure 1.1.

Figure 1.1 Flow of argument for Text 1

The argument is rational because it depends on facts that can be observed and verified. As a reader, you can go to the relevant sources to check that in 1995 Brazil had a large international debt. You might also search for government documents that show Brazil will benefit financially from selling logging concessions. If you are unable to find these documents, you can check to see that other researchers have done so.

The argument is also impersonal. (We will look at how to introduce the personal in Chapter 9.) Because it is impersonal, both the writer's feelings and emotions are not relevant, and the writer does not put him or herself into the text. Instead, he or she bases the argument on evidence that can be checked and verified.

All this means that we as readers can argue with what the writer is claiming. Because the argument is logical, rational and impersonal, we can indicate sections of the argument that are problematic. For example, we could point out that governments often receive very little money for logging concessions, so there must be other reasons why they are selling logging concessions.

Now look at Text 2. The purpose of this text is to describe somebody's personal experience of logging and their feelings about it. The tone is therefore personal and subjective. The writer does not attempt to build a logical, rational argument. Instead he tells us directly and indirectly how he feels about logging. However, this does not mean that the text is irrational or illogical; rather, the purpose of the text is not to present a logical, rational argument. We can see this if we look at the last paragraph:

> The hardwood from these ancient trees is not even being used for fine furniture or the like, it is being chipped to make paper in Japan.

The writer implies that using timber for fine furniture is better than using it for paper, but he does not explain why this is so. The result is that it is difficult to argue with what the writer is saying. Even if we showed that some of his facts were wrong, this would not affect him, because he has a right to feel as he does. Text 2 is not an academic argument.

Verifiable claims and precise information

There are two more features of academic argument that we need to identify. First, these claims are supported by evidence and secondly, the facts are as precise as possible. When writers do not have precise evidence, they indicate this by using qualifying words.

Text 3, another section from the same deforestation article as Text 1, deals with the effect of deforestation on biodiversity. In this text, the writers qualify several of their facts and we learn, for example:

- Of the tens of millions of species <u>believed</u> to be on Earth, scientists have only given names to <u>about</u> 1.5 million of them.
- <u>Many</u> of the rain forest plants and animals can only be found in small areas, because they require a special habitat.
- If their habitat is destroyed, they <u>may</u> become extinct.

 **TEXT 3**

Worldwide, 5–80 million species of plants and animals comprise the 'biodiversity' of planet Earth. Tropical rain forests – covering only 7% of the total dry surface of the Earth – hold over half of all these species. Of the tens of millions of species <u>believed</u> to be on Earth, scientists have only given names to <u>about</u> 1.5 million of them, and even fewer of the species have been studied in depth.

Many of the rain forest plants and animals can only be found in small areas, because they require a special habitat in which to live. This makes them very vulnerable to deforestation. If their habitat is destroyed, they may become extinct. Every day, species are disappearing from the tropical rain forests as they are cleared. We do not know the exact rate of extinction, but estimates indicate that up to 137 species disappear worldwide each day.

Urquhart G., Chomentowski, W., Skole, D. & Barber, C., (n.d.)
Tropical deforestation fact sheet. Page 3. Earth Observatory, NASA.
http://earthobservatory.nasa.gov/Library/Deforestation

Notice how the underlined words qualify the claim that the writers are making. For example, they do not say that there <u>are</u> tens of millions of species on Earth. This is because we do not know how many species there are – they have not been counted. The writers do not say that <u>all</u> rainforest plants are found in small areas, nor do they say that if the habitat of rain forest animals is destroyed, they <u>will</u> become extinct. In each case, the writers recognise that there may be exceptions. Some rainforest plants are found over large areas. Even if one habitat is destroyed, some animals may be able to adapt to a different one.

You can see that scholars are usually very careful about what they claim. They want to make sure that the evidence they have supports the conclusion they reach, so they qualify their claims in different ways. Here are some ways in which the sentence about the extinction of rain forest animals might be modified:

- If their habitat is destroyed, rain forest animals <u>will</u> become extinct.
- If their habitat is destroyed, rain forest animals <u>may</u> become extinct.
- If their habitat is destroyed, <u>some</u> rain forest animals <u>may</u> become extinct.
- If their habitat is destroyed, <u>some</u> rain forest animals <u>may</u> become extinct in <u>some areas</u>.

However, while it is important not to make claims that the evidence does not support, it is also important to be precise where possible. For example, we learn that tropical rain forests cover only 7% of the total dry surface of the Earth. The exact figure is known, and so it is used. Notice also that the dry surface of the Earth is specified, rather than the total area of land and sea together.

Giving verifiable and precise information are important features of academic texts because they support the development of knowledge through debate and discussion. If a scholar does not qualify his or her argument, others will criticise it. On the other hand, if scholars are not precise when it is possible to be so, their argument will also be criticised. We will examine how to make our arguments precise in Chapter 15.

 SUMMARY

1. Attitudes and values lead to ways of behaving.

2. Academic culture = attitudes + values + ways of behaving that are shared by university staff.

3. New students have to learn new knowledge, new skills AND new attitudes, values and ways of behaving. That is, they have to learn a new academic culture.

4. Many features of academic culture are common to all disciplines, but each discipline also has its own expectations.

5. Academic knowledge develops through debate and argument.

6. There is more than one way to approach an academic issue or question.

7. Theories are refined and developed over time.

8. More recent theories build on earlier theories and develop them.

9. Academic arguments are usually logical, rational and impersonal.

   ■ They are logical, so the reader can see their reasoning.

   ■ They are rational, so evidence for the argument is observable and verifiable.

   ■ They are impersonal, so the argument is based on verifiable evidence and not on personal feeling.

10. Academic arguments only claim what the evidence will support.

11. Academic arguments are precise when there is clear evidence.

 SKILLS PRACTICE

Task 1

■ Text 4 is another extract from the same article on deforestation. What features tell you that this is an academic article?

TEXT 4: AFTER DEFORESTATION

What happens after a forest is cut is very important in the regeneration of that forest. Different cutting techniques and uses of the land have diverse effects on the ground and surviving organisms that make up a rain forest.

In a tropical rain forest, nearly all of the life-sustaining nutrients are found in the plants and trees, not in the ground as in a northern, or temperate forest. When the plants and trees are cut down to sow the land, farmers usually burn the tree trunks to release the nutrients necessary for a fertile soil. When the rains come, they wash away most of the nutrients, leaving the soil much less fertile. In as little as 3 years, the ground is no longer capable of supporting crops.

When the fertility of the ground decreases, farmers seek other areas to clear and plant, abandoning the nutrient-deficient soil. The area previously farmed is left to grow back to a rain forest. However, just as the crops did not grow well because of low nutrients, the forest will grow back just as slow because of poor nutrients. After the land is abandoned, the forest may take up to 50 years to grow back.

Urquhart G., Chomentowski, W., Skole, D. & Barber, C. (n.d.).
Tropical deforestation fact sheet. Page 4. Earth Observatory, NASA
http://earthobservatory.nasa.gov/Library/Deforestation)

Task 2

Write a short description of academic culture for a brochure about university life that will be given to all new students at your university. You will need to:

- explain what culture is
- define academic culture
- describe how many scholars in English-speaking universities believe academic knowledge develops.

Task 3

Write a second paragraph for the brochure about university life. Identify the major features of academic culture and illustrate these features with examples taken from the extract on deforestation that you looked at in Text 4.

2 ABOUT UNIVERSITY

✸ LEARNING OBJECTIVES

When you have finished reading this chapter, you will understand:

- How a university is structured
- The different titles that academic staff have and how to address them
- The different areas and levels of study
- How to find out about the structure of your program of study
- The meaning and use of unit/module guides

✓ WORD LISTS

Do you know the meaning of these words? Many have special meanings in academic culture. You can check their meaning in the glossary at the back of the book.

- [ ] academic
- [ ] apprentice
- [ ] bibliography
- [ ] chancellor
- [ ] department
- [ ] doctorate
- [ ] facilitator
- [ ] faculty
- [ ] honours
- [ ] humanities

- [ ] lecturer
- [ ] literature
- [ ] PhD
- [ ] professor
- [ ] reference
- [ ] seminar
- [ ] social sciences
- [ ] school
- [ ] source
- [ ] vice chancellor

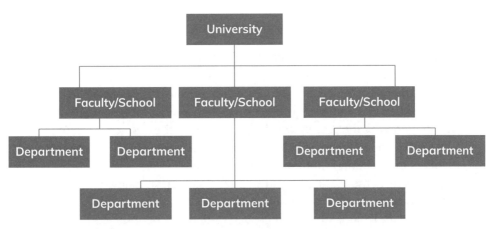

Figure 2.1 General map of the structure of a university

We have examined some of the concepts that describe approaches to knowledge and learning in many universities in English-speaking cultures. We now need to understand the titles that lecturers have, which means we also need to understand how universities are organised. Most universities are organised into a number of faculties and/or schools – different universities use different names. A faculty or school generally groups together a number of departments. Your university may use different terms, but the general principle is the same: Each department involves one or more disciplines. A general outline looks something like Figure 2.1.

For example, your university may have a faculty of economics that includes the departments of accounting, marketing, international business, and so on. The faculty of health sciences may include the departments of nursing, physiotherapy and orthoptics. At some universities, a department combines a number of related disciplines. For example, a department of history might be divided into sections studying and teaching ancient history, Asian history, modern history and world history. No two universities are organised in the same way. It is worth understanding how your university is organised, as there will be times when you are expected to know in which faculty or school and which departments you are studying, especially when you are completing official university forms.

THINK ABOUT THIS

How is your university organised? If you are not sure, you can probably find an organisation chart on the university's website, in the section giving general information about the university.

- Is your university divided into faculties, schools or something else?
- Do you know what department your studies fall under?
- Where does your department fit within the university structure?

What do the titles of academic staff mean?

Now that you have a general idea about how a university is organised, we can look at the meaning of the titles carried by different members of the academic staff.

Starting at the top, the head of the university is called a vice chancellor. He or she is basically the chief executive officer (CEO) and is responsible for running the university. You may be wondering why the vice chancellor, rather than the chancellor, is the CEO. Most, if not all, universities have a chancellor, but this is an honorary position – the chancellor is not usually involved in the actual running of the university.

There are several other senior administrative positions in a university, but as a student you are not likely to get involved with them. However, you will certainly be in contact with the research and teaching staff. Remember that most academics both teach and do research: When you are on holiday, they are not! The times when you are on holiday are usually the times when your lecturers are doing their research or going to conferences to liaise with colleagues from other universities.

The academics who teach you may have one of the following titles:

- Professor
- Associate professor
- Senior lecturer
- Lecturer
- Associate lecturer
- Tutor

Professor is the title given to the most senior academics in a department. Unlike in the United States, where most academic staff have the title of Professor, in countries such as Australia, the United Kingdom, New Zealand and Canada, only a few people in a department have this title.

An *associate professor* is one step down from a professor. Associate professors are also senior members of the academic staff.

Senior lecturers and *lecturers* occupy the middle ranks of the academic departmental hierarchy. The majority of a department's staff are likely to be senior lecturers and lecturers.

Associate lecturers are more junior staff, and are usually in the early years of their academic career.

Finally, many departments also use *tutors*, especially for teaching tutorials. Tutors are often very senior students – that is, they are completing a doctoral degree, usually a PhD, which is the highest academic qualification.

While senior academics may focus on teaching students in the later years of their studies, this is by no means certain. Many professors enjoy teaching first-year students. During your university career, you are likely to be taught by junior, middle-ranking and senior academics.

Another term you are likely to come across is *unit* or *subject coordinator*. Each subject that you study in your degree will have a coordinator who organises the content of the unit (what is taught and in what order) and makes sure that it runs efficiently. The coordinator is also likely to give some or all of the lectures and coordinate the work of other lecturers or tutors involved in the course. If you have a problem, for example with accessing unit materials or with your tutor, the unit coordinator is the person to contact. Coordinators may have either of the titles that we have just examined; their title does not affect the work they do as coordinator.

THINK ABOUT THIS

- Do you know the names and contact details for the unit or subject coordinators for each of the subjects you are studying?
- If you are not sure, you will probably find the details on the website for each unit or subject.

How are academic staff addressed?

In general, most academic staff prefer to be called by their first or given name. This is especially so in Australia as there is a strong cultural preference for treating people equally regardless of title. So, for example, Mary Jones is called Mary and David Smith is called David. However, if you are addressing a member of the academic staff for the first time, especially by email, it is polite to call them by their title and family name.

If, generally, you don't want to use the first name, then you can use a person's title and their family name. There are four main titles:

- **Professor:** Only use this title if your lecturer is a professor. If you're not sure, check the departmental website for a list of staff. This usually indicates the position held by each staff member.
- **Doctor (Dr):** This title indicates that the person has obtained a PhD, often called a doctorate – the highest academic qualification available. Most academic staff have PhDs, but not all of them. It depends when and where they completed their academic studies.
- **Ms:** This is used for a woman.
- **Mr:** This is used for a man.

Thus, a woman named Mary Jones can be called Professor Jones if she is a professor, Dr Jones if she has a doctorate or Ms Jones. However, she cannot be called Professor Mary, Dr Mary or even Ms Mary. In the same way, a man called David Smith is Professor Smith, Dr Smith or Mr Smith, but never Professor David, Dr David or Mr David. If you are not sure what to call your lecturer, just ask them what they prefer to be called!

THINK ABOUT THIS

- Do you know how to address each of the academic staff who teach you?
- If you are not sure, check the website for each of your subjects.

How is my course organised?

How your course is organised will vary depending on what you are studying. Firstly, you may need to decide whether you wish to study for an honours degree. An honours degree involves an extra year of study, usually at a higher level of difficulty. Honours degrees are very competitive, and often you are not expected to apply until your final year of study in a standard degree.

More importantly, you need to decide whether you want to study in the humanities, the social sciences or the sciences, or whether you wish to complete an employment-related qualification in, for example, medicine, law or nursing. If you are interested in studying the humanities – subjects examining human culture, such as history, literature, philosophy, art and music – you are likely to have a wide choice of subjects. The main consideration will be the level of each subject, often divided into entry level (usually designated as 100-level units), mid-level (200-level) and senior (300-level) units. A subject with a 100-level code may include knowledge and skills that need to have been completed prior to taking 200- or 300-level units, and so may be a prerequisite.

Rather than studying the humanities, you may be interested in the social sciences, that is, subjects examining human relationships in a social context. Psychology, economics, and sociology are all social sciences. Choice in these disciplines is variable. If you want to study sociology, you are likely to have some choice, but students of economics or psychology are likely to find that there is very little room for choice of subjects in their degree.

Students in the sciences tend to have more choice of subjects, but need to make sure that they have completed the prerequisites for more advanced study in their favourite subjects. Finally, students enrolled in employment-related courses such as medicine, law or nursing are likely to find that they have very little choice of subjects indeed. All subjects are compulsory.

How do I find out the structure of my course?

The way in which your course is structured is usually listed on your university's website. The site will list the subjects, or units, that you are required to complete and those that you can choose from as optional components.

 THINK ABOUT THIS

■ Do you understand the structure of your degree? If not, check your university's website.

What is a syllabus and why is it so important?

Every unit you study at university has been planned by a convenor, and a key part of this planning is the development of a *unit or module guide* or *outline*, the *study guide* or a *syllabus*. You are likely to be given a copy of the unit/module guide or syllabus for each of the subjects you are studying at the commencement of a semester, and it can also usually be found on the website for each subject.

For many lecturers, the website is the central point of contact for a unit, though some lecturers simply use it as a place to make lecture slides available. However, it should be your first port of call if you need information about the unit, such as the requirements for an assessment, the schedule of lectures, the reading list or the assignment deadlines.

Regardless of the way it is accessed, the syllabus tends to use terms like:

- Unit description
- Learning outcomes
- Mode of delivery
- Schedule
- Readings
- Assessment

The unit description is usually a simple description of the topics covered in the unit.

The learning outcomes are a set of goals that set out the skills and knowledge that a successful student will have acquired after completion of the unit. An example of a learning outcome is:

> *Students will be able to critically compare a range of methodologies used in the study of group dynamics in social psychology.*

Unit convenors often start designing a unit by specifying the learning outcomes, then developing the assessment that will test or facilitate these and the content that students need to learn in order to complete the assessment.

Units are likely to be taught through a combination of lectures and tutorials or with a combination of online and classroom learning activities. The syllabus is where you will find out what you need to attend, when, where and what preparation you are expected to do. There is also likely to be a list of the topics that will be covered each week and the associated reading that is required. There is also usually a specification of the assessment used to determine your grade for the module. Finally, the syllabus usually also includes the attendance policy, what to do if you are unable to submit your coursework on time and how you should contact your lecturer.

THINK ABOUT THIS

- Do your subjects have a unit or study guide?
- What does the guide tell you about attendance at lectures and tutorials?
- How does it suggest you contact your lecturer?
- Do your lecturers have office hours? If so, when?
- What are the learning outcomes for your subjects? Do you understand them?

SUMMARY

1. Most universities are divided into faculties or schools, and each faculty or school is divided into departments.

2. All academic staff have titles: professor, associate professor, senior lecturer, lecturer or associate lecturer. Academic staff are usually addressed by their first or given name. If a title is used, it is always linked to the family name.

3. The amount of choice you have in subjects depends on your area of study. If you are studying in the humanities, you are likely to have a lot of choice, but if you are studying in an employment-related area such as medicine or nursing, almost all your subjects will be compulsory.

4. Information about the aims of the unit, the content and the assessment is contained in the module or unit guide. This guide will also tell you about attendance and how to contact the lecturer.

SKILLS PRACTICE

Task 1

■ How do you think you should address a senior member of the academic staff who does not teach you? What about a member of the academic staff who is only a few years older than you?

Task 2

■ Write a short description of the role of a unit guide to give to people who do not understand its role.

3 LECTURERS AND STUDENTS

✵ LEARNING OBJECTIVES

When you have finished this chapter, you will understand:

- the ways that lecturers understand their roles
- how ideas about the development of knowledge influence lecturers' conceptions of their roles
- how ideas about independent learning influence lecturers' conceptions of their roles
- how ideas about how the development of knowledge influence lecturers' expectations of students
- what a 'good student' is
- the role the audience plays in creating electronic texts
- the correct way to address your audience
- the purpose and structure of emails

✓ WORD LISTS

Do you know the meaning of these words? Many have special meanings in the academic culture. You can check their meaning in the glossary at the back of the book.

- ☐ academic
- ☐ apprentice
- ☐ bibliography
- ☐ doctorate
- ☐ facilitator
- ☐ humanities
- ☐ lecturer

- ☐ literature
- ☐ PhD
- ☐ reference
- ☐ seminar
- ☐ source
- ☐ LMS

Perhaps the most important issue in understanding university life is to understand the roles of lecturers and students, and particularly the way lecturers understand their roles and their expectation regarding what makes a good student. In this chapter we will examine these issues, comparing what lecturers tend to think with the attitudes that many students bring with them to the university. We will also look at how you should address lecturers, especially with regard to email.

What is the role of a lecturer?

Having explored the various titles used by academic staff, and what you should call them in Chapter 2, we can now look at how they see their roles. Although you may be taught by professors, lecturers or tutors, in this book we will use the word 'lecturer' to refer to them all.

THINK ABOUT THIS

■ Before you continue reading, take a moment to decide what you think the role of a lecturer is.

How do lecturers see their role?

We will explore the way lecturers see their role by looking at an extract from a set of course notes (Text 5). The lecture is part of a course on contemporary Australia and deals with the topic of national identity. It asks the question, 'What do Australians think about themselves?' and explores how the idea of an 'Australian' has changed over the decades.

The lecturer begins by asking, 'Do Australians think about themselves today in the same way as they thought about themselves in the past?' He then outlines the ways in which ideas about Australian identity have developed, beginning with Australia's convict past and continuing through the nineteenth century. However, note that he does not treat the subject fully. He outlines major features and then gives a reference to further reading. (Because this course is on the web, the references are given in the form of an underlined link to a web page. Alternatively, a list of further readings is provided and these readings are available in the library or via the library website.)

TEXT 5

Note: The extract is taken from 'National Identity', a unit in an Australian Studies course entitled 'Contemporary Australia' developed by the National Centre for Australian Studies at Monash University in conjunction with Open Learning Australia. The notes below have been greatly abbreviated and simplified.

2.4   THE 'AUSTRALIAN TYPE'

What then are the dominant images of Australia's national identity that continue to have appeal today?

Early representations

Australia's convict origins have been valued in different ways at different times. Once it was a shameful admission to have a convict ancestor, but today it is more likely to be seen as a badge of honour.

After the transportation of convicts stopped, the gold rushes of the 1850s and the influx of free settlers resulted in a view of Australians as 'born colonists' emerging. The Australian 'born colonist' was always male, and regarded as a hardy type, adaptable, independent, sport loving and resolute. He was egalitarian and valued mateship more highly than respect to authority. The anti-authoritarian character of the 'Australian Type' was perpetuated by images of bushrangers, and by the independence and resolve of miners on the gold digging fields and the unionists of the late 19th century. Explore visions of life on the goldfields.

White, male larrikins

The 'Australian Type' was always portrayed as Anglo-Celtic. This partly reflected the make up of the population at the time, but it was also a cultural suppression of the identities of Aborigines, Torres Strait and Pacific Islanders, Chinese, Germans and many more. Even though the vast majority of Australians lived in urban environments in the late 19th century, the 'Australian Type' was also a pioneer of the bush. The literature of writers and poets such as Henry Lawson and Banjo Paterson portrayed the bushman as a resourceful larrikin who tamed the landscape, was resilient in the face of hardship and heroic in overcoming the odds, which were inevitably stacked against him. Click here for more information

Relevancy today?

Contemporary manifestations of these myths by dominant political and cultural institutions continue to shape our imagining of national identity. Prime Minister Howard's attempts to include 'mateship' to describe contemporary Australia in the Preamble to the Constitution during the 1999 Republic Referendum made clear reference to the past. The debate that ensued and the consequent removal of the word 'mateship' is perhaps an indication that past notions of Australian identity are not perceived as relevant or inclusive enough anymore. Read more about the preamble debate

2.5   THE 'AUSTRALIAN WAY OF LIFE'

The 'Australian Type' was not just a character but embodied a 'way of life' that we think of as Australian. The 'Australian way of life' is seen as reflecting traditional virtues of egalitarianism, classlessness, 'a fair go', stoicism and mateship. It is sometimes referred to as the 'national ethos'.

How do contemporary visions of the diversity of Australian multiculturalism fit into this construction of the 'Australian way of life'? Do representations of the 'Australian way of life' incorporate cultural difference? A wave of critique by Australian feminists, Aboriginal activists, and ethnic community leaders has challenged the dominant representation of what it means to be an Australian. They argue for an acceptance of diversity and choice over all aspects of lifestyle, culture and religion. Has multiculturalism as an official government policy led to the imagining of a multiplicity of identities in Australia? Consider the views of youth in Australia in a report commissioned by the Victorian Multicultural Commission

Adapted from Cousins, S., National identity. In Contemporary Australia, Monash University. Retrieved from www.radioaustralia.net.au/australia/pdf/national_id.pdf

Another thing to notice is that the lecturer not only outlines major ideas, but also indicates areas of debate or disagreement. For example, in section 2.5, he suggests that for some people, traditional ideas about Australian identity are still relevant today. However, he then points to the debate that took place when Australia was considering changes to its constitution in the late 1990s. At that time, some people wished to include a reference to the concept of 'mateship', while other people did not. This debate shows that some people believed that mateship was an important part of Australian identity, while others did not. The lecturer indicates this disagreement, but does not say which is the 'correct' opinion. It is up to each student to analyse the evidence and decide for themselves which position they think is strongest.

Finally, and perhaps most importantly, the lecturer raises a number of questions but does not answer them. The last paragraph raises three questions:

- How do contemporary ideas about the diversity of Australian multiculturalism fit into the idea that there is an 'Australian way of life'?
- Does the 'Australian way of life' incorporate cultural difference?
- Has multiculturalism as an official government policy led to the possibility of many different identities all being considered Australian?

Students are left to think about these questions and to supply their own answers, based not only on the lecture but more importantly on the readings.

What is the lecturer's intention?

What is the lecturer doing in this lecture? Why, for example, does he raise questions without answering them? To answer this question, we need to understand how lecturers see their role and how it relates to the ideas about academic culture that we have already explored. Firstly, we need to distinguish between two different roles – the role of teacher and the role of facilitator. For many people, teachers are responsible for transmitting knowledge. They are a student's main source of knowledge and are responsible for organising and presenting that knowledge in ways that help the student to learn.

Facilitators, on the other hand, have a wider range of responsibilities. They help students to learn by:

- identifying major ideas and trends in the field being studied
- encouraging students to explore important issues in greater depth
- fostering the development of students' critical and analytical skills
- assisting them to develop their own voice
- helping them to identify and use different sources of knowledge.

You will see that the role of facilitator fits closely with the idea of the independent learner that we outline in Chapter 4, so it is not surprising that most lecturers see themselves as facilitators rather than teachers.

How do lecturers see their responsibilities?

Most lecturers believe that it is their basic responsibility to develop their students' ability to analyse arguments critically and to present and support positions of their own; that is, to express their own voice. Here is how one lecturer expressed it:

> *I don't want students who just write down everything I say, then give it back to me in exams. I want them to look at things critically, to argue. I want them to develop other ways of looking at things.*

You can see that this lecturer expects students to take an active part in discussion and debate. Most lecturers echo this point of view. They do not believe that students should first develop an understanding of the subject and then develop their critical and analytical skills. Instead, they believe that in order to develop understanding, students need to use critical and analytical skills. In other words, they see students as apprentice academics, learning to think and act in the way that academics do – debating, arguing and analysing.

Most lecturers also expect their students to be independent adults with their own interests and abilities. While they believe that they need to identify the major issues in a field clearly and concisely, they expect that students will select issues that interest them and explore these issues in depth. This is partly because they recognise that it is not possible to cover all topics in depth in the time available, but more importantly because of their belief that students need to develop their own research and analytical skills.

We call the opposite to encouraging the development of these skills 'spoon feeding'. You give a baby food on a spoon because the baby cannot feed him or herself. In the same way, lecturers believe that if they give students all the information that they need, they would be treating students as babies and, as a result, students would never develop analytical and independent learning skills.

For this reason, most lecturers see their role as providing a general map of the area being studied, rather than a detailed guide. They do not see themselves as the student's main source of knowledge – firstly because the amount of knowledge in any field of study is so vast that no lecturer could possibly present it all. More importantly, however, they believe that students must learn to use the many sources of knowledge that contribute to academic life, including books, journals and databases. They therefore outline the major theories, concepts and ideas in a field and expect students to use the library and other resources to deepen their understanding. By using such resources, students not only function as independent learners, they also develop skills in identifying relevant information and evaluating its relevance in relation to specific problems.

Why do lecturers raise questions without answering them?

We saw in Chapter 1 that there are many different ways of answering a question. There are, for example, several different ways of explaining how people learn language. None of the theories offers a complete explanation. Instead, each focuses on an aspect of the process. In other words, there is seldom one 'right' answer to an academic question. This is especially so in the social sciences and the humanities. Lecturers expect that students will evaluate different approaches to a question and decide which approach is most useful for his or her purposes. To do this, students need to use their critical and analytical skills to compare and contrast different positions and to evaluate the evidence that supports each different position. By doing this, they also develop their understanding of the whole field. In other words, lecturers attempt to give students opportunities to practise and display their academic skills and understanding.

In the sciences, and in disciplines such as business and economics, there may be less emphasis on evaluating different approaches to a question and more on problem solving: that is, applying the concepts and ideas presented by the lecturer to solving practical problems. Students are still expected to use critical and analytical skills, but these are displayed though identifying the most suitable way of solving a specific problem and to appropriately applying the method.

However, having said all this, the role of lecturers has changed a great deal over the last 20 years, so you are likely to encounter lecturers who want a more interactive classroom. These lecturers may use the classroom as a forum for discussion of some activity or text that you need to complete prior to class. This is referred to as the 'flipped classroom' and you will need to take an active role in the discussion to make best use of your time. Other lecturers will expect you to be active on the discussion board. While some lecturers no longer stand in front of the class and talk, you are still likely to find that the majority of your lecturers do this' to 'you are likely to find that some lecturers do still do this.

THINK ABOUT THIS

- What do you think are the responsibilities of a lecturer?

Discuss this with a partner.

What is the role of a student?

Now that we have explored the lecturer's expectations regarding critical thinking and independent learning, we can ask what role you, as a student, are expected to play. What do you need to do in order to be considered a successful student? We can examine the expected role by considering a student as an apprentice.

THINK ABOUT THIS

- How would you describe your role as a student?

Think about that, then compare your ideas with the description below.

Students as apprentices

An apprentice is a person who learns knowledge and skills in a particular field from someone who is already experienced in that field. The essential thing about an apprentice is that they learn by doing. From the beginning of their apprenticeship, they are involved in activities that demand the use of both knowledge and skills. While part of their training involves learning a body of knowledge, they are constantly expected to apply what they are learning in real situations.

As a student at a university, you are in a similar position. You have to acquire a great deal of knowledge, but you also have to use that knowledge in many different ways. For example, you may have to compare and contrast different approaches to an issue, and identify the strengths and weaknesses of these approaches. You may have to apply your theoretical knowledge to concrete situations. You may find yourself interviewing managers regarding their views on leadership, and comparing these views with the different theories of leadership that you read about in texts on management.

You are also expected to take an active part in tutorials, seminars and workshops. If you are presenting a paper, your job is not to summarise the readings. Instead, you need to present a position – that is, your own view of the issue – together with evidence to support it. This means that you need to develop your own voice. (We will examine this further in Chapters 12, 13 and 16.) Even if you are not presenting, you need to ask questions, agree or disagree with the presenter, bring in additional information and so on.

The apprenticeship role also includes writing. When you are given a written assignment, you are likely to be assessed in two different ways. One aspect of the assessment will involve your understanding of the issues involved, the amount of reading that you have done, the position that you present and the way that you use evidence to support your position. As with presenting a paper in a tutorial or a seminar, this involves expressing your voice.

The other aspect will relate to the way you write up your assignment. If you are a student of business or economics, you are likely to have to write reports, because these are common in business. You will therefore have to show that you know how to structure a report, and how to use the language of reports. In the same way, students in most science subjects have to write laboratory reports, and students in both the sciences and the social sciences often have to write research reports. Each of these texts has a specific structure and as a student you are expected to use that structure appropriately. You are also expected to understand technical issues, such as how to acknowledge the writings of other scholars, and how to write bibliographies and reference lists.

Students as independent learners

Your role as an independent learner is particularly important with regards to the technical aspects of locating and referring to sources and writing in an appropriate style. Most lecturers will indicate the required and recommended readings for an assignment, but they usually expect that you will supplement these with readings that you locate yourself. They will expect that you know how to identify and locate relevant and appropriate texts. Of course, most first-year students do not know how to do these things, but they are expected to find, and to enrol in, the courses that all university libraries arrange in these areas. If you are not clear about how to write a research report or how to refer to the writings of other scholars, you are expected to find out what courses in academic writing, speaking and study skills your university offers. Academic councillors and/or the website of your university can help you.

To summarise, a good student is:

- a critical thinker
- a problem solver
- an independent learner.

A good student is also:

- active
- organised
- self-motivated.

A good student is able to:

- identify their areas of weakness and find ways to develop them into strengths
- identify the resources available
- use a range of resources to locate and evaluate different sources.

THINK ABOUT THIS

- Are you a good student?

Evaluate yourself as a student by comparing your own actions with those described in this chapter.

Communicating with your lecturer

Using email

It is hard to imagine a time when we only discussed things with people in person or over the telephone, and when people had to read a book or go to a library to access information. Today, we can interact in real time without needing to be in the same place or use a telephone, and we can access enormous amounts of information from anywhere with an internet connection.

Access to the internet has changed many aspects of academic culture. University staff and students can communicate over the internet using email or discussion forums using email, discussion forums or even online classrooms. Modern Australian academic culture exists as much online as it does offline.

However, email tends to be the most frequently used form of electronic communication for communicating with your lecturer. For students, the most useful aspect of email is that it allows you to have greater access to academic staff. However, you should be aware that while your lecturer may be one of three or four lecturers you work with in a semester, you will be one of three or four *hundred* students your lecturer works with in that same semester. They will be receiving a lot of emails! Because of this imbalance, it is important that you understand how to write your emails appropriately.

When you send an email, make sure you use your official email address. An official university email address usually takes the form of FirstName.LastName@university.edu.au. It is often official policy that all email communications between staff and students are sent using your official university email and the lecturer's official email address. Even if it is not the policy of your institution, remember that personal email addresses can be quite obscure, and it can be difficult for your lecturer to identify who you are. Also, university junk email detection programs, or spam filters, can be very strict and unrecognised email addresses are often sent to junk mail folders, meaning that your lecturer may not even see your email.

Who is the audience of your email?

With email, you have control over who your audience will be. Remember that the relationship between a student and an academic is a formal one, and your email should be written in a formal style. This is important to keep in mind, as the speed of online communication means that you can often send off an email as soon as you have a question or encounter a problem without really considering what you are doing.

What is the purpose of your email?

Usually, students email academic staff with questions about their unit or course. Lecturers try to make sure that all information is provided in course guides and on the LMS, so make sure you have checked all other sources of information before you send your email.

Emails to academic staff can sometimes be for less than positive reasons. If you are unhappy about something, whether with the teaching material or the behaviour of another student or staff member, remember that the person receiving your email cannot always fix your problem immediately. You should be polite and respectful, just as you expect them to be polite and respectful to you.

Email structure

Text 6 is an example of an email from a student to their lecturer asking for information about an assignment.

The email includes a subject line, an appropriate address term, the email body and a sign off.

- Subject line:

  A subject line should be short and clear, and should always include the unit or course code the email is in relation to. This is for two reasons. First, your lecturer can see quickly what your email is about. Second, most email clients only show the first few

TEXT 6

Subject: ECON123 Research Report

Harada Smith <harada.smith@youruniversity.edu.au>   16:30 (1 hour ago)
To Dr Josh Jones <josh.jones@youruniversity.edu.au>

Dear Dr Jones,

I am a student in ECON123. I am writing to ask about the Research Report. I was wondering if you could tell me how many people we should survey to collect an appropriate set of data? I have asked on the discussion forum and none of my fellow students seem to know either.

Thank you for your time,

Harada Smith
(Student number 12345678)

---

words of the subject, meaning that the person you are emailing will not see a longer subject line. The subject appears before or after the place where you type in the email address of the intended recipient.

- An appropriate greeting:

  Always begin your email by first greeting the person you are emailing. Remember that you are emailing your lecturer, and while they may be friendly and approachable, you need to greet them in a way that acknowledges the formal relationship between student and teacher. Try 'Dear' and if you feel that that is too formal, try 'Hi'. Avoid 'Hey' and other informal forms. Remember that if you are unsure, address lecturers by their title and their family name. If you don't know their title, search the university staff directory. When you do address your lecturer by their title, do not use their first name. So, if your lecturer is Professor Brian North, you would address him as Professor North, not as Professor Brian.

- Email body:

  Remember that your lecturer will have many emails to respond to, so keep your message short and clear. If you have many issues to cover, include only a short overview in the email body and include the detail in a word processing document and attach that to the email.

- Sign-off:

  You should finish your email by thanking the person for their time. In very formal situations, you may want to sign off by saying, 'Yours faithfully' or 'Kindest regards'. For a less formal sign-off, you could use 'Best' or 'Regards'. End your email by using your full name and student identification number.

 SUMMARY

1. Most lecturers see themselves as facilitators rather than teachers. Their most important responsibility is to:
   - develop students' ability to critically analyse arguments
   - encourage students to express their own voice and relate to the opinions of others.

2. As facilitators, lecturers help students to learn by identifying major trends and issues in the field being studied. They do not expect their lectures to be a student's main source of information.

3. Lecturers expect students to:
   - identify specific issues that interest them and explore those issues in depth
   - use a variety of sources to explore issues
   - identify different approaches to issues
   - critically analyse differing approaches to decide which is most useful for a given purpose
   - apply the information and theories that they study in their courses to solving real world problems.

4. Students are expected to show that they can use the knowledge they acquire, for example by:
   - comparing and contrasting different approaches to a problem
   - evaluating different approaches to a problem
   - applying a particular approach in a concrete, real world situation.

5. Students are apprentices in that they learn by doing. They are expected to use knowledge, rather than show that they understand it.

6. Students are expected to apply their knowledge by:
   - taking an active part in tutorials, seminars and workshops
   - presenting tutorial or seminar papers that present a position on the issue and analyse it in depth
   - asking questions about the presentations made by other students
   - agreeing or disagreeing with the positions put by others
   - writing in the style appropriate to the discipline.

7. Students are expected to act as independent learners by:
   - locating different resources and referring to them appropriately
   - identifying their own weaknesses
   - identifying and using resources that will help them overcome their weaknesses.

8. Email is the most common way for a student to contact a lecturer. The email should use formal language and clearly specify the unit or module the student is enrolled in, and the question or issue involved.

Task 1

Text 7 is an example of an email sent to a lecturer.

(a)   What changes would you make to the email?

(b)   Justify each of the changes you suggest.

 TEXT 7

	New	Reply	Delete	Archive	Junk	Move to
Search	H-S <h-s-email@email.com> 23:30 (11 hours ago)					
Inbox	to Dr Josh Jones<josh.jones@ youruniversity.edu.au>					
Drafts	Hey – Jonzie					
Sent	so look im gunna b up front with u. ive got work things going on & i'll be					
Deleted	away for a bit. i get back the day U want the report and TBH I live quite far from uni, submitting my assignment on time wld mean taking 2 buses and a train out to uni – thats a total travel time round trip equalling over 3 hrs solely to put a piece of paper in a box.: (Reckon I could send just a submit it a day late?					
	Cheers					

Task 2

Think about your own previous learning experiences. Were the expected roles of teachers/ lecturers and students similar to those described in this chapter or different?

- Discuss this question with a partner.

Task 3

- What do you think the characteristics of a good student are?
- To what extent do you agree with the description of a good student presented in this chapter?
- In what ways does this description match your previous learning experiences? In what ways is it different?
- Summarise your ideas on a sheet of paper and be ready to explain them.

Task 4

Evaluate the description of a lecturer given in this chapter. Would you change anything that has been written here? Would you add anything?

■ Discuss these questions with a partner.

4 INDEPENDENT LEARNING

LEARNING OBJECTIVES

When you have finished this chapter, you will be able to:

- explain the concept of independent learning
- explain what an independent learner does
- explain how the concepts of individuality and independence contribute to the concept of independent learning
- identify the resources that support independent learning
- identify ways of improving independent learning skills.

WORD LIST

Do you know the meaning of these words? Many have special meanings in academic culture. You can check their meaning in the glossary at the back of the book.

- ☐ audience
- ☐ independent learning
- ☐ independent learning skills
- ☐ individual
- ☐ journal article
- ☐ learning style
- ☐ plagiarism
- ☐ seminar presentation
- ☐ tutorial
- ☐ voice

What is independent learning?

If you ask lecturers what qualities they expect from their students, they usually mention the ability to learn independently. What do they mean by this and why do they expect it?

Fundamentally, independent learning involves taking responsibility for your own learning. Before we explore more fully what 'taking responsibility for your own learning' involves, we need to discuss two key expectations that underlie the notion of responsibility. These relate to the concepts of the student as an individual and as an independent adult.

What is meant by 'individual'?

Most English-speaking cultures stress the role of the individual in society. This means that people in English-speaking cultures tend to see society as composed of separate individuals, each of whom has their own unique interests and talents. They believe that one of the major features of a healthy society is that it allows each member to develop their talents and interests as fully as possible. This attitude is reflected in the education system. From pre-school onwards, children are encouraged to express themselves in many different ways, and they are expected to explore activities, subjects and ideas that interest them.

Individuals not only have their own unique interests and talents, they also have individual learning styles and preferences. In general, individuals learn most effectively when using their preferred learning styles. Some may prefer to learn *visually* and rely mainly on written texts while others prefer to learn by *doing*, that is, through active engagement with their environment. Still others learn most effectively by *listening* to others or by taking part in *debates* and *discussions*.

The concept of independent learning is closely related to the idea of the unique individual. Because each individual has his or her own interests, talents and learning styles, most people believe that each person should have as much control as possible over their own learning situation. They believe that the more control a student has, the better they will be able to choose a course that suits them and the better they will learn. Also, because people learn in different ways, they need to be given the opportunity to choose how they will learn.

THINK ABOUT THIS

- In Chapter 3, we discussed how lecturers see their role. How do you think your lecturers see your role as a student?

What is an independent adult?

To understand the concept of independent learning, we also need to understand what people mean by an independent adult. In most English-speaking countries, people are considered to be adults at age 18. At this age, they are expected to know what they want and to be able to choose from a number of different alternatives. They may seek advice from different people about the best choice to make, but they expect to make the actual decision themselves. In fact, if parents, advisors, friends or other adults attempt to make decisions for them, most people feel angry. If someone makes a decision on behalf of another person, that implies that the person is incapable of making the decision for themselves. Most English speakers would experience this as insulting and would feel that they had lost face.

Almost all university students are over the age of 18, so they are considered to be adults. They are also individuals with their own interests and talents, and they are independent, so they expect to make decisions for themselves. This way of thinking about a university student contributes to the idea of the independent learner. Independent learning attempts to allow students some choice in *what* they will learn, *when* and *where* they learn and the *learning skills* and *strategies* they employ.

THINK ABOUT THIS

- Do you think of yourself as an independent adult?
- How does the concept of an independent adult affect your understanding of what a good student is?

What choices do we make as independent learners?

Now that we understand why university students are considered independent adults, we can examine what 'taking responsibility for your own learning' means by looking at the choices you must make.

What you study and why

Before you even start your university studies, you have to decide what course you want to study. This often involves selecting from a wide range of options. For example, you may decide that you want to study business. You may then find that you have to decide whether you want to study Business Administration or Business Accounting, or whether you want to combine two subject areas such as Business and Information Technology or Business and Psychology. Once you have made this choice, you will find that there are certain subjects that you must study, and others that you select from a list of options. You may also find that one or two subjects can be chosen from other fields altogether. It is your responsibility not only to select subjects but also to check that the subjects you select allow you to qualify for the degree that you wish to gain.

The wide range of courses available and the degree of subject choice within those courses reflect the ideal of the independent learner who tries to select courses that fit his or her individual interests and needs. However, it means that the process of choosing a course and selecting subjects may be quite difficult and so many universities have student advisers to help you choose appropriately. These advisers will not choose for you; their job is to help you decide what you want to do. In order to help you, they will expect that you can answer three questions:

- Why do you want to study this course?
- What type of job do you want when you graduate?
- What are your interests?

Because students are expected to choose both the course they study and the career that they eventually want to follow according to their interests and talents, advisers expect students to know what type of activities interest them, and to be able to link these interests to possible careers. So your answers to the three questions above will allow them to make suggestions about possible courses and subjects. If you have not thought carefully about these questions, your adviser will find it very difficult to help you. In fact, advisers usually see their job as clarifying the options available. Once the options are clear, then the student – as an adult individual – is able to make an informed and independent choice.

When and where you study

Taking responsibility for your own learning also involves developing the ability to organise your studies and manage your time. One of the major differences between school and university is that students are expected to take responsibility for attending class, completing assignments on time and so on. If you consistently fail to attend lectures or hand work in, your lecturers will not usually check up on you. However, you will be expected to accept the consequences – which may involve failing the subject.

Another aspect of time management involves arranging your assignments so that you do not have to complete several in one week. This may involve finishing some assignments before the due date. Furthermore, if you realise that you are unlikely to be able to complete an assignment on time, you are expected to ask for an extension before the submission date.

Again, the underlying expectation is that students are adults, and so they are able to behave rationally and logically. This means organising their time appropriately, looking ahead to identify possible problems (such as having several assignments due at the same time) and taking action to solve the problem (for example, completing some assignments ahead of time).

How you study

Perhaps the most significant aspect of independent learning involves the development of learning skills and strategies. These are seen as important because they allow each person to continue learning even in situations where no teacher is available. In today's world, where technological change is taking place at an ever-increasing pace, it is very likely that much of the knowledge that you learn in your course will be regarded as out-of-date in ten years' time. This means that it is not enough to learn a body of knowledge about a subject. You also need the skills and strategies that will allow you to update your knowledge throughout your life. In other words, you need to develop independent learning skills.

THINK ABOUT THIS

- As an independent adult, which of the following do you feel will likely be easy?
  - ☐ what you study
  - ☐ when and where you study
  - ☐ how you study
- Which are likely to give you some trouble?

What are independent learning skills?

Independent learning skills cover a number of different areas such as monitoring your own learning, organising your own learning and mastering specific skills. We will discuss each of these in turn.

Monitoring your own learning

You need to be able to monitor your own learning and identify areas in which you are weak. As an independent adult, most lecturers will expect you to be able to recognise your own weaknesses and to do something about them. Some of the areas in which you might be weak include:

- not understanding how to use library resources such as search engines and databases
- not being able to use common word processing and spreadsheet programs such as Word or Excel
- difficulty with basic statistics (especially if you are studying the social sciences or related disciples)
- problems with the demands of academic reading and writing
- difficulties with tutorial or seminar presentations, or with participating in discussions
- difficulties in understanding the content of the courses.

Once you have identified problem areas, you then need to be able to locate and use resources that can help you improve. As an independent adult learner, it is your responsibility to decide which resources, such as the following, might help you and then to use them:

- **The library:** Most university libraries offer a range of courses to help students use their resources effectively. These include library-focused courses teaching you how to use resources such as databases, and also more general courses on, for example, word processing skills.
- **The writing centre:** Most universities also have writing centres, often called academic literacy centres or independent learning centres, which offer courses in academic reading and writing, grammar, discussion skills and so on.
- **The mathematics unit or numeracy centre:** Again, most universities have units or courses that assist students who have problems with basic mathematics or statistics.
- **Student counsellors:** Student counsellors assist students with a wide range of personal and academic problems. While lecturers may refer a student to a counsellor, the general expectation is that you will realise that you need help and will go yourself.

However, not all resources are provided by the university. Many students organise informal study groups so that they can help each other with their problems. This is a very useful strategy, as long as it does not mean that you work on an assignment with other students and all hand in identical papers. We discuss plagiarism, a serious academic offense, in Chapter 14.

THINK ABOUT THIS

- What are your strengths in terms of learning skills?
- What are your weaknesses?
- Make a list of each, then use your university website to look for services that might help you improve in these areas.

Organising your own learning effectively

The second aspect of independent learning skills involves being able to organise your own learning effectively. This involves the following skills:

- **Identifying your learning style:** Do you learn best by listening to lectures and taking part in discussion, or by reading books and articles? Do you prefer to learn by actively experimenting or by thinking about what you observe? By knowing how you learn, you can use your time and focus your energy more effectively.

- **Setting your own learning aims:** Most university courses involve a large number of subjects, and each subject involves a huge range of skills and knowledge. You need to be able to decide which subjects and which areas to focus maximum attention on, and which require less attention. In making this decision, you need to first decide how important each subject or topic is for understanding the subjects or topics that you will study in the future. However, you also need to consider your own interests and goals. A subject that is vital to one person's career goals may be less important to another.

- **Deciding when to work alone, when to work in a group and when you need to seek help:** This involves being able to identify the demands of the assignment or task and your own strengths and weaknesses as they relate to the task.

- **Assessing your own progress in relation to your aims:** It is true that your lecturer will assess your progress by marking your assignments and examinations. However, you also need to constantly assess your own progress so that you can decide where to concentrate your efforts, and whether you need to ask for help.

Mastering specific skills

The third aspect of independent learning skills involves mastering the specific skills involved in analysis, critical thinking and problem-solving. Some of the most important of these involve the ability to:

- select sources of information that are reliable and appropriate for the task

- recognise that there are a number of different ways of reading texts and choose the one that is most appropriate to the text and the task

- compare different approaches to an issue, topic or problem and identify their strengths and weaknesses

- relate theory to practical problems and use appropriate theories to solve problems

- select the type of text to use in relation to its purpose and audience
- express your own voice and distinguish it from the voices of others.

We will find out more about these skills in the following chapters.

Evaluating your own needs

Finally, the concept of independent learning focuses on recognising yourself as a person who is able to make your own decisions and evaluate your own needs. By developing your ability to learn independently, you are preparing yourself for a life of ongoing learning in a world where knowledge is developing rapidly. This is one of the most important things that you can learn at university.

 **SUMMARY**

1. Most lecturers in English-speaking cultures expect students to be independent learners.

2. The concept of an independent learner is built on recognising two other learner characteristics:
   - learners as individuals
   - learners as independent adults.

3. As an individual, each learner has:
   - unique interests and talents. They learn best when they follow these interests and talents unique ways of learning, or learning styles. They learn best when they use their preferred learning style.

4. As independent adults, learners are expected to:
   - choose what they want to study in relation to their interests and talents
   - manage their learning effectively.

5. In order to manage their own learning, students need to:
   - identify areas where they are weak
   - use the library, the writing centre, student counsellors and other resources to improve their learning
   - manage their time effectively so that they fulfil the requirements of all their courses
   - use appropriate study methods.

 **SKILLS PRACTICE**

Task 1

How well do you know your university library?

- Can you use the library catalogue to find books on a particular subject?
- Do you know what a database is?
- Which databases are most relevant to your own areas of study?
- Do you know how to locate specific journal articles?
- Do you know how to get help in using the library?

If the answer to any of these questions is 'no', you should go to the information desk at your university library and ask about the training programs the library offers.

Task 2

Take a tour of your university library. Use the information that you learn on this tour to prepare a brief guide to the library that would be suitable for new students.

Task 3

Use the Internet to find out about the training classes for students offered by your university library. Select one training class and prepare an advertisement giving the following information to your fellow students:

- the aim of the training class
- the time and place it is held
- the reasons for enrolling in this class.

Task 4

Does your university have a Study Skills Centre, a Writing Centre or other means of assisting students with the demands of academic life?

- Where is the centre located?
- What type of courses does it offer?
- Are the courses for credit?
- Select one course and explain why this course would be useful to you.

Task 5

Does your university have a Numeracy Centre to assist students with mathematics and statistics?

- Where is the centre located?
- What type of courses does it offer?

- Are the courses for credit?
- Select one course and explain why this course would be useful to you.

Task 6

- What type of problems do you think a counsellor might help you with?
- Where are the counsellors located in your university?
- How do you make an appointment?
- Does your university have international advisors for students from overseas?
  - ☐ If so, what type of problems might they assist with?
  - ☐ Where are they located?

Task 7

What is your learning style? There are several different ways of analysing learning styles. One common method involves identifying the senses that you use in learning. Look at the four brief descriptions below. Which type of learner do you think you are? You may find that your learning style involves more than one sense. This means that you have a mixed learning style.

LEARNING STYLES

- **Visual learners** learn best when information is presented in tables, graphs, flow charts and other figures. They also find diagrams which use symbols to illustrate how different concepts relate to each other useful.
- **Oral/aural learners** learn best when information is presented through activities which involve listening and discussing. They find lectures, group discussions, tutorials and study circles of friends most useful.
- **Reading/writing oriented learners** learn best by using text books, journal articles, and other texts and from writing essays, reports and so on.
- **Kinaesthetic learners** learn best through hands-on experience and physical activity. They like using personal experience and examples.

Once you have identified your general learning style, go online and find a learning style questionnaire to check your response.

Hint: Some online questionnaires ask you to pay for the results. However, most questionnaires on university websites are free. You can identify a university web site by the *edu* in its URL.

Task 8

How might knowing your learning style help you study more effectively? Discuss with a partner.

Part 2
TAKING PART IN UNIVERSITY LEARNING

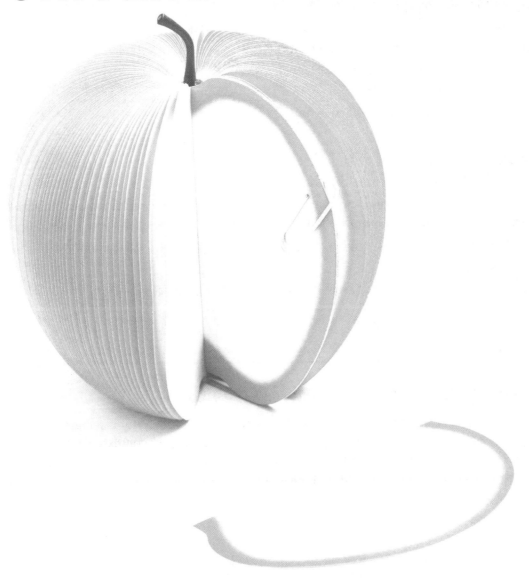

5 ACADEMIC LISTENING

★ LEARNING OBJECTIVES

When you have finished this chapter, you will be able to:

- explain the function of academic listening
- understand how academic listening and academic reading support each other
- use readings and PowerPoint presentations to support your listening
- understand how to be an active listener
- use handouts of PowerPoint slides to guide your note-taking
- understand how to take effective notes.

✓ WORD LIST

Do you understand the meaning of these words? Many have special meanings in the academic culture. You can check their meaning in the glossary at the back of the book.

- ☐ approach
- ☐ concept
- ☐ lecture
- ☐ PowerPoint presentation
- ☐ readings
- ☐ technical language

Listening, lectures and university study

One of the first activities that you are likely to encounter at university is lectures, so you probably already realise how important they are in the university context. However, they do not stand alone. They go hand in hand with other ways of teaching and learning which together make up a complete 'learning package'. This package includes:

- participating in lectures
- reading

- participating in tutorials, seminars and laboratory sessions (if you are a science student)
- completing written assignments individually or in groups.

You can think of these four ways of teaching and learning as four pillars on which your knowledge and understanding are built. If you take away any of them, the building, and your understanding, falls down.

THINK ABOUT THIS

- Why are lectures such an important part of university study?
- How do you find them: Useful? Interesting? Boring? A waste of time?
- What makes a good, or an interesting lecture?

What is the function of lectures?

You may remember that in Chapter 3 we saw that most lecturers see themselves as facilitators of student learning, and expect students to be independent and critical in their approach to learning. These expectations strongly influence the function that lectures play in the learning package. These functions include:

- providing an outline of the essential knowledge involved in the subject
- identifying the major approaches, theories and concepts involved in the subject
- exploring how these approaches, theories and concepts relate to daily life
- demonstrating how these approaches, theories and concepts are used to solve problems
- comparing and contrasting different approaches, theories and positions.

In general, most lecturers will attempt to provide an outline of the essential knowledge in the subject, and may also carry out one or more of the remaining functions, depending on the subject in question and the lecturer's preferences.

The important point to remember is that lectures do not present all the knowledge and understandings involved in a subject. Lectures go together with readings, either in the form of a textbook or involving required and recommended readings. These are usually articles from academic or professional journals or individual chapters from scholarly books. This is good news, as it means that you do not have to rely entirely on your listening abilities in order to understand the content of a subject. The knowledge that you gain from lectures supports the knowledge that you gain from reading, and conversely, the knowledge that you gain from reading makes lectures easier to understand.

Developing listening skills
Preparing for a lecture

Lack of familiarity with topics and concepts is probably the most important factor that makes listening to lectures difficult. Unfamiliar material is always more difficult to understand than familiar material, and if you don't prepare, the lecture material is likely to be unfamiliar. This means that you need to be proactive in your listening; you need to prepare.

There are two main resources that can help you prepare for lectures. The first is PowerPoint presentations. Most lecturers use PowerPoint presentations to outline their major points, and, depending on the lecturer, these are often available in advance. You can print them out and read through them before you go to the lecture, paying particular attention to definitions and technical language.

Technical language is language that has a special meaning in a particular subject. For example, Figure 5.1 shows a slide from a lecture in macroeconomics. You may already know the common meaning of the word 'commodity': something that is useful for a particular purpose. However, in macroeconomics, this meaning is expanded to include three different types of things, goods, services and assets. So on this slide there are four different technical terms, each of which is defined. By reading this slide and making sure that you understand the technical meaning of these four terms, you will be ready for them when they come up in the lecture. Consequently, your understanding of the lecture will be greatly improved.

The second resource that will help you get more out of lectures is the textbook or the readings that are set down for the subject. Most subjects that you study at university involve either a textbook or a number of recommended readings, usually one or two for each topic. (We will look more closely at recommended readings in Chapter 6.)

Try to read either the chapter or one of the readings that are set down for the topic of the lecture. As with the PowerPoint slides, take particular note of any definitions or technical

Commodities

There are three different types of commodity:

- **Goods:** physical objects which are produced and exchanged.
  Examples: food; clothing; machinery; coal.
- **Services:** activities. Unlike goods, activities do not have an ongoing existence.
  Examples: hairdressing; banking; tourism; hospitality.
- **Assets:** owned by people and constitute wealth.
  Examples: houses; factories; jewellery; money.

Figure 5.1 Example of a PowerPoint slide

language, but also note the main ideas, which, in the case of a textbook, are often summarised at the end of the chapter, as they are in this book. The more you know about the topic before you listen to the lecture, the more you will gain from the lecture itself.

Active listening

If you look back at the four pillars of the learning package, you will see that the first pillar is not 'listening to lectures' but 'participating in lectures'. You may think that attending a lecture is rather a passive activity, as there is usually very little opportunity to comment or ask questions, but this does not mean that you are a passive listener. Being an active listener is another key to getting the most out of lectures.

THINK ABOUT THIS

- What strategy will you use to take notes? Will you use your mobile phone, laptop, or other device, or will you use a notepad and paper?
- Look at some of the notes you have taken in the past. What note-taking strategy did you use, and how effective was it?

The most important aspect of active listening is selective note-taking. A selective note-taker does not write down everything that the lecturer says. This is a very bad strategy for two reasons. Firstly, you will inevitably miss some of the lecturer's points, as while you are trying to note down one point, the lecturer has already moved on to the next. More importantly, however, if you try to note down everything, you will not have the time to think about what the lecturer is saying, identifying the main ideas, considering how the information in this lecture relates to the information in the previous lectures and in your reading and so on.

As an active listener, you need to identify the main ideas that are being presented, and distinguish between these main ideas and the evidence, examples and so on that are used to support them. Your notes should focus on the main ideas, but if your lecturer is using slides, then part of your job is already done for you. This is because, as we have already noted, most lecturers use slides to summarise the main points of their lecture. If your lecturer makes the slides available before the lecture, you can print them out as a handout. (If you are not sure how to do this, consult the Help function on your word processing program or type 'PowerPoint handouts' into your search engine.)

Figure 5.2 shows an example of a PowerPoint handout. The slide is reproduced on the left of the page and a space is available for your notes on the right.

You can use the right-hand column to note the extra details that the lecturer presents; details that are not included on the slide. These might include examples, or consideration of how the point relates to everyday life, or how it might be used to solve problems. In other words, if PowerPoint handouts are available, they can to guide your note-taking, giving you time to think a little about the implications of what you are hearing.

If the slides are not available, do not despair! There are other ways of identifying the main ideas.

Commodities

There are three different types of commodity:

- **Goods:** physical objects which are produced and exchanged.
  Examples: food; clothing; machinery; coal.
- **Services:** activities. Unlike goods, activities do not have an ongoing existence.
  Examples: hairdressing; banking; tourism; hospitality.
- **Assets:** owned by people and constitute wealth.
  Examples: houses; factories; jewellery; money.

Figure 5.2 Example of a PowerPoint handout

Many lecturers indicate the main points that they intend to cover in the first 5 min of the lecture. This is a good reason to get to the lecture on time. Most lecturers also clearly indicate each new point in the lecture. They may do this using words:

- First ..., Second ..., Third ...
- Now I'm going to look at ...
- Let's turn to ...

However, they may just pause, or use a 'filler', such as 'OK', or 'Right', or even 'Um'. If the lecturer is using slides, each new point will usually be indicated by a new slide.

Main ideas also tend to get repeated, and some lecturers will slow down and speak very clearly to make sure that everyone understands and has time to note the point down. If you have done some preparatory reading, you should also be listening for the main ideas that you identified in that reading.

Active listening is not limited to identifying main ideas. You also need to be able to identify whether the lecturer is giving examples or considering how the information applies to daily life or is used to solve problems. He or she may also be trying to make the lecture more interesting by telling stories or anecdotes that are related to the main point of the lecture. These are often funny, but you don't need to write them down!

Active listening also involves mentally comparing the information in the lecture with information in previous lectures and with information in the readings. This is especially so when the lecturer is exploring different positions or approaches to an issue. In this case, it is quite possible that the positions being discussed in the lecture differ in some ways from the positions you read in the textbook or readings. Remember that academic knowledge involves debate and argument, and there are often several different approaches to an issue, each of which has strengths and weaknesses, none of which is absolutely correct or absolutely wrong.

Remember also to note down any references that the lecturer gives you so that you can look them up and read them.

Finally, as an active listener, you should be noting down things that you don't understand or are not sure of so that you can follow them up after the lecture.

After the lecture

After the lecture, you should go over your lecture notes again. Because these days most lectures are recorded and can be downloaded from the university website, you can do this while listening to the lecture again. As you do so, you can fill in any important details that you missed, and check up on things that you did not fully understand the first time. You may find it useful to listen together with a friend, so that you can compare your notes and help each other with difficult concepts.

Finally, you need to organise your notes logically, recording the title of the lecture and the date on which it was given and placing them, together with any handouts that you were given, into a folder. You will then have a valuable resource to use when you are preparing written assignments or revising for an exam.

THINK ABOUT THIS

Think about the way you listen to lectures.

- What might stop you from being an active listener?
- What might you change about your listening practice to become more active?

Other tips for developing your listening and note-taking

- Sit near the front of the lecture hall rather than at the back, and preferably in the middle, so that you can hear well.

- Don't panic if at first you find the lecturer's accent difficult to follow. This is a common problem in the first two or three weeks of a course, but most students adjust fairly quickly. The more you prepare for the lecture, so that you are familiar with the content, and the more you follow up by listening again to the recorded lecture, the more quickly this adjustment is likely to take place.

- Learn some common note-taking abbreviations so that your note-taking is efficient. Some common abbreviations are:

    c.f. = compare
    i.e. = that is
    e.g. = for example
    NB = note well
    no. = number
    etc. = et cetera, and so on.

- Symbols can also be used to make your note-taking more efficient:

    ∴ therefore
    = equals; is the same as
    ≠ does not equal; is not the same as
    > greater than
    < less than
    ↓ decrease
    ↑ increase.

SUMMARY

1. Lectures form one part of a 'learning package' that includes:
   - participating in lectures
   - reading
   - participating in tutorials, seminars and laboratory sessions (if you are a science student)
   - completing written assignments individually or in groups.

2. The function of lectures is to:
   - provide an outline of the essential knowledge involved in the subject
   - identify the major approaches, theories and concepts involved in the subject
   - explore how these approaches, theories and concepts relate to daily life
   - demonstrate how these approaches, theories and concepts are used to solve problems
   - compare and contrast different approaches, theories and positions.

3. Lectures do not present all the knowledge and understandings involved in a subject. They go together with reading textbooks, articles and other texts.

4. Lectures may be difficult to understand because the content is unfamiliar. This means students need to prepare.

5. Preparation for lectures may involve:
   - reading PowerPoint slides and identifying main ideas
   - identifying technical terms and checking their definition
   - reading recommended readings (chapters in textbooks, journal articles, etc.).

6. Active listening involves:
   - selective note-taking
   - distinguishing between main ideas and supporting evidence
   - comparing the ideas and concepts presented by the lecturer with those in the readings
   - using PowerPoint handouts to guide note-taking
   - recognising the ways in which lecturers indicate the main ideas of a lecture, and the change from one idea to the next
   - noting down references
   - noting down points that are not clear for future follow-up.

7. After the lecture you should go over your notes, identifying missing information and locating that information by listening again to the lecture, reading or talking with friends.

8. Learn common note-taking symbols to make your note-taking more efficient.

 **SKILLS PRACTICE**

There are many sources of authentic academic lectures on the internet. Some of the most useful are:

- Many universities make their courses available free on-line. Lectures usually consist of both audio and video material which can be downloaded from YouTube or iTunes U. This is an excellent source of authentic lectures in a very wide range of fields

  Some of the universities that do this are:

  The Massachusetts Institute of Technology: http://ocw.mit.edu/courses

  Stanford University: http://itunes.stanford.edu/

  Harvard University: http://online-learning.harvard.edu/

- Many universities in Australia and internationally offer MOOCs (Massive Open On-line Courses). These are courses of study that individuals can follow without charge, although if you want credit for a subject, a fee is usually charged. MOOCs offer lectures on a very wide range of subjects. A list of Australian MOOCS and other free on-line courses is available from: https://www.mooc-list.com/countrys/australia?static=true

- YouTube has a wide range of audio and audiovisual academic and professional lectures: http://youtube.com/education?b=400

Task 1

Select an academic lecture in your area of interest from one of the sites above, making sure that it has accompanying PowerPoint slides.

a. Read the slides.

- What is the topic of the lecture?
- What are the main points that the lecturer makes?
- Identify the key technical terms that he or she uses?

b. Use a good dictionary to check the meaning of:

- the technical terms
- any other words or phrases that you do not understand

c. Listen to the lecture and take notes, using the PowerPoint slides as a guide.

d. Compare your notes with a partner and identify areas where you have missed important information. Listen to the lecture again and complete your notes.

Task 2

Select an academic lecture in your area of interest from one of the sites above.

a. Listen to the first five minutes of the lecture.

- What is the topic of this lecture?
- What are the main points that it will deal with?

b. Make a list of 1–2 questions related to each of the points that the lecture will discuss.

c. Listen to the lecture.

- Are your questions answered?

Task 3

Select an academic lecture in your area of interest from one of the sites above.

a. Listen to the lecture.

- What is the topic of the lecture?

- What are the main points that the lecturer makes?

- Identify the technical terms used in the lecture and note their definitions.

6 ACADEMIC READING

LEARNING OBJECTIVES

When you have finished this chapter, you will be able to:

- explain the function of academic reading
- identify the most common types of academic text
- understand the function of databases
- identify the different purposes of academic reading
- relate reading purpose to reading strategy
- understand what is involved in both summarising and paraphrasing
- understand how to read critically and effectively.

✓ WORD LIST

Do you know the definitions these words? Many have special meanings in academic culture. You can check their meaning in the glossary at the back of the book.

- ☐ collection
- ☐ edited collection
- ☐ field
- ☐ hypothesis
- ☐ key words
- ☐ logical connectors
- ☐ position
- ☐ recommended reading
- ☐ supplement
- ☐ textbook
- ☐ validity

Why read?

Many new students ask why they are expected to read so much in their university courses. 'Isn't it enough,' they ask, 'just to read a textbook?' To understand why a textbook is not enough, we need to ask questions about the purpose of reading at university. The first question is: Why read? There are several answers to this question.

If you have read the preceding chapters, you will understand that we develop academic knowledge through debate. Scholars take part in this debate by writing journal articles, research reports, books and so on. One of the aims of university study is to give you the skills and knowledge to join the debate yourself, so when you read academic writing, you are taking the first step in this direction. Textbooks can give you a basic understanding of the major issues in a particular field, but they cannot give in-depth coverage of specific topics. They also cannot tell you about the most recent developments, which are usually found in journal articles. Most importantly, however, they do not provide you with the opportunity to join in the world of academic debate. You can compare reading a textbook to reading a short account of a football game in a newspaper a week after the game. On the other hand, reading a journal article is like being in the stands watching the game. If you want to continue this metaphor, then writing an essay or report is like playing a game in the junior competition!

Another reason for reading is, as you already know, that lecturers do not aim to give you complete information about a topic. Instead, they want to give you a general map of the area being studied, and they expect that you will deepen your understanding through extra reading. This expectation is based on the belief that you are an independent learner who can make decisions about what you need to learn. It also recognises that it is not possible to cover topics in depth in the few hours that are spent in lectures each week.

Ways of reading

Having discussed why we should read, we can now examine two important ways of undertaking academic reading. They are:

- reading to understand the main concepts, ideas and so on in the field
- reading to understand a specific topic in depth.

Reading to understand the field: textbooks and recommended readings

Reading to understand the main concepts in a field is the type of reading you do before and after lectures. Most subjects nominate a textbook or required readings, which all students are expected to read because they support and develop the information given in lectures. You may also find that the lecturer has listed a number of supplementary readings, which are often called recommended readings. Supplementary readings may present a different view of the field from the main text, or they may provide an in-depth view of a particular aspect of the topic. In Text 8 the convenor of one first-year subject in business studies at an Australian university discusses the recommended reading for the course. Notice that the course *textbook* is an American publication, and so the first book on the *recommended reading* list gives an Australian view of the same field. The other two references are to specific chapters rather than whole books, and each deals with an important aspect of management: planning and human resources. Again, students are given both American and Australian perspectives on these topics.

So by reading the textbook (or the required readings if your course does not nominate a textbook), you should gain a broad and basic knowledge of what the subject is about. You can supplement this by reading the recommended texts to develop your understanding in specific areas.

TEXT 8: BUSINESS ORGANISATION PRINCIPLES

The text for this unit is:

- Jones, G., George, J., & Hill, C. (2000). *Contemporary Management*, 2nd ed. McGraw-Hill: New York.

Recommended Reading:

- McKenna, R. (1999). *New Management*. McGraw-Hill: Sydney.
- Rue, L. W., & Byars, L.L. (1997). *Management: Skills and Applications*, McGraw-Hill: Chicago. Chapter 8 'Operations Management and Planning'.
- Bartol, K., Martin, D., Tein, M., & Matthews, G. (1997). *Management: A Pacific Rim focus*, 2nd ed. McGraw-Hill: Sydney. Chapter 11 'Human resource management'.

The McKenna text is highly recommended, as it takes a contemporary approach to managing and is Australian in authorship and content. Rue and Byars gives an American perspective, and while Bartol et al. is similar it presents an Australian slant on the American perspective.

Department of Business. (2005). BBA102 Business Organisation Principles. Macquarie University, Sydney. Retrieved from http://www.bus.mq.edu.au/units/bba102/index.htm

---

THINK ABOUT THIS

Choose one of the subjects that you are studying.
(You may need to read the next section before you answer this question.)

- Is a core reading specified for the subject? Is the core text a textbook?
- Is the core text supplemented by other readings?
- How do the supplementary readings relate to the core text?

Reading on a specific topic: books, articles and reports

While the textbook and recommended readings will usually give you a good overview of the subject, they will not give a deep enough understanding for you to write an essay or report. In order to write an assignment, you need to include other types of text. Some of the most common are described below.

Textbooks

Textbooks are written by academics for a student audience. They outline the main ideas relating to the subject you are studying. While you do not necessarily have to read the whole of the textbook, if you do so, you should have a very good grasp of the main ideas relating to the subject.

Specialised academic books

Specialised academic books are written for an academic or professional audience and deal with technical or academic topics.

You don't usually have to read the whole of an academic book. Instead, use the chapter headings to select chapters that are relevant to your assignment and read them. You may also read the introduction, because that gives you an overview of the whole book and helps to put the chapters that you read in context.

Edited collections

An edited collection is a book that deals with a specific topic, but each chapter is written by a different person. If you are using an edited collection, you should select the chapter or chapters that are relevant to your assignment and read them. As with specialised academic texts, you do not need to read the whole book.

Journal articles

A journal contains articles on specialised academic topics written for academic or professional audiences. Most journals are published quarterly, and because they are published so frequently, the articles they contain are usually the most up-to-date sources available. In order to find journal articles that are relevant to a specific topic, you need to use one or more databases. You can read more about databases in the section below.

Research reports

Research reports describe how and why a piece of research was done, and discuss the results and their significance. Most research reports are published in journals, and you find them by using databases in the same way as you find journal articles.

Annual reports

If you are studying accounting, business or economics, you may have to consult the annual reports of listed companies or other business-related information. An annual report is a record of the financial condition of a publicly listed company. It is written to inform shareholders about the financial performance of the company. Annual reports are usually located on a company's website, but may be more easily accessed using a business database.

Official reports

In the later years of your academic study, you may be expected to consult reports put out by official bodies, including government departments and international organisations such as the World Health Organisation (WHO), the Organisation of Economic Co-operation and Development (OECD) and the World Bank. Other sources of official reports are non-government organisations (NGOs) such as the Red Cross and Oxfam. Official reports usu-ally collect data, analyse problems and present solutions. As with annual reports, official reports can usually be accessed via the organisation's website or by using a database.

THINK ABOUT THIS

- Select one of the subjects you are studying. What type of texts do you have to read for that subject?

What are databases?

Every year, thousands of academic journals are published in English alone. Most of these journals are printed four times a year and each contains many articles. How can you find articles that are relevant to your area of interest? The answer is that you use databases. Databases are online indexes that list journal articles, conference papers, book chapters and so on in a particular discipline. For example, if you want to find articles on a particular topic in computing science, you could use a database such as Inspec. Inspec lists journal articles, books, conference papers and so on in the fields of computers and computing and information technology as well as in other engineering-related disciplines. In economics, you might use Econlit, while if you are an accounting student you may need to use Datastream Advance, a database that provides stock market and company data as well as listing articles and reports on international finance and economics.

Once you have decided which database (or databases) you want to consult, you enter keywords regarding your specific topic. You will get a list of articles, reports and so on that relate to your keywords. Many databases also give a short abstract or summary of the content of the article so that you can decide if it is relevant to your needs. If you are access-ing the database through your university library, you should have free access to the full text of the article as well. Otherwise, you may be able to locate the article that you want through Google Scholar, but this is more common in science than in other disciplines.

TEXT 9: EXCERPT FROM ECONLIT SEARCH USING KEY WORDS 'MOTIVATION THEORY'

Why Motivation Theory Doesn't Work, By Fitzgerald, Thomas H.; Harvard Business Review, July–Aug. 1971, v. 49, iss4, pp 37–44

Linked Full Text

Motivation Theory and Job Design; By Gallagher, William E., Einhorn, Hillel J.; Journal of Business, July 1976. v. 49, iss. 3, pp. 358–73

Linked Full Text Check Library Holdings Check Library Holdings

Motivation Theory Revisited: A Theoretical Framework for Peripheral Tasks; By Killmer, Annette B. C.; Ramus, Catherine A.; Rivista di Politica Economica, Jan–Feb, 2004, v. 94, iss. 1–2, pp 101–132

Check Library Holdings

Text 9 presents three of the articles that were found by a search of the Econlit database for the keywords 'motivation theory'. You can get a copy of the first article online. The second article is available online and may also be in the university library. The third article may be available in the university library in hard copy, but is not available electronically.

When you conduct a search of a database, the keywords that you enter are extremely important. If they are not appropriate, you may not find the resources that you want. Training in how to use databases appropriately is beyond the scope of this book. However, almost all university libraries offer training in this field both online and in person. As an independent learner, you should make sure that you find out about the training available at your university and complete the relevant courses. This is especially important in the later years of your undergraduate degree and essential if you are a postgraduate student.

THINK ABOUT THIS

■ Which database or databases do you think will be most useful to you in your studies?

Summarising and paraphrasing

Of course, reading and note-taking are very closely linked. Two words tightly linked to note-taking are summarising and paraphrasing. Though they are widely used words, not everyone knows what they mean. Summarising involves identifying the main ideas in a text and expressing them in your own words. This means that you need to pay particular attention to the topic sentence of each paragraph. You can combine different ideas in a single sentence, but it is important not to include any of your own ideas or judgments, or to include information not present in the text you are summarising. You need to continually remind the reader that you are summarising the ideas of someone else: 'the author says ...', 'the text states ...', and you need to cite your source. (If you're not sure how to do this, read Chapter 12.)

When you paraphrase, however, you are trying to note the all the thoughts of the author, not just the main ideas, Of course, you still have to be careful that you don't include ideas and judgements of your own, but a paraphrase is very likely to be longer than a summary. But, just as you do with a summary, when paraphrasing you need to remind the reader that the ideas are those of someone else, and you need to cite your source(s).

Summarising and paraphrasing are note-taking strategies, they are not assignment writing strategies. In the latter, you are expected to express an opinion (you will read more about this below). Summarising and paraphrasing focus on what the writer of the article said, rather than on what you think of what he or she said.

What is effective reading?

Many students complain that they have too much reading to do, and not enough time to do it. As one student said:

> It takes me a long time to read each article because I'm afraid that I will miss some important points. I waste a lot of time because I read things carefully and sometimes they are not very useful.

This student is wasting time because she does not understand that there are different ways to read a text. How you read depends on why you are reading and what you want to find out. A good reader is flexible and uses different ways of reading at different times.

The 4-S system of academic reading

One of the most useful ways of approaching academic reading is the 4-S system.[1] This system helps you to decide which texts you should spend time reading closely, and which you should leave aside. It also allows you to use reading strategies that are related to your reading purpose. It involves a four-stage process of Searching, Skimming, Selecting and Studying. These stages are briefly outlined below.

Searching

Searching allows you to identify the purpose and audience of a text, what it is about, and the order in which information is presented.

- Use the title, the description of the book given on the back cover, the Table of Contents or the abstract (if you are reading an article) to identify the purpose and audience of the text. For example, is the text aimed at an academic or a popular audience? Is it a textbook or a journal article? The five tests that we will discuss later in Chapter 11 will help you here.

---

[1] The 4-S Strategy is presented in Boddington, P. and Clanchy, J. (1999), *Reading for study and research*. Australia, Addison Wesley Longman.

- Also use the title, the back cover description and the Table of Contents or abstract to give you a general idea of what the text is about.
- Use the headings and subheadings to identify the major aspects of the topic that the text covers.
- Use any tables, graphs, diagrams or other figures to get more information about what the text covers.

After you have searched a text in this way, you need to decide whether it is suitable for your needs. This means that you need to have a clear idea of why you are reading the text. You need to ask yourself, for example, 'Is this a reliable academic text?' and 'Is the information in it relevant to my assignment?' Some texts will be suitable, but you must not be afraid to decide that some are not useful and to stop reading them.

Skimming

Skimming allows you to identify the main points that the writer is making, and the type of evidence that is being used.

- Use the introduction and the conclusion to identify the position being presented, the hypothesis being tested or the problem being examined.
- Use the topic sentences to identify the way the argument develops, the main points that are being made and the type of evidence being presented.

After you have skimmed the text, you should have a very clear idea of the main ideas being discussed in the text, so you will find it easier to understand when you read it carefully. You may also decide that the text is not relevant to your specific purpose and stop reading.

Selecting

The first two stages of the reading process help you to identify the main ideas of the text and allow you to reject texts that are not relevant for your purpose. Now you need to select the texts or the parts of texts that you will read intensively. You do this by analysing your assignment topic and deciding which texts or parts of texts give you the information that you need.

Studying

You can now read your selected text carefully and efficiently. Efficient reading in this stage means that you know what you are looking for. For example, you may want to:

- get an overview of the topic
- find specific information about the topic
- identify what different writers have said about the topic
- identify how these different positions relate to each other
- identify the strengths and weaknesses of each position.

When you know what you are looking for, you are more likely to understand the content of the article and be able to relate it to other writing in the field.

However, effective reading involves more than identifying the topic the writer is discussing or the facts that he or she is presenting. You also need to pay attention to the way facts and concepts relate to each other and to the judgements the writer makes. By paying special attention to these three aspects of the text, you will greatly improve your reading. Focus on:

- key content words and phrases
- the words and phrases indicating the logical relationship between concepts
- the evaluative words and phrases that indicate the author's judgement about the concepts being discussed.

Using the 4-S system

Let's examine how the 4-S system works by reading a short passage from Young Yun Kim's discussion of how people adapt to living in a new and unfamiliar culture, which is presented in Text 10.

TEXT 10: ADAPTING TO A NEW CULTURE

Young Yun Kim

Stress, adaptation and growth

Individuals move to another country for varied reasons, under differing circumstances, and with differing levels of commitment to the host society. Most immigrants plan the move as permanent in the sense that they now expect the host society to be the primary setting for their life activities. For many short-term sojourners, <u>on the other hand</u>, contacts with new cultures are mostly peripheral, requiring less overall engagement. Foreign students, <u>for example</u>, can limit their adaption to the bare minimum required to fulfil their role as students and can confine their informal social contact to fellow students from their home country.

<u>Despite</u> such differences in the degree of adaptive demands, most people in a foreign land begin life in the host society as **strangers** (Gudykunst & Kim, 2003). Many of their previously held beliefs, and routine behaviors are no longer relevant or appropriate. Faced with things that do not follow their unconscious 'cultural script', strangers must cope with high levels of uncertainty and anxiety (Gudykunst, 1995). They are challenged to learn at least some new ways of thinking, feeling and acting – an activity commonly called **acculturation** (Berry, 1990; Padilla, 1980; …). <u>At the same time</u>, they go through a process of **deculturation** (Bar-Yosef, 1968), of unlearning some of their previously acquired cultural habits, <u>at least to the extent</u> that new responses are adopted in situations that previously would have evoked old ones.

The experience of acculturation and deculturation <u>inevitably</u> produces **stress** (Kim, 1995) in the form of temporary discomfort or even 'breakdown' in extreme circumstances. Stress is particularly acute during the initial phase of relocation, <u>when</u> strangers face severe difficulties, amply documented in studies of 'culture shock' and related issues (Adler, 1987; Furnham, 1988). Internally, strangers are undergoing a struggle between the desire to retain their original identity and the desire to forge a new identity more in harmony with the changed environment (Ford & Lerner, 1992). Strangers often cope with this conflict through various 'defense mechanisms' <u>such as</u> selective attention, denial, hostility and withdrawal (Lazarus, 1986).

<u>Yet</u> the stress strangers experience also assists the **adaptation**. In time, most strangers manage to achieve a new level of learning that helps them to meet the demands of the host environment and work out new ways of handling their daily activities. Strangers <u>gradually</u> modify their cognitive, affective and behavioural habits and acquire increasing proficiency in expressing themselves, and understanding new cultural practices. The interplay between stress and adaptation <u>gradually</u> leads to an internal *growth* – a transformation which increases their ability to fit in to the new society both socially and psychologically.

Stress then is necessary for a stranger's adaptation and growth over time. Together, the three elements – stress, adaptation, and growth – help define the nature of strangers' psychological development, increasing their chance of success in meeting the demands of the host environment. As shown in Figure 6.1, the stress-adaptation-growth dynamic plays out <u>not</u> in a smooth arrow-like linear progression, <u>but</u> in a cyclic and continual pattern similar to the movement of a wheel. Each stressful experience <u>results</u> in a 'draw-back' (temporary disengagement) which then activates adaptive energy to help strangers reorganise themselves and 'leap forward' (temporary engagement). This internal process reflects a dialectic relationship between new cultural learning (acculturation) and unlearning of old cultural habits (deculturation). As strangers work through difficulties, they develop an ability to see others, themselves, and situations in a new light and to face new challenges. Failure to work through this process results in prolonged feelings of inadequacy and frustration.

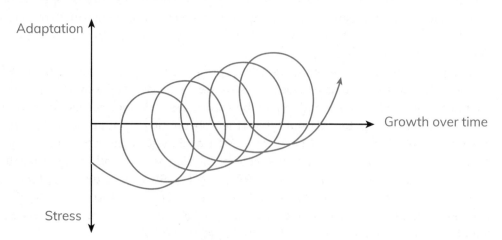

Figure 6.1 Stress adaptation-growth dynamics of adaptive transformation. (Source: Kim, 1988, p. 56)

Young Yun Kim. (1997). Adapting to a new culture, In L. Samovar & R. Porter. Intercultural communication: A reader. (Eds.). Belmont: Wadsworth, pp. 405–406.

Searching the text

As we saw in the previous section, searching involves looking at aspects of the text such as the title of a book and the information on its back cover, the title of an article, the headings and subheadings it uses and any graphs and tables, all of which allow you to get a general idea of what the article is about.

The passage in Text 10 is taken from:

> Samovar, L., & Porter, R. (1997). Intercultural communication: A reader. (Eds.).
> Belmont: Wadsworth. pp. 405–406.

The description of the book on the back cover states,

> In this Eighth Edition, 42 readings ... introduce the practice and the underlying theories of intercultural communication.

This book is a textbook, aimed at introducing the major issues in intercultural communication to an academic audience of students. It also tells us that the book is a collection of 42 readings, each written by a different academic author or authors. In other words, it is an edited collection and passes the fives tests that establish it as a reliable academic text.

The chapter we are interested in is 'Adapting to a new culture', by Young Yun Kim. The chapter heading indicates the specific aspect of intercultural communication that is addressed – the ways that people adapt to a new culture. The passage starts with a subheading that introduces three concepts which are likely to be key concepts – stress, adaptation and growth. We can guess that stress, adaptation and growth are involved in the process of adapting to a new culture. This impression is strengthened by the figure, which you can see towards the end of the passage. It indicates a close relationship between stress and adaptation, with growth, shown on the X-axis, occurring over time.

Skimming the text

Skimming involves using the introduction and the topic sentences of each paragraph to identify the main ideas that the writer is developing.

At the end of the introduction to her chapter (not reproduced in Text 10), the writer presents her position, specifying exactly what she will be talking about.

> This essay presents a brief account of [the experiences of people who move into an unfamiliar culture] in confronting the difficult task of adapting to a new cultural and communication system (p. 404).

The topic sentences (or the first sentences) of each paragraph give you a good idea of the main points that the writer makes and the order in which they are discussed. (If you want more information on topic sentences, read Chapter 17.)

Here are the topic sentences from our passage:

1. Individuals move to another country for varied reasons, under differing circumstances, and with differing levels of commitment to the host society.

2. Despite such differences in the degree of adaptive demands, most people in a foreign land begin life in the host society as *strangers* (Gudykunst & Kim, 2003).

3. The experience of acculturation and deculturation inevitably produces *stress* (Kim, 1995) in the form of temporary discomfort or even 'breakdown' in extreme circumstances.

4. Yet the stress strangers experience also assists the *adaptation*.

5. Stress then is necessary for a stranger's adaptation and growth over time.

You can see that the concepts presented in the subheading – *stress, adaptation and growth* – all occur in the topic sentences, which indicates that these are key concepts. You might also notice the use of the word *strangers* in topic sentences 2, 4 and 5, and that topic sentence 5 links these four concepts together:

Stress then is necessary for a stranger's adaptation and growth over time.

As you can see, the topic sentences give a good general idea of the major point or points that the writer is making.

Selecting the text

The selected passage is Text 10.

Studying the text

Studying the text involves careful reading, paying particular attention to the key words, to the logical connectors between sentences and clauses, and to words that indicate the writer's judgment.

Because this passage is taken from a textbook, the key words are printed in bold type.

- strangers
- acculturation
- deculturation
- stress
- adaptation.

We have already noted that three of these key words are presented in the subheading. Subheadings often pick up the key words in a text. However, notice that key words that the author thinks the reader will not understand are defined. Here is an example:

[People] are challenged to <u>learn at least some new ways of thinking, feeling and acting</u>—an activity commonly called **acculturation**.

… they go through a process of **deculturation** (Bar-Yosef, 1968), <u>of unlearning some of their previously acquired cultural habits</u>

Words that the author believes readers will understand are not defined.

Having identified the main concepts being discussed, you need to see how these concepts relate to each other. This involves paying close attention to words or phrases that indicate logical connections. In our passage, these are underlined:

on the other hand	for example	despite
at the same time	when	such as
yet	not ... but	results

If we take the first as an example, you can see that the author is contrasting people who move to a new culture meaning to stay for the rest of their lives with people who move for a short time.

> Most immigrants plan the move as permanent in the sense that they now ex- pect the host society to be the primary setting for their life activities. For many short-term sojourners, <u>on the other hand</u>, contacts with new cultures are mostly peripheral, requiring less overall engagement.

Many students who are new to the university environment ignore the logical connectors in the texts they are reading, and as a result (note my logical connector!) they misunderstand the points the writer is making.

As well as paying particular attention to the logical connectors in a text, you also need to notice the words that indicate the writer's judgement. We will consider this in more detail in Chapter 13. However, in this passage, notice the way the writer uses the words and phrases that are double-underlined:

at least to the extent   inevitably   gradually

[Strangers] go through a process of **deculturation** (Bar-Yosef, 1968), of unlearning some of their previously acquired cultural habits, <u>at least to the extent</u> that new responses are adopted in situations that previously would have evoked old ones.

Notice how the writer claims that newcomers to a culture (strangers) unlearn their original culture, which is a very strong claim, and one that most people would disagree with. She therefore modifies the claim, using the phrase 'at least to the extent', to indicate that the unlearning only occurs in some situations and involves responding to a situation in a way appropriate to the new culture rather than the original one.

Recognising the judgements a writer makes is as important as recognising the logical connections between concepts and facts, and both are essential to the process of critical reading, to which we turn next.

THINK ABOUT THIS

- How do you read?
- Are there any differences between the way you read and the 4-S System described here?
- What advantages can you see for the 4-S System?

What is critical reading?

In Chapter 3, we heard from a lecturer who said:

> I don't want students who just write down everything I say, then give it back to me in exams. I want them to look at things critically, to argue. I want them to develop other ways of looking at things.

To begin developing your critical ability, you need to start with reading. Academic reading carried out to write an essay is not a passive activity. It is not just underlining important points or making notes. You need to do this early on, when you are summarising and paraphrasing articles and taking notes rather than when you are preparing an assignment. Academic reading in order to write an assignment is an active process that involves evaluating what you read.

Some students say, 'But I'm just a student. I don't know enough to criticise all these important scholars.' Wrong attitude! Remember what we have been saying about academic knowledge developing through debate and discussion? Also remember that most lecturers believe that people learn by doing; so you learn to be critical by practising being critical.

Reading critically is largely a process of asking questions. The sorts of questions that you need to ask are:

- What position is the writer presenting?
- What evidence is the writer giving to support his or her position?
- Is the evidence presented accurately?
- Has the evidence been collected using appropriate methods?
- Is the writer basing his or her position on a particular theory or approach?
- Are the writer's claims reasonable?
- How does the writer's position compare with the positions of other writers in the field?
- Do I agree with the position the writer is presenting? Why or why not?

We can examine how to ask some of these questions by doing some critical analysis ourselves, as well as by seeing how others have done it. To do this, we will look at the writings of Bjorn Lomborg, author of *The Skeptical Environmentalist* (2001), *Cool It* (2007), *Smart Solution to Climate Change: Comparing Costs and Benefits* (2010) and other works. In these writings, Lomborg initially claimed that environmentalists were exaggerating the extent of the world's environmental crisis, and more recently that the cost of moving to a carbon-free environment would outweigh the benefits of capping greenhouse emissions. (Clearly, Lomborg does not live in Tuvalu or Kiribati!)

Text 11 is one reader's critical analysis of some of Lomborg's claims. You can see some of the questions that this reader asked himself in order to critically analyse the argument. And from these questions, and his answers, you can see that Lowe read very actively. Not only did he ask questions, but he also compared Lomborg's claims with the findings of other authorities. He identified weaknesses in Lomborg's method of analysis and pointed out that Lomborg's approach was economic rather than environmental.

To be a critical reader, you need to start with a critical attitude, as Lowe's analysis demonstrates. You can't accept something just because it is written in a book. You also can't accept it because it is written by someone well known or knowledgeable. Before you can accept or reject an academic claim, you need to evaluate it through careful questioning and comparison.

TEXT 11: ONE READER'S CRITICAL ANALYSIS OF LOMBORG'S CLAIMS

Bjorn Lomborg is neither sceptical nor an environmentalist

By Ian Lowe – posted Wednesday, 8 October 2003

Danish statistician Bjorn Lomborg has written a controversial book called *The Skeptical Environmentalist*. In fact, Lomborg is neither sceptical nor an environmentalist. A better title might have been *The Gullible Economist*.

Q: Does the writer base himself on a particular approach?
A: Yes. Lomborg takes an economic approach.

In fairness, the book has some good points. It correctly points out that some environmentalists are either selective in their use of evidence or not rigorous in their thinking. If Lomborg had applied the rigorous thinking he advocates, he would have extended that criticism to some industrialists, many economists and most politicians – but he didn't. He is very selective in his scepticism. For example, he analyses the limits of global climate models, but accepts uncritically the much shakier claims of economic models.

Q: Does the writer use evidence appropriately?
A: No, he is selective. He criticises climate models, but not economic models.

In some cases, Lomborg is just wrong. He claims that the 1972 Club of Rome report *Limits to Growth* predicted we would run out of resources. It actually said that limits to growth would be reached within a hundred years if all of the trends of increasing population, agricultural output and production of waste were to continue, before showing that it is possible to re-direct development onto a sustainable path. Lomborg claims that the UN climate projections are 'worst case' scenarios, when the scientific panel said its estimates could be wrong in either direction.

Q: Does the writer summarise sources accurately?
A: No. He mis-quotes sources.

Lomborg lists the broad litany of environmental problems: 'forests are shrinking, water tables are falling, soils are eroding, wetlands are disappearing, fisheries are collapsing, rangelands are deteriorating, rivers are running dry, temperatures are rising, coral reefs are dying, and plant and animal species are disappearing'. He then claims to have refuted them. In fact, almost all of those statements are true for Australia. Most of them are also true globally. The CSIRO's *Australian State of the Environment 2001 Report* (2001) noted some good signs before stating that the environment 'has improved very little since 1996, and in some critical aspects has worsened', blaming the compounding pressures of growing population and increasing material demands per person.

Q: Do other authorities agree with Lomborg?
A: No. For example, reports by the CSIRO and the UN disagree.

The UN report *Global Environmental Outlook 3* (2002) found 'indisputable evidence of continuing and widespread environmental degradation'. It said policy measures have not been able to counter the pressures of unsustainable consumption levels in rich countries and increasing numbers of desperately poor people in the developing world. It specifically noted problems of water stress, species extinction, depletion of fish stocks, land degradation, forest loss, urban air pollution in developing countries and increasing greenhouse gas emissions.

Q: Does Lomborg understand the evidence he presents?
A: No. He does not understand how serious the extinction rate is.

Lomborg also argues that we are not losing biodiversity because the lowest of the credible estimates for species extinction is only 1500 times the planet's long-run average. Biologists like Lord Robert May, President of the Royal Society, say that figure is typical of major extinction events.

Q: Is the writer's position reasonable?
A: No. It relies on a discredited theory.

The fundamental belief driving Lomborg's argument is that 'it is imperative that we focus primarily on the economy' – the environmental equivalent of the discredited trickle-down model of economic development. It suggests our environmental problems will be solved if we get rich enough. Lomborg claims that wealthier countries are more likely to have clean environments. The actual data reveal that some nations with a GDP below $1000 per head have better environmental quality than others with over $20 000 per head. So there isn't a simple link between wealth and a cleaner environment.

Q: Is the writer's position reasonable?
A: No. He draws inappropriate conclusions from data.

Lowe, I. (2003). *Bjorn Lomborg is neither sceptical nor an environmentalist. Online opinion.* Retrieved from http://www.onlineopinion.com.au/view.asp?article=773.

THINK ABOUT THIS

- Before you read something, do you identify several questions you want the author to answer in the article, book or post?
- If you do, do you find doing so helps you understand the author's points more quickly?
- If you do not already do so, choose an article or chapter that is specified in one of your subjects and identify several questions before you read it.
- Did you find the procedure useful? Why or why not?

SUMMARY

1. Reading is important in academic life because:
   - Academic discussion takes place through articles, research reports and books. By reading these, you find out what the debates are about.
   - Reading prepares you to take part in academic discussion through your own essays and reports.
   - Students need to read widely because lectures only outline issues. Lecturers expect that students will deepen their understanding through reading.
2. Using textbooks and recommended readings:
   - Textbooks present basic information in the field, but do not consider issues in depth and may not include recent debate.
   - Recommended readings provide alternative views of an issue, or treat issues in greater depth.
3. Different types of text:
   - Specialised academic books are written for an academic or professional audience and deal with technical or academic topics.
   - Edited collections are books that deal with a specific topic, but each chapter is written by a different person(s).
   - Journal articles are published in journals that appear regularly, usually one every 3 months.
   - Research reports describe a piece of research and discuss its significance. They usually appear in journals.
   - Annual reports are records of the financial condition of a publicly listed company.
   - Official reports are produced by bodies such as governments or international organisations. They analyse problems, collect data and suggest solutions.
4. Databases are online indexes that list journal articles, conference papers, book chapters and so on in a particular discipline. They are usually accessed through university libraries and allow you to find articles on a specific issue.

5. The 4-S system of academic reading helps you to read more efficiently. It involves four stages:
   - searching
   - skimming
   - selecting
   - studying.

6. Critical reading involves evaluating what you read by asking questions and seeking answers as you read.

 SKILLS PRACTICE

Task 1

Text 12 is a critical analysis of Lomborg's claims regrading biodiversity.

- What questions do you think the writer, Thomas Lovejoy, asked?
- What criticisms does he make?

 TEXT 12: BIODIVERSITY: DISMISSING SCIENTIFIC PROCESS

The chapter on forests also suffers from superficial research and selective use of numbers. Lomborg starts by displaying Food and Agriculture Organization (FAO) data from 1948 to 2000. However, in the early years, the FAO reported 'official data' given by governments. Such data are notoriously uneven in quality and frequently overestimate forest stocks. Subsequently, the FAO adopted different definitions and methods to estimate forest stocks. Because of these differences, any statistician should know they cannot be used for a valid time series.

Lomborg's discussion of the great fire in Indonesia in 1997 is still another instance of misleading readers with selective information. Yes, the WWF (World Wide Fund for Nature) first estimated the amount of forest burned at two million hectares, and Indonesia countered with official estimates of 165 000 to 219 000 hectares. But Lomborg fails to mention that the latter were not in the least credible and that in 1999 the Indonesian government and donor agencies, including the World Bank, signed off on a report that the real number was 4.6 million hectares. ...

The central question of the book – Are things getting better? – is an important one. The reality is that significant progress has been made in reducing acid rain, although much still needs to be done. And major efforts are under way to stem deforestation and to address the tsunami of extinction. But it is crucial to remember that whereas deforestation and acid rain are theoretically reversible (although there may be a threshold past which remedy is impossible), extinction is not. A dispassionate analysis, which Lomborg pretends to offer, of how far we have come and how far we have yet to go would have been a great contribution. Instead we see a pattern of denial.

The pattern is evident in the selective quoting. In trying to show that it is impossible to establish the extinction rate, he states: 'Colinvaux admits in *Scientific American* that the rate is "incalculable,"' when Paul A. Colinvaux's text, published in May 1989, is: 'As human beings lay waste to massive tracts of vegetation, an incalculable and unprecedented number of species are rapidly becoming extinct.' Why not show that Colinvaux thought the number is large? Biased language, such as 'admits' in this instance, permeates the book.

In addition to errors of bias, the text is rife with careless mistakes. Time and again I sought to track references from the text to the footnotes to the bibliography to find but a mirage in the desert.

Far worse, Lomborg seems quite ignorant of how environmental science proceeds: researchers identify a potential problem, scientific examination tests the various hypotheses, understanding of the problem often becomes more complex, researchers suggest remedial policies – and then the situation improves. By choosing to highlight the initial step and skip to the outcome, he implies incorrectly that all environmentalists do is exaggerate. The point is that things improve because of the efforts of environmentalists to flag a particular problem, investigate it and suggest policies to remedy it. Sadly, the author seems not to reciprocate the respect biologists have for statisticians.

Lovejoy, T. (2002). Biodiversity: Dismissing scientific process. Scientific American, 286(1), 69.

Task 2

Imagine that you have been asked to write a report on the following topic:

What is intercultural communication? In what ways do differing concepts of management impact on the conduct of business internationally?

Text 13 is the reading list for this report.

1. Use the reading list to answer the following questions:
   - Which of the publications on the reading list are books?
   - Which are edited collections?
   - Which are journal articles?
2. Which of the readings in Text 13 would you expect to include:
   - a general overview of the important issues in intercultural communication
   - information about common difficulties in intercultural communication
   - a discussion of the management styles most common in East Asia
   - a discussion of the problems faced by Western managers in China
   - a discussion of different approaches to the training of managers in effective intercultural communication.

3. Arrange the titles in the order in which you would read them. Be ready to explain why.

4. Are there any publications on the list which you probably wouldn't read for the report? Why or why not?

TEXT 13

Gudykunst, W., & Kim. Y.Y. (Eds.). (1992). *Readings on Communicating with Strangers.* New York: McGraw-Hill.

Hodgetts, R., Luthans, F., & Doh, J. (2005). *International Management Culture, Strategy And Behavior* (6th ed.). Boston: McGraw-Hill.

Barna, L. A. (1997). Stumbling Blocks in Intercultural Communication. In L. Samovar & R. Porter, R. (Eds.). *Intercultural Communication: A Reader* (8th ed.). Belmont: Wadsworth Publishing.

Bjorkman, I., & Schaap, A. (1994). Outsiders in the Middle Kingdom: Expatriate managers in Chinese-Western joint ventures. *European Journal of Management, 12*(2), 147–153.

Faure, G. (2000). Negotiations to Set up Joint Ventures in China. *International Negotiation, 5*(1).

Harris, H & Kumra, S. (2000). International Manager Development: Cross-Cultural Training in Highly Diverse Environments, *Journal of Management Development, 19*(7).

Chen, G. M., & Chung, J. (1994). The 'Five Asian Dragons': Management Behaviours and Organisational Communication'. *Communication Quarterly.* Spring 1994, 93–105.

Task 3

Text 14 is an abbreviated table of contents from an edited collection on intercultural communication. (If you are not sure of what an edited collection is, re-read this chapter.)

■ Which chapters would you read for the report from Task 2? Why?

TEXT 14

PART 1: Intercultural communication: Theories and approaches

1. Understanding intercultural communication, *Richard Duckmanton*

2. Communicating in a multilingual setting, *William Stevens and Catherine Stevens*

3. Identity and intercultural communication, *David Nation*

4. Language and social life: An introduction, *Robert Bottomly*

5. Understanding behaviour in a globalised world, *Thomas Lang.*

PART 2: Influences on intercultural communication

6. Cultural influences on communication, *Alexandra Geddes*

7. Individualism and collectivism in social life, *Bradley Eades*

8. Cultural dimensions of educational practice, *Karen Simpson*

9. Cultural differences in framing: A comparison of Australian and Korean management practice, *Kim Kyung-min*

10. Listen to what I'm not saying: Indirection and direction in negotiations, *Muhammad Al Shammery*

11. Confucian influences on business practice in China, Japan and Korea, *Jin Baoli*

12. Nonverbal behavior: The role of gesture in inter-cultural communication, *Amjad Hussein*

PART 3: Intercultural interaction

13. Organisational behaviours in four cultures: China, Germany, Saudi Arabia and the United States, *George Milner and Margaret Murray*

14. By indirections find directions out: Negotiating styles in China, Japan and Australia, *Alison Grey*

15. Diversity is strength: Developing an effective intercultural working environment, *Phillip Johnson*

16. Intercultural interaction in the classroom, *Tony Large*

17. Negotiating intercultural understanding in the health care system, *Lyn Robertson*

18. Study abroad: Exchange students' expectations of the sojourner experience, *Lisa Accosi*

19. Personal space in intercultural interactions, *Deepa Mehta*.

PART 4: Developing effective communication in a globalised world

20. Diversity is strength: Developing a culturally diverse workplace, *Jeremy Long and Susan Childs*

21. Effective intercultural pedagogy, *Li Jianguo*

22. Learning language/Learning culture, *David Long*

23. Culture shock: Adjusting to an unfamiliar environment, *Tomoko Watanabe*

24. A theory of intercultural adaptation, *Barbara Levy and Jan-Louis Leroux*

25. Developing intercultural communication competence, *Barry Schmidt*

26. Developing effective communication skills through role-play, *Lisa Miller*.

Task 4

Select a journal article or a chapter in an edited collection. Read it using the 4-S strategy. After you have read it, discuss the strategy with a partner.

- Did you find the 4-S strategy useful? Would you recommend it to a friend? Why or why not

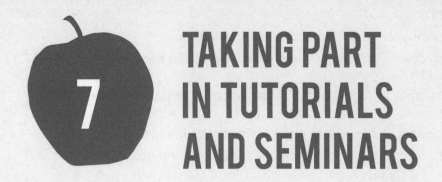

TAKING PART IN TUTORIALS AND SEMINARS

7

LEARNING OBJECTIVES

When you have finished this chapter, you will be able to:

- identify the types of tutorials found in different disciplines
- understand the difference between seminars and tutorials
- understand the general aim of tutorials
- understand the specific aims of different types of tutorials
- understand the ways in which tutorials assist in the development of critical and analytical skills
- understand how spoken presentations differ from written essays and reports.

✓ WORD LIST

Do you know the meaning of these words? Many have special meanings in academic culture. You can check their meaning in the glossary at the back of the book.

- [ ] analytical
- [ ] deductive
- [ ] discussion
- [ ] position
- [ ] presentation
- [ ] seminar
- [ ] tutorial

What happens in tutorials and seminars?

Many students find that taking part in tutorials and seminars is one of the most difficult and confusing things they have to do at university. They find it difficult because they don't like speaking in front of other people. They find it confusing because, as one student said, 'I'm a student. The lecturer knows much more than me, so why do I have to give the paper? Isn't that the lecturer's job?'

So, why are tutorials and seminars so important in university study? And how can you participate in them successfully?

THINK ABOUT THIS

'I'm a student. The lecturer knows much more than me, so why do I have to give the paper? Isn't that the lecturer's job?'

- Do you agree with this student?
- Why or why not?

What do students do in tutorials?

Before we discuss the purpose of tutorials, it is important to understand that what you do in tutorials depends on the subject you are studying. You may have to:

- make a presentation on a specific topic, then answer questions and discuss the topic with other students
- work through a series of problems with the help of a tutor
- take part in practical sessions in a laboratory or workshop.

While the form of tutorials varies with the subject, the overall purpose of all tutorials is similar.

What is the difference between a tutorial and a seminar?

Seminars are similar to the first type of tutorial on the list above; that is, students have to give a presentation on a specific topic followed by questions and discussion. The main difference is that papers given in seminars are usually more complex and treat a subject in greater depth than papers given in tutorials. Most undergraduates only take part in seminars if they are studying at the Honours level, usually in fourth year. If you are a postgraduate student, however, participation in seminars is likely to be common.

As the purpose of seminars and tutorials is very similar, we will refer to tutorials, but most of what we say refers equally to both.

THINK ABOUT THIS

- Does your university refer to tutorials, seminars or both?
- If both terms are used, what is the difference between them?

What is the purpose of a tutorial?

Tutorials allow you to practise applying the knowledge and skills that you have been learning. In Chapter 3, we talked about students as apprentices. Apprentices learn knowledge from books and from other people, but they also have to show that they can use the knowledge they learn. We can put this another way by saying that apprentices learn by doing. They are not expected to be able to do something perfectly the first time; instead, they are given many opportunities to practise so that they gradually get better. Tutorials provide these opportunities for students. However, different types of tutorial provide different types of practice. We will examine each type in turn.

What is a presentation tutorial?

This type of tutorial occurs most often in the social sciences and the humanities; that is, in subjects such as education, sociology, economics, history and so on. The major aims are to allow time to explore a topic in depth and to give you practice in academic debate. As we have seen, debate and discussion are the most important ways in which knowledge is developed. Tutorials of this kind may involve one student presenting a paper on a specific question or topic, followed by questions and discussion involving everyone in the tutorial. Alternatively, they may involve a group discussion of questions or issues set by the lecturer. You need to prepare for this type of tutorial by reading the chapters or articles nominated by the lecturer. If you don't do so, you will not be able to contribute to the discussion, and you will probably find that tutorials are very boring. If you do the reading first, however, you are far more likely to enjoy the experience and develop your ability to discuss issues critically.

Presentations share many of the features of essays and reports, and in fact when you write up your presentation, it is usually in the form of an essay or a report. Table 7.1 indicates some of the common features.

When you are the presenter, you are developing your critical and analytical skills in two ways. Firstly, your presentation will usually involve arguing a position or analysing a problem and/or suggesting solutions. Tutorial presentations, like essays and reports, allow you to study a specific topic or question in depth, comparing and evaluating what different scholars have said about the topic, and developing a voice of your own.

Asking questions and taking part in discussions

In the questioning and discussion that follow a presentation, you may be asked to clarify or to expand on your points. You may also be asked to comment on a different position, or to consider something that you had not previously thought about. This is the second way in which you are developing your skills. Some students worry about this aspect of the tutorial because, as one student said, 'What happens if I can't answer the question? Everyone will think I'm stupid!'

The first thing to remember is that you are the expert on this particular topic. You know more than anyone else in the tutorial, except perhaps for the tutor. You have done the read-

Table 7.1 Common features of essays/reports and tutorial presentations

Feature	Essay/report	Presentation
Presents and defends a position or analyses a problem and/or presents and evaluates solutions	✓	✓
Analytical rather than descriptive	✓	✓
Uses deductive rather than inductive organization	✓	✓
Writer's voice is dominant voice	✓	✓
Writer's voice states the position; voices of other scholars support the position	✓	✓
Writer's voice evaluates the positions of other writers and identifies strengths and weaknesses	✓	✓

ing and developed a position, so it is likely that you will be able to answer most of the questions that are asked. Secondly, if someone asks you a question that you don't think you can answer, this is not a disaster! Indicate that you are unsure how to answer the question and that you will investigate it further.

It is acceptable for both lecturers and students to say that they are not sure about something. This is because knowledge is expanding very rapidly, and it is not possible to keep up with all new developments. In addition, people specialise in specific areas, and while they may know a great deal about their own area, they may not be so well informed in related areas. In other words, while it is important to understand a subject well, it is just as important to be able to recognise areas where you know less.

However, it is not enough just to say that you do not know how to answer a particular question. You must know how to find out! This means that you should know which resources are likely to help you, and how to locate those resources. This usually involves finding books in the library and using databases to locate relevant articles, but it may also involve asking your lecturer or tutor for guidance or suggestions. Remember that they expect you to be an independent learner – they will usually be happy to suggest books and articles to read, but they will expect you to develop your own answer.

If you prepare for questions and discussion in the same way as you prepare your presentation, you will probably find it easier to cope. One strategy is to take the initiative and ask questions yourself. Make a list of two or three questions to ask the group. For example, indicate an area where scholars disagree and ask what others think about it. In some subjects, especially in fields such as education and psychology, you can ask about the implications of the topic for peoples' work.

Contributing to a tutorial

While the presentation is important, the questions and discussion that follow are just as important, because they allow everyone in the tutorial to develop their critical and analytical skills. Many students find this difficult because they are afraid that others will laugh at them. These students often believe that they should only make a comment if they have something really valuable to say. Wrong attitude! You don't have to show that you are already a master of analysis and you don't have to put forward a carefully thought out position. You do have to develop your critical and analytical skills, and this involves practice. You learn to be a critical thinker by practising being a critical thinker; that is, by making comments and asking questions.

If you listen to other students in the tutorial, you will find that their questions and comments are not usually especially clever, but these students know that they develop their skills and understanding more effectively by being active than by being passive.

What is the difference between speaking and writing?[1]

THINK ABOUT THIS

- Is spoken academic language the same as written academic language?
- How do you think they differ?

Check your answer by reading the next section.

While presentations share many features with essays and reports, they are not the same – because essays and reports are written texts, and presentations are spoken. Spoken and written language are rather different, so when you are making a presentation, you cannot just read your paper aloud. You have to change your language.

Text 15 presents two versions of a text on the causes of the water shortage in the world today. (You can read the full essay in Chapter 13.) One version is written, the other a spoken version as it might have been presented at a tutorial. Which version uses spoken language and which is the written text? How can you tell?

---

[1] This discussion draws on Hood, S., Solomon, N., & Burns, A. (1996). *Focus on reading* (New ed.). Sydney: National Centre for English Language Teaching and Research.

TEXT 15

VERSION A

Overuse of water resources is a major problem all over the world. The crisis is particularly acute in relation to groundwater reserves which lie deep under the surface in aquifers. One-third of the world's population depends on these aquifers, which have taken thousands of years to develop. Because the reserves of water they hold are large, they have been used without any thought of the future. Payal Sampat states that worldwide, people use about 200 billion cubic metres more water than can be replaced. In other words, the world's water capital is being steadily used up.

VERSION B

People use too much water all over the world, but the real problem is groundwater. Groundwater is under-ground water which is stored in aquifers and they are usually very deep down under the surface. About a third of the people in the world use water from aquifers, but they take thousands of years to develop. Because there is a lot of water in aquifers, humans have been using it without thinking about the future. Payal Sampat says that around the world, we use 200 billion cubic metres more water than we can replace, which means that we are steadily using up our water reserves and we will run out.

You are right if you identified version A as the written text. What are the differences between the two?

Verbs

Version A has fewer verbs than Version B. In fact, Version A, the written text, has 10, while Version B has 15.

Speech tends to use more action-oriented verbs than writing does, while writing tends to use more nouns or groups of nouns. For example, in the first sentence, the spoken form is *people* use *too much water*, while the written form is *overuse of water resources*. Notice how the verb has completely disappeared in the written form. Instead we have a phrase containing three nouns 'overuse', 'water' and 'resources'. (Note that 'water' is functioning as an adjective.)

This means that instead of using a verb to talk about an action, written texts tend to use a noun or a nominal group. You can see this in the example we examined above: *people* use *too much water*. The written version becomes *overuse of water resources*.

Pronouns

Version A of Text 29 uses fewer personal pronouns than Version B. For example, Version A states:

Payal Sampat (cited in Brown, 2001) states that worldwide, people use about 200 billion cubic metres more water than can be replaced. In other words, the world's water capital is being steadily used up.

Version B, on the other hand, says:

Payal Sampat says that around the world, we use 200 billion cubic metres more water than we can replace, which means that we are steadily using up our water reserves and we will run out.

Context

Another important difference between speech and writing is that spoken language can easily refer to the context where it is being used. For example, you can say *Look at this* and point to a figure in your PowerPoint presentation. However, when you are writing, you have to spell out exactly what you want your readers to look at, so you write *Table 2 shows ...*

Audience

Speakers and listeners are close to each other, so they can check that they understand and show that they are following by using body language, while readers and writers are distant, meaning that writing needs to be more precise. It needs to spell things out.

Why can't I just read out my written text?

These differences explain why you should not read your presentation aloud. When you read written academic language aloud it is difficult to understand because it uses written ways of expressing things. Give your presentation from notes using spoken language.

Some students who do not speak English as their native language worry that they will make too many grammar mistakes if they do not read their paper aloud. If you are in this situation, remember that everyone finds written academic English difficult to understand when it is read aloud. You may make more mistakes by speaking from notes, but more people will understand you!

Table 7.2 sets out some of the main differences between written and spoken language.

Table 7.2 Differences between speech and writing

Speech	Writing
Generally uses verbs to talk about actions	Often uses nouns to talk about actions: i.e. actions are often represented by nouns or nominal groups
Uses more pronouns	Uses fewer pronouns
Generally more dependent on context	Generally less dependent on context
Speaker and listener close	Speaker and listener distant

Using slides to support your presentation

 THINK ABOUT THIS

- Why use slides in your presentation?
- What makes a good slide?

Most presentations involve using slides to support your argument. Using slides and other visual aids can be very helpful in communicating your ideas to your audience, but they can also be damaging if you do not think carefully about them. You need to consider what the purpose of each slide is, and how their design will assist in getting your point across.

The purpose of your slides is to *support* the argument that you are making, not to make the argument for you. Therefore you should include only your major points and use bullet points so that they are clear and easy to understand. Whatever you do, don't try and put the entire content of your talk on your slides – your audience is likely to find this very boring! Make your bullet points brief (about 5–7 words per point) and limit each slide to 6 or 7 bullet points at most. You want your audience to listen to you, and not be distracted by slides that are difficult to read, so use plain fonts in conservative colours, with a good contrast between the writing and the background. Be careful not to go overboard with fancy transitions and animations.

Slides need to be professional. Many students have lost marks because of careless spelling mistakes, dot points that are difficult to read and graphics that do not support the points you are making. To avoid falling into this trap, make sure that you begin preparing well ahead of time. That way, you will have plenty of opportunities to improve before the big day.

Making group presentations

A very common form of presentation at university is the group presentation. The aim of a group presentation is to give you practice working as a team, which is a highly valued life skill, both at university and beyond. While preparing your presentation with other students can be a lot more fun than preparing an individual presentation, working as a part of a team brings with it new responsibilities. Of course, any presentation requires planning, careful preparation and a good presentation structure. Working as a group means you also need to manage each person's contribution and maintain good group relations. (See Chapter 8 for more information on working in groups.)

Good communication among all group members is key to a successful group presentation. From the outset, make a commitment as to how you will communicate (text, email, Facebook group and so on) and also make a commitment as to how quickly each of you will respond to group messages. Coming to a mutual understanding early on can save a lot of problems later. Early in your planning phase, work out your presentation structure and then allocate roles to each speaker. Preferably each speaker's section should be approximately equal and it is usually best if each speaker speaks only once. When each group member has prepared their section, allow yourselves enough time to rehearse as a group, checking presentation structure, timing and smooth transitions between sections.

When you are happy that you have a clear, well-structured and professional presentation, check the location of the presentation. Think about how you want the room to be set up, where in the room you will stand when you present and where other group members will be located when not presenting. Check the technology in the room and make sure that your slide file is readable. It's a good idea to bring a backup copy of your slides in PDF format just in case your slide file is unreadable on the day.

In making your presentation, keep in mind that audiences will be more engaged and interested if you speak with enthusiasm, making frequent eye contact with them. It is usually okay to use brief, tidy notes to prompt you but don't just read from your report. This is boring for the audience and makes it look as if you under-prepared and under-rehearsed. The first speaker should clearly state the aim of the presentation and introduce the other group members. Make an effort to hand over from one speaker to the next and remember that it shows good consideration of your audience if each speaker clearly states what they will be talking about at the beginning of their section. Wrap up the presentation with a clear conclusion.

THINK ABOUT THIS

- Have you participated in a group presentation?
- Did you find the experience useful? Why or why not?
- If you did not find it useful, how might you improve the process next time so that it is more useful?

What is a problem-solving tutorial?

Problem-solving tutorials are common in subjects in the pure and applied sciences, and in disciplines such as accounting, economics and business studies. The aim of this type of tutorial is to explore how the theory that you have learned in your lectures can be applied in practical situations. The types of problems that you may be expected to solve vary widely, depending on the subject, but all will demand analysis and critical thinking. For example, in some subjects you may work with mathematical formulae, but the problems you work with will usually involve more than the straightforward application of formulae. You will need to decide both which method to apply and how to apply it.

Other subjects may call for the development of computer programs or the use of mathematics to decide where a road should be built or what the loads on a bridge should be. In the social sciences and in disciplines such as business studies or nursing, you may have to identify real situations and explore how the theories that you have been studying apply to a particular situation.

What about laboratory and workshop tutorials?

Tutorials in laboratories or workshops are common in the pure and applied sciences. Their aim is to train you in the practical business of designing and carrying out experiments, setting up equipment, and recording and discussing results. While they form a very important part of many subjects, a discussion of successful laboratory practice is beyond the scope of this book.

 SUMMARY

1. Tutorials and seminars in different disciplines involve different types of tasks. They may involve:
   - a presentation on a topic, followed by questions and discussion
   - a group discussion of an issue
   - working through a set of problems with the assistance of a tutor
   - practical sessions in a laboratory or workshop.
2. All tutorials seek to develop students' critical and analytical skills and to provide opportunities to practise them.
3. Tutorial presentations often involve presenting and defending a position or analysing a problem and/or evaluating solutions, followed by questions and discussion.
   - Presenters are not expected to be able to answer all questions.
   - Listeners are expected to participate through asking questions and contributing to discussion.
   - Because speech differs from writing, presenters should not read their paper, but should speak from notes.

4. Problem-solving tutorials involve applying theory to practical situations.
  - Students develop analytical skills by deciding which theories, concepts or formulae can be applied to a particular problem.
5. Laboratory and workshop tutorials develop the ability to design and carry out experiments and to record and discuss results.

 SKILLS PRACTICE

Task 1

Read the essay on the water crisis in Chapter 13. Imagine that this paper has just been presented in a tutorial.

- Work with a partner to develop four questions to ask the writer of the paper.
- After you have identified the questions, ask and answer them with your partner.

Task 2

- Working in pairs, make a list of characteristics of a good tutorial participant.
- Interview a lecturer or tutor at your university and ask them to identify the five characteristics they look for in tutorial participants
- Compare your list with the qualities identified by the lecturer or tutor.

Task 3

Many books and web sites on study skills and English for Academic Purposes (EAP) give suggestions on how to improve your tutorial participation. Working in pairs, select at least five of these resources and use them to prepare and present a tutorial. Your presentation should include two sections:

1. Preparing the presentation
  - Carrying out research
  - Organising your ideas
  - Identifying your position
  - Writing your paper
  - Developing presentation notes
2. Giving the presentation
  - Using appropriate language
  - Using visual aids
  - Body language
  - Dealing with questions
  - Promoting discussion

Task 4

Choose one of the following and write a set of notes to use in a presentation:

- Text 40, the sample essay in Chapter 13
- Text 87, the sample report in Chapter 20
- Text 96, the research report in Chapter 21.

8 DOING GROUP ASSIGNMENTS

LEARNING OBJECTIVES

When you have finished reading this chapter, you will be able to:

- explain why group work is widely used in universities
- understand how to organise group work effectively
- understand the most common problems that arise in groups
- develop a range of strategies to cope with these problems.

WORD LIST

Do you know the meaning of these words? Many have special meanings in academic culture. You can check their meaning in the glossary at the back of the book.

- ☐ minutes
- ☐ process
- ☐ product
- ☐ timeline

Why have group work?

In recent years, many subjects have introduced group work as an important means of assessing students. In this chapter, we will look at why group work is used and at how to participate in a group project effectively.

Many students complain bitterly about group work. They say it is much easier just to do the work themselves, and that usually one or two people do all the work for the group. Others point out that if one person doesn't pull his or her weight, it can result in a reduced mark for everyone. It is true that getting several busy people together for meetings can take a lot of time and effort. It is also true that some people don't work well in groups for a number of reasons, only one of which is laziness. So why work in groups?

THINK ABOUT THIS

- What is your own experience of group work?
- Has it been a positive or a negative experience?
- What aspect of group work influenced your answer?

The development of team skills

The first reason is that much of the work in modern companies involves teamwork rather than individual work. So group work during your studies helps develop many of the skills that you are likely to need in your future employment.

To work effectively in a team, you need to be flexible and able to negotiate and compromise. You also have to work with people from different backgrounds and with different expectations and experience. This means that you need to be able to resolve disagreements and to handle criticism. You need to experiment with ways of coping with lazy people, with quiet people, with people who don't want to compromise, and with people who believe that they know better than everyone else. Group work also tests your organisational skills, as teams need to set deadlines and ensure that everyone meets them. Tasks and responsibilities need to be allocated and the work of different team members coordinated.

An effective learning tool

The second reason is that, as the saying goes, two heads are better than one. In other words, working in groups allows you to help others and to receive help in areas where you need it. When you have to explain something to another student, or when another student explains something for you, it is usually easier to understand. In fact, there is a lot of evidence suggesting that learning is more effective when it involves people working together. Because every person has different strengths and weaknesses, group work allows everyone to use their strengths to help others while receiving assistance in the areas in which they are weak.

Getting large jobs done

Finally, group work allows you to work on projects that would be too large for an individual to carry out by themselves. It allows you to develop specialised skill areas and to relate different specialisations together in a meaningful whole. This type of cooperation is common in the world of work, and many employers seek graduates who can demonstrate experience with such teamwork.

How do I work effectively in a group?

The process of group work is as important as the product. Your lecturers will expect you to develop and display good group-working skills even if they don't say this explicitly. They know that you may encounter problems, but they expect you, or rather everyone in the group, to find ways of solving these problems, or at least coping with them.

Groups don't work well by accident: you have to put effort into making them work. Below are a number of suggestions that can help establish a successful and productive group.

Get to know everyone

At the first group meeting, you need to get to know each other. Of course, you may know each other already, but often lecturers like to mix people up and create groups containing students from different backgrounds and with different interests. This is useful because it opens up new ways of looking at things and encourages new ways of working together. In fact, it is often better to work with people you don't know because if a conflict arises it can be handled without the personal relationship suffering. Friendships have been damaged or destroyed by the pressures of group work.

Even more importantly, one of the most common problems that teams encounter in the world of work is the problem of incompatible team members. It is highly likely that in your future work you will sometimes find yourself having to work with someone you find difficult. If you have experience in working together with people you don't know, even with people you don't particularly like, you will have developed some of the skills necessary to cope with this situation.

In order to minimise the possibility of conflict, however, it is important that all group members feel comfortable from the beginning, so make sure that everybody knows everyone's name and that you all have each other's contact details. Remember to exchange social media or email addresses, which are often used more frequently than telephones. It's a good idea to make sure that you have at least two ways of contacting each group member, in case one method doesn't work. Make sure that no one is left out of the discussion. You may need to make extra effort to involve people who are naturally quiet, or who do not have English as their first language. You may find that your group includes only one man or one woman, or someone who has a job that requires unusual hours, and you will need to consider how to include them fully. It may be useful to meet informally at least once, in the cafeteria or the local coffee shop, for example. Be careful about meeting in a pub, as Muslim students and many young women from socially conservative backgrounds would find this difficult, if not impossible.

THINK ABOUT THIS

- Have you experienced feeling left out in a group situation?
- What did you do?
- If your answer is 'nothing', what might you try in the future?

Analyse the task

Once you have gotten to know each other a little bit, you need to analyse the assignment so that all agree on what needs to be done. You then need to divide the task up, so that each person in the team has responsibility for part of the task. It is important to make sure

Table 8.1 Example of a timeline for group work

Week	Task	Person(s) responsible
Week 1	Meet group members Analyse task Allocate individual responsibilities Establish time frame Establish time and place of meetings	Whole group: Harada, Kim, Hamid, Carmen
Week 2	Present main ideas from readings Discuss readings Draft survey	Carmen Whole group Kim
Week 3	Finalise survey Carry out survey	Kim Whole group
Week 4	Carry out survey Analyse results	Whole group Hamid
Week 5	Discuss results Identify conclusions	Whole group
Week 6	Write first draft of report Discuss first draft with group Write, edit and proof final draft	Harada Whole group Harada

that the work is divided fairly so that everyone has approximately the same amount of work to do. As you allocate tasks, try to take people's abilities and previous experience into consideration.

After allocating tasks, you need to work out a timeline that shows each task, the date by which it must be completed and the person or people who are responsible for doing it. Table 8.1 presents a simple example of such a timeline. You also need to decide when you are going to meet and where. You may find that at some points in the project you meet once a week, but that at other times you need to meet more frequently.

Create a group agreement

Once your group has allocated tasks, you may want to set up a group agreement. A group agreement asks all members to verify that they agree to the responsibilities and the tasks assigned to them. Table 8.2 shows one way you could set out your group agreement. As part of the agreement, decide what action will be taken to support any member who falls behind in meeting their commitments. One solution may be to negotiate a new deadline for the task's completion. Or, you may agree to let the group know you are delayed, and negotiate to swap tasks with another group member.

Table 8.2 Example of a group agreement

Group project title: Group Report Project		
Members	**Contact details**	
Harada	Harada@emailaddress	
Kim	kim@emailaddress	
Hamid	hamid@emailaddress	
Carmen	carmen@emailaddress	
Person	**Agreed task**	**Timing**
Carmen	Present main findings from readings	Week 2
Kim	Draft survey	Week 2
	Finalise survey	Week 3
Hamid	Analyse survey results	Week 4
Harada	Write first draft of report Write, edit and proof final draft	Week 6
Whole group	Analyse task Allocate individual responsibilities Establish time frame Establish time and place of meetings	Week 1
	Discuss readings	Week 2
	Carry out survey	Week 3
	Carry out survey	Week 4
	Discuss results Identify conclusions	Week 5
	Discuss first draft before final draft is written	Week 6
I agree to complete the above tasks by the agreed times. If I fall behind in completing my individual tasks, I will let the group know and negotiate a new time. If I choose to swap my agreed task with another member, I agree to discuss it with the whole group first.		
Group member name:	Signature	

Allocate roles

You may find that your group operates more effectively if you allocate roles for your regular group meetings, including chairperson, timekeeper and task manager. These roles can be rotated during the project so that, for example, a different person chairs each meeting. The chairperson's job is to keep the discussion focused and to make sure that everyone's voice is heard. He or she should also try to prevent the group getting stuck on one point or being dominated by one voice. The timekeeper is responsible for keeping the meeting moving forward so that all business is covered. He or she may also time members' contributions to prevent one person dominating. The task manager makes sure that everyone is keeping up with their task between meetings. If someone is having difficulties with their part of the project, the task manager should identify this and call on other group members for help. Finally, some groups also appoint a secretary to record any decisions that the group makes.

Keep records

Take minutes of your meetings, recording all decisions. Minutes are notes recording who attended the meeting, what is said, who said it, and what decisions were made as a result. You can use minutes to make sure that everyone knows what they have to do and when. It is a good idea to have all group members agree that the minutes are correct soon after each meeting. If the group then starts experiencing problems, you have an objective record of group decisions.

Contribute fully

Your group will only function well if everyone contributes by fulfilling their commitments. Firstly, this means that everyone completes their section of the project well and on time. If someone in the team does not cooperate, try to find out what the problem is. He or she may be struggling with personal difficulties. See how you can help them complete their task without just doing it yourself. One of the hidden aspects of group work is learning to cope with difficulties such as non-performing members of the team. Contributing fully also means taking part in discussions. If you find this aspect of group work difficult, read Chapter 7 on tutorials and seminars for some suggestions.

Remember that at the conclusion of the project, the group should meet to review the process, discuss any issues that were experienced, and celebrate their achievement in completing their project!

THINK ABOUT THIS

- Use the procedures described here to organize your next group work task.
- Once you have completed the task, evaluate the process. Do you think it improved the functioning of the group? If so, how?
- If not, why do you think it failed?

How do I cope with difficulties?

The main difficulties that are likely to arise in group work are:

- coping with team members who do not complete their share of the project
- coping with a dominant team member
- coping with silent team members
- writing up the final report.

Coping with non-cooperative team members

Try to find out why the team member is unable to complete his or her section of the project. It may be that they need assistance from other team members. They may also, as has already been mentioned, be facing a difficult personal situation. Whatever the problem, it is preferable to help the person complete their task rather than have other team members complete it for them.

It is never appropriate to complain to the lecturer or tutor about an uncooperative team member. One of the reasons for assigning group work is to provide opportunities for students to develop group-working skills, therefore most lecturers do not react favourably to complaints about individual team members. In other words, most lecturers regard the need to cope with difficulties as part of the assignment. If you are having problems, talk to a student advisor or study skills tutor.

Coping with dominant team members

Some groups may find that one or two group members dominate the group, especially during discussion. This needs to be addressed directly in order to give everyone a chance to participate equally. The chairperson or other group members should point out that everyone needs to be heard, and ask quieter members for their ideas. It is also possible to politely indicate to the dominating person that he or she is taking more than their fair share of time.

Coping with silent team members

Give silent team members the chance to speak by asking them for their ideas. Leave a space after each person's contribution so that quieter team members have time to indicate that they have something to say. Pay attention to everyone as they speak and acknowledge the contributions of others, even if you disagree with it. You might say, for example: 'That's very interesting, but have you thought about X?'

Writing up the final report

In many ways, writing up the final report is the most difficult stage of any group project because it involves summarising each team member's contribution and incorporating them into a coherent whole. This task is probably best done by one person, but only after discussion involving the whole team, in which the general line of argument and conclusions are agreed on.

If one person is chosen to write up the report, they should have less responsibility in the earlier stages of the project. They should also be given adequate time to complete the report, including time for editing, redrafting and proofreading. Ideally, they will present a draft of the report to the group for discussion before writing the final draft.

THINK ABOUT THIS

- Do you think you are a responsible and productive team member?
- If so, what do you do that makes you one?
- If not, how might you improve?

How can I be an effective group member?

You can improve your effectiveness as a group member by paying attention to the following points. Good team members:

- listen carefully to others
- show that they are listening
- find ways of encouraging other group members
- take responsibility
- relate their ideas to the ideas of others
- don't reject the ideas of others; they suggest alternatives
- are ready to compromise.

SUMMARY

1. Group work is widely used in universities because:
   - it develops students' ability to participate effectively in a team
   - working in groups is an effective way of learning
   - teams can undertake large projects that one person could not complete alone.
2. The process of working together as a group is as important as the final product.
3. To establish a group that works effectively, you need to:
   - make sure that everyone in the group knows how to contact each other
   - analyse the assignment or task
   - allocate tasks to all members of the group clearly and fairly
   - establish a timeline for completion of different aspects of the task
   - record tasks and a timeline in a group agreement
   - establish group roles (chairperson, time keeper, minutes taker and so on)

- keep a record of group decisions
- encourage everyone to contribute fully.

4. The most common problems arising in group work are:
   - team members who do not complete their tasks
     Coping strategy: Do not complain to the lecturer; instead, discuss the issue with the team member and solve the problem in the group
   - dominant team members
     Coping strategy: Provide opportunities for quiet members to be heard
   - silent team members
     Coping strategy: Provide opportunities for all to speak. Be accepting.

5. Good team members:
   - listen carefully and show they are listening
   - encourage other group members
   - take responsibility
   - relate their ideas to the ideas of others
   - suggest alternatives
   - compromise.

6. Writing up the final report:
   - involves summarising all contributions into a coherent whole
   - is best done by one person after discussion with the team to agree on a line of argument and conclusions
   - should be done by someone with less responsibility in the early stages, with adequate time allowed for editing, redrafting and proofreading
   - should allow time for the whole team to read the draft before the final version is produced.

 SKILLS PRACTICE

Task 1

Below are some of the personal qualities that are involved in group work. Rank them in order of importance and be ready to explain your reasoning.

(a) Being able to meet deadlines

(b) Being able to set goals

(c) Being able to disagree politely

(d) Being able to accept criticism

(e) Being ready to compromise

(f) Doing the best job possible

(g) Getting on with other people

(h) Being able to write well

(i) Being able to get others to do what you want them to do

(j) Being able to delegate responsibility

Task 2

You are part of a team of four developing a new student parking scheme for your university. You have four weeks to complete the project.

- Draw up a list of the tasks that need to be done in order to complete the project.
- Draw up a timeline showing when each task will start and when it will be completed.
- Identify who will carry out each task.
- Identify the major problems that you might face and some of the ways that you might solve these problems.

Task 3

Think about your own previous experience of working in groups.

- Did you find the experience useful or not?
- What were the positive aspects of the experience?
- What problems did you face and how did you solve them?
- What do you think are your own strengths in participating in group work?
- What are the things that you find difficult to do? How might you improve your group working skills?

Part 3
BECOMING CRITICAL

9 OPINIONS, POSITIONS AND BIAS

⊛ LEARNING OBJECTIVES

When you have finished this chapter, you will be able to:

- identify an opinion
- identify a position
- explain the difference between an opinion and a position
- understand the difference between a position and bias.

✓ WORD LIST

Do you know the meaning of these words? Many have special meanings in academic culture. You can check their meaning in the glossary at the back of the book.

- ☐ categorical statement
- ☐ finding
- ☐ information literate
- ☐ paper
- ☐ reference
- ☐ research
- ☐ statement
- ☐ study
- ☐ subject
- ☐ technology

What is an opinion?

I remember being approached by a very distressed first-year student who had just failed an essay, despite having put a great deal of effort into writing it. His lecturer had stressed the importance of presenting his own ideas and opinions and that is what the student had done. He felt therefore that the lecturer had failed him because he did not agree with what the student had to say. As I talked to this student, I realised that he and his lecturer understood the word 'opinion' in different ways.

In everyday life, we take it for granted that everyone is entitled to their own opinion on any topic. If you want to believe that the world is flat, or that the pyramids were built by aliens from another galaxy, you may do so. You may have excellent evidence to support your opinion or you may have none at all – it doesn't matter. You are entitled to your opinion, no matter how strange that opinion is.

In the academic world, however, not all opinions are acceptable or appropriate.

We saw in Chapter 1 that an academic argument is generally:

- logical
- rational
- impersonal
- precise
- qualified.

Opinions and positions

Let's now compare an opinion (Text 16) and an academic argument (Text 17) to identify the differences between them. Both Text 16 and Text 17 give answers to the question 'Do mobile phones pose a health risk to users?' Text 16 presents the opinion that mobile phones have a negative effect on health.

TEXT 16

I think that mobile phones have a negative effect on health. Mobile phones emit radiation, and we all know that radiation causes cancer. Also, children who live near high-tension wires often die of cancer, even though the wires are several hundred metres away. When you use a mobile phone, you put it right next to your head, so the radiation is more concentrated.

Scientists have proved that radiation causes birth defects in chickens and reduced production of milk in cows. Also, many humans who develop brain cancers have used mobile phones.

Therefore, I think the evidence shows that mobile phones have a negative effect on people's health.

You can see that this argument is very personal and subjective because it uses phrases like 'I think' and 'we all know'. You can also see that it makes many claims without any evidence to support them. Let's examine some of these claims.

- *We all know that radiation causes cancer.*

  This statement is much too strong. If it were true, everyone would suffer from cancer because of radiation from televisions, microwave ovens and computers, among other things. This claim needs to be qualified.

- *Children who live near high-tension wires often die of cancer.*

  This statement is also too strong and the writer provides no evidence to support the claim.

- *Radiation from mobile phones is more concentrated than the radiation from high-tension wires.*

  The writer supplies no evidence for this claim either. In fact, it is not true. The radiation from mobile phones is different from the radiation associated with high-tension wires.

- *Experiments with animals suggest that radiation causes birth defects in chickens and reduced production of milk in cows.*

  Which experiments? Who carried them out? When? What exactly did they do? We need a reference to these experiments so that we can check this claim.

- *Many humans who develop brain cancers have used mobile phones.*

  Again, this claim is much too broad. A reader could point out that many people who develop brain cancer have also drunk milk!

Now let's look at Text 17, which answers the same question as Text 16. One of the first things to notice about this text is that the answer is not personal. The writer does not refer to himself or herself, so there is no 'I think' or 'we know'. But this does not mean that the writer has no opinion. The first sentence tells us that there is some evidence that mobile phones may affect peoples' health, so we know what the writer thinks.

TEXT 17

There is some evidence to suggest that the use of mobile phones may have a negative effect on health. Mild (1998) studied radiation risk in 11,000 mobile phone users and found that headaches and fatigue were reported more often by people who made longer phone calls. Braune (1998) reported a rise in blood pressure in a group of 10 mobile phone users. Animal studies on the effects of electromagnetic radiation have suggested that exposure to high levels of radiation may be associated with birth deformities in pigs (Smith, 1999).

However, studies of the effects of radiation are difficult to interpret because of the effects of background rates of disease. For example, as Foster and Moulder (2000) point out, every year brain cancer affects approximately 6 people per 100,000 in the US regardless of exposure to mobile phones. Studies need to be carefully designed to distinguish between background rates of the disease and elevated occurrence related to the use of mobile phones.

More studies need to be carried out before the negative effects of mobile phone use on health can be confirmed.

You should also notice that the writer provides evidence for each claim that he or she makes. The evidence in this case is provided by scientific studies carried out by different researchers. Notice, also, that the names of the researchers and the dates when their studies were published are provided. These are called *references*. It means that the writer has based his or her argument on things that we can check. For example, we can read Mild's

Table 9.1 Categorical and qualified statements

Categorical statements	Qualified statements
All English people speak English.	Many English people speak English.
Smoking causes cancer.	Smoking may cause cancer.
Women are shorter than men.	In general, women are shorter than men.
Watching violence on TV causes children to become violent.	Watching violence on TV may cause some children to use violence in certain situations.

study to see how it was carried out and to check its findings. We can then decide whether it is a reliable study, which we should take notice of, or an unreliable study. If it is unreliable, we can explain why it is so. Another way of expressing this is to say that the evidence the writer uses is verifiable – it can be checked.

Another point to note is that each statement is qualified. For example, Mild found that headaches and fatigue were reported *more often* by people who made longer phone calls. He did not find that people who made long phone calls *always* suffered from headaches and fatigue. Statements that are not appropriately qualified are called *categorical statements*, and they are usually avoided in academic writing. Some examples of categorical statements, together with a qualified version of the same statement, appear in Table 9.1.

What is a position?

By now, you can probably see that an academic opinion is not the same as a personal opinion. In this book, we will call an academic opinion a *position*, and we will refer to a personal opinion simply as an *opinion*. Most of the writing that you do at university is likely to involve presenting a position, although you may find that in certain subjects, you have to read personal opinions, especially if you are reading newspapers aimed at the business community, such as the *Financial Times*, or websites such as www.Fortune.com.

Table 9.2 sets out the major differences between an opinion and a position.

Table 9.2 Comparison of opinion and position

Personal	Impersonal
Subjective	Objective
Doesn't need evidence	Needs evidence
Evidence not necessarily verifiable	Evidence is verifiable
Categorical claims may be used	Claims are qualified

THINK ABOUT THIS

Which of the following is an opinion and which a position? How did you decide?

■ It is clear to me that claims about global warming were created by the Chinese in order to make U.S. manufacturing non-competitive.

■ NASA data (https://climate.nasa.gov/vital-signs/global-temperature) shows that global averages were 0.99 degrees C warmer than the mid-20th century average, making 2016 the third year in a row with record-setting surface temperatures

What is bias?

Some students confuse presenting a position with bias. One student, who was a strong supporter of the use of genetic modification to increase global food supplies, asked me whether he could defend this position in an essay without being accused of bias. This student believed that an essay was biased if it did not present both sides of the story. While this is a common belief, it is not a good definition. If it were true, we would not be able to say that the pyramids were built by the ancient Egyptians. We would also have to indicate that some people believe they were built by aliens!

A better definition, and the one that is used in the academic world, is that a position is biased if it 'cherrypicks' the evidence. You cherrypick the evidence if you refer only to the evidence that supports you, and ignore the majority of evidence that does not. You are also biased if you claim that a researcher said something that he or she did not say. This is called misrepresentation. To avoid the charge of bias, you need to make sure that you support your position with evidence, and that if your position is a minority one – that is, if most of the evidence does not support you – you indicate that and show why it is not important.

Let's look at an example. The issue of whether or not humans are causing global warming and climate change has attracted a lot of attention over the last few years. Although the huge majority of scientists agree that the climate is warming and that human activity is responsible, there are some who insist that this is not so. Text 18 is a short article written by someone who denies global warming. What aspects of the argument indicate that this article is biased? (Sentences are numbered to help you refer to specific sentences.)

TEXT 18

[1]Over the last 30 years, public debate about climate change has been dominated by discussion of global warming. [2]However, 95 per cent of the climate models that predict global warming resulting from human CO_2 emissions are wrong. [3]While it is true that 97 per cent of the world's scientists agree that climate change is caused by human activity, these scientists ignore the research of a number of scientists. [4]In fact, there has been an unexplained pause in global warming over the past 18 years. [5]Physicist Paul Brekke claims that temperatures are likely to fall over the next 50 years. [6]Some Russian scientists claim that the world is in for a cooling period that will last for 200–250 years. [7]Sebastian Luning and Fritz Varen believe that temperatures could be to one-fifth of a degree cooler by 2030 as a result of reduced radiation from the sun. [8]The research of these scientists proves that the current campaign against the use of fossil fuels is a conspiracy by left-wing activists who wish to destroy the major companies engaged in mining and oil production and exploration.

Notice that in sentence 2, the writer states that 95 per cent of the models that predict global warming are wrong. However, he gives no evidence to support this claim. He admits that close to 100 per cent of scientists agree that human activity is causing global warming, but he ignores this huge body of evidence. Instead he 'cherrypicks' the evidence, quoting some of the very few scientists who believe that the climate will cool rather than heat up. He finishes by claiming a conspiracy by left-wing activists to attack the coal and oil industry. Again, he offers no evidence to support this claim.

Overall, this is a clear example of bias. The writer presents a position, and appears to back it up with evidence, but the evidence he uses is not representative of the total. In addition, he makes claims that he makes no attempt to back up.

THINK ABOUT THIS

Which of the following statements represents a position, and which suggests that it is biased? What features allowed you to decide?

- The International Union for Conservation assessed 71,576 mostly terrestrial and freshwater species and reported that the percentages of threatened terrestrial species ran from 13 per cent for birds to 41 per cent for amphibians and gymnosperms (Abell, 2011). Twenty-three per cent of mammals and fish face extinction, as do 39 per cent of reptiles (TROPICOS, 2014).

- Many scientists claim that the world is on the brink of the sixth mass extinction of life, that is, a catastrophic loss of biological diversity. This is alarmist. I believe the true rate is closer to 0.7 per cent over the next 50 years.

Can we ever use 'I' in academic writing?

We have just stated that when you present a position in academic writing, you need to be impersonal. This does not, however, mean that you can't refer to yourself and your experience in your writing. You can do so, but there are particular ways in which you should do it. These ways vary from discipline to discipline, and even, in some cases, from lecturer to lecturer. Look at the following two examples.

TEXT 19

In this paper I present examples of students' difficulties in writing academic texts, and show how these difficulties relate to misunderstanding about the basic values of academic culture. The examples involve students who came to see me for advice on how to improve their writing. I have separated the difficulties into two groups. The first group deals with problems encountered in the research phase of the writing cycle, while the second group includes problems in the process of writing itself.

Nevile, M. (1996). Literacy culture shock: Developing academic literacy at university. The Australian Journal of Language and Literacy, 19(1), 41.

TEXT 20

There are many psychological researchers who believe that television violence is a cause of real violence. However, I remain unconvinced that television has anything to do with real-world violence.

Milavsky, J. (1988). Television and aggression once again. In S. Oskamp (Ed.), Television as a social issue. Social Psychology Annual 8. Newbury Park: Sage.

Text 19 is the section of a research report where the writer explains what she is going to do in the report. The writer uses 'I' because she is taking responsibility for her claims. She is saying, 'This is my position: I believe that this report has something useful and valid to say.'

Text 20 involves controversy. Notice that the writer points out that many researchers believe that watching violence on television can cause some people to act violently in real life. Then he says he disagrees with these people. In this example also, the writer is taking responsibility, but here he does so because his position is controversial. He disagrees with the majority of other researchers working in the same field.

Another time when it may be appropriate to use 'I' is when you participate in a research project both as a subject and as a researcher. For example, you may be involved in researching how management motivates staff in the company that you work for. In this case you might report on what managers and staff members say about motivation, and also refer to your own experiences as a staff member in the company.

Although it is possible to use 'I' in the situations described above, you should remember that some disciplines and some individual lecturers oppose its use. It is always a good idea to check with your lecturer before you use it yourself. You can read more about using pronouns, including 'I', in Chapter 13.

SUMMARY

1. Academic opinions and personal opinions are not the same. An academic opinion, or position, needs evidence to support it. A personal opinion may or may not be supported by evidence.

2. Academic opinions, or positions, are:
   - logical
   - rational
   - impersonal
   - precise
   - qualified.

3. A bias is an opinion that ignores large amounts of contrary evidence and focuses on the small amount of evidence that does support the opinion. Bias may also involve misrepresenting someone else's ideas; that is, indicating that they said or wrote something that they did not actually say or write.

4. While academic writing is usually impersonal, 'I' or 'we' may be used in some circumstances, such as:
   - when you want to take responsibility for your research or your position
   - when your position is controversial, and contrasts with the positions of most other researchers in the field
   - when you take part in research as either a researcher or a participant in the study.

5. Attitudes to using 'I' or 'we' vary from discipline to discipline. You should check with your lecturer before using either.

SKILLS PRACTICE

Task 1

Look at your own assignments.

(a) Do you think you are presenting positions or opinions?

(b) What makes you think so?

Task 2

Have you come across any texts that you consider biased? If so:

(a) Where were they published?

(b) What makes you think they are biased?

(c) What changes might make them less biased?

Task 3

Text 21 is an extract from an article on climate change. Identify the words and phrases that qualify the claims the writer makes.

TEXT 21

Climate change ultimately affects us all. But our capacity to withstand its consequences can come down to economics. If you are poor you are far more likely to live in an ecologically vulnerable region. This is true of both rural and city folk. Poor people tend to have less solid houses which are more likely to be destroyed or submerged by storms or mudslides. And they are unlikely to be insured. If global warming brings drought and crop failure, poor communities may have nothing to fall back on.

Baird, V. (2003, June). 'The big switch'.
New Internationalist, 357.
Retrieved from www.newint.org

Task 4

Texts 22 and 23 are two short essays written in response to the following question:
Discuss the evidence regarding the effects of vaccination in children.

■ Which text represents a position and which an opinion?

■ Does either text show evidence of a bias?

TEXT 22

The issue of vaccination has attracted a great deal of discussion in recent years. Anti-vaccination campaigners claim that vaccination harms children's health and should be avoided. In this essay, I will examine some of the arguments presented by anti-vaccine advocates, focusing on claims that vaccination itself causes diseases, that it overloads a child's immune system and that it is unnecessary in the modern world.

Many people opposed to vaccination state that vaccination causes autism in children. It is true that *The Lancet*, a highly respected medical journal, published a study stating this in 1998. However, the author, Andrew Wakefield, was shown to have falsified the data, and the paper was withdrawn (*The Lancet*, Vol 375, No 9713). Many other papers have found no link between vaccination and autism (Madsen et al., 2002; Uchiyama et al., 2007; Mrozek-Budzuyn et al., 2010).

Some opponents argue that vaccination is unnecessary because the diseases we vaccinate against have largely disappeared. However, cases of whooping cough have greatly increased in recent years because not enough children are being immunised (Australia Government Department of Health, 2015).

Overall, the arguments raised by anti-vaccination campaigners are one-sided and ignore the huge amount of evidence that supports the beneficial results of vaccination.

TEXT 23

The question of whether or not children should be vaccinated against common illnesses has aroused a lot of argument. I think that vaccination harms children's health and should be avoided. Firstly, think about some of the ingredients that are used in vaccines. These include aluminium, which is associated with Alzheimer's disease, glycerine, which is toxic to the kidneys, and acetone, which is used in nail polish remover. These ingredients are injected deep into the child's body where the toxins are absorbed by the blood. This cannot possibly be healthy for the child.

Talk to your friends and neighbours and they will tell you that the unhealthiest kids are those who have been vaccinated. In fact, I know of many mothers who have some children who have been vaccinated and some who have not. They will tell you that their vaccinated children have far more health problems that their unvaccinated children.

This is supported by a very well-known study published in the medical journal *The Lancet*, which conclusively proved that measles vaccination causes autism.

Finally, many of the diseases that children are vaccinated against have almost disappeared. Nobody gets diphtheria these days, but we are still vaccinated against it. Whopping cough and measles are quite rare, and anyway are normal childhood diseases, so there is no real reason to insist on vaccination.

Overall, the danger from vaccination is far higher than the danger from the diseases that we vaccinate against.

10 CRITICAL THINKING, PROBLEM-SOLVING AND DESCRIPTION

✳ LEARNING OBJECTIVES

When you have finished this chapter, you will be able to:

- understand the difference between description and analysis
- understand the characteristics of critical thinking
- understand the characteristics of problem-solving
- distinguish between questions that need a descriptive answer and questions that need an analytical answer
- understand the difference between descriptive and analytical problem-solving
- recognise texts that display critical thinking.

✓ WORD LIST

Do you know the meaning of these words? Many have special meanings in academic culture. You can check their meaning in the glossary at the back of the book.

- ☐ analysis
- ☐ analytical
- ☐ case study
- ☐ critical thinking
- ☐ information
- ☐ method
- ☐ theory

Critical thinking

You have probably heard the term 'critical thinking' before. You may also have heard the term 'analysis', or 'critical analysis', which refer to the same thing. Together with its close relative 'problem-solving', critical or analytical thinking is usually found high on the list of the abilities or qualities that universities want to develop in their students. So what is involved in critical thinking and problem-solving?

THINK ABOUT THIS

■ Before you continue reading, what do you think critical thinking involves?

What is critical thinking?

The easiest way to understand critical thinking is to consider what a critical thinker does. A critical thinker can:

- evaluate the reliability of sources of information
- distinguish between relevant and irrelevant information
- compare and contrast ideas, concepts and theories
- make connections between ideas and concepts in different disciplines.

Let's take these one by one.

Evaluate the reliability of sources of information

We are surrounded by huge amounts of information, but not all this information is reliable. The information may not be based on evidence, or the evidence may have been collected or analysed in inappropriate ways. We will look at how to recognise reliable sources of information in Chapter 11.

Distinguish between relevant and irrelevant information

It is not enough that the information that we have is reliable, it must also be relevant. This means that it has to be appropriate to the purpose it is used for. Suppose that you are writing an essay about the effects of television violence on children's behaviour. You read an article telling you that a large percentage of the world's televisions are made in China. While this information is on the topic of television, it is not relevant because it does not relate to your purpose: discussing the effects of watching violent television programs on children's behaviour.

It is easy to see that this example is not relevant. Now consider a second example. You read that the number of households in which children have television in their bedrooms has tripled in the last five years. Is this relevant? The answer is that you have to show *how* it is relevant. If you merely state this as a fact, it is not relevant. However, what about this:

> The number of households in which children have televisions in their bedrooms has tripled in the last five years (Smith, 2004). As a result, parents are less able to monitor what their children are watching, potentially giving children access to greater amounts of violent programming.

Notice how the writer shows why the increase is important by indicating its implications with regard to the amount of violent television children watch. Greater exposure to television violence may lead to increased aggression.

You may think that the reader can see the implications without you having to point them out. However, this is not the reader's job. It is your job as the writer to guide the reader, showing how the ideas, concepts and evidence you discuss relate to the argument or position that you are developing.

Compare and contrast ideas, concepts and theories

We have already seen that there is seldom only one way of addressing an issue or a problem. As a student, one of your main tasks is to understand the major approaches and theories in the disciplines that you are studying. However, not only do you have to understand them, you also have to be able to recognise both the similarities and the differences between them. In Chapter 1, we saw that some economists believe in the free market, while others think that governments need to intervene to manage problems such as excessive lending or unemployment. You need to compare the assumptions that these two approaches make and to recognise how these assumptions result in different conclusions.

In the same way, when you read research studies, you need to recognise how these studies relate to each other. You might ask, for example:

- Do the studies use the same theories to guide the research?
- Do they use similar data? If not, how does it differ?
- How do the findings of each study relate to each other? Do they support, partially support or contradict each other?

Your ability to point to similarities and differences between theories, concepts and research studies is crucial in demonstrating that you are a critical thinker.

Make connections between ideas and concepts in different disciplines

This is an aspect of critical thinking that develops over the whole course of your university career. As you learn more about the disciplines that you are studying, you will begin to see that there are times when approaches and concepts that you consider in one discipline might have application in another. Of course, you also have to recognise when an approach or concept that is very useful in one discipline is not relevant in another.

THINK ABOUT THIS

- Has your understanding of what critical thinking involves changed as a result of reading this explanation?
- What do you think is the most important thing you have learned about critical thinking?

Demonstrating critical analysis

In evaluating your assignments, your lecturers will look to see if you demonstrate critical analytical skills. We have just examined some of the ways you can do this, but your lecturer will also be looking to see if you can:

- make appropriate generalisations from evidence
- recognise contradictions
- evaluate ideas, concepts and theories
- identify assumptions and evaluate them
- explore implications and consequences.

Making appropriate generalisations

When you make a generalisation, you apply your conclusion about a specific situation to a wider context. However, there are good generalisations and bad generalisations. To put this in more academic language, there are appropriate generalisations and inappropriate generalisations.

Let's go back to our imaginary essay on the effects of watching violent television on children's behaviour. You read a study that reports on one person's viewing habits over a ten-year period. This person watched a lot of violent television and was himself violent. Can you make a generalisation that watching television violence makes people more aggressive? Quite clearly you cannot, because this is based on one particular person, whose aggression may be caused by many other factors.

A second study reports on the viewing habits of 1000 people over a ten-year period. This study found that many of those who watched a lot of violent television were themselves violent. Can you generalise from this study? Yes, you can, as long as you do so appropriately. An appropriate generalisation might be:

> *Watching violent television over a long period may cause people to be more aggressive.*

We will look at how you can use words such as 'may', 'might' or 'likely' to make appropriate claims in Chapter 16. Here, we just need to note the importance of appropriate generalisations. If you make a generalisation based on insufficient evidence, your lecturer is likely to criticise you for simplifying the situation, which means making a complex situation or process appear simpler than it really is. Your generalisation needs to be carefully related to the evidence that supports it.

Recognising contradictions

Many students find it surprising that the results of research are often not consistent. One study or group of studies may make one finding, while others make a different or even contradictory finding. This does not mean that any of these studies are wrong. The researchers may have started with different theoretical assumptions, or defined their concepts in different ways. They may have used different methodologies, or selected their participants differently. Your job as a student is firstly to recognise contradictions.

This means that you need to show that you are aware, for example, that study A and study B do not come to the same conclusions. The same applies to theories and concepts: you need to indicate that you are aware of any differences and conflicts between them. For example, going back to our essay on the effects of television violence on children's behaviour, you might read some studies that conclude that watching violence leads to greater aggression, and other studies that conclude the opposite. In your essay, you need to indicate that you are aware that the studies do not support each other. Here is how one student did this:

> While some researchers claim that watching television violence has little or no effect on real-world aggression (Smith, 2005; Jones, 2007) others have reported real results. Thomas (2004) followed 1000 people over a ten-year period ...

Usually, you will spend more time discussing the studies that you think are most reliable or useful. This brings us to the next aspect of critical thinking: evaluation.

Evaluating ideas, concepts and theories

We have already seen that you need to compare and contrast different theories, concepts, studies and so on. You also need to evaluate them. This may involve several different processes. One way of evaluating involves deciding which of the different approaches, theories or studies are useful for your purposes. Another is to examine how a particular study was carried out, deciding if the methodology was appropriate, or whether the generalisations reached by the researcher are appropriate. The common thread is the need for judgment: as a critical or analytical thinker, you are required to state which approach, theory, concept or study you find most convincing and why.

Identifying assumptions and evaluating them

While you need to evaluate different ideas, concepts and theories, you also need to recognise the ideas, concepts and theories that others are using, and to see how these affect their conclusions. Often these assumptions are implicit; that is, they are not stated openly. So, for example, you might read an article discussing the future of the euro in which the writer claims that the euro will collapse. What he or she does not say is that he or she is a euro-sceptic, that is, a person who opposes the integration of Europe, usually because they believe European integration undermines national sovereignty.

This does not mean that hidden assumptions are bad. It is, however, important to be able to recognise them. At the beginning of your studies, this will be difficult, but as you learn more and more about your field, you will find it easier to do.

Exploring implications and consequences

Finally, a critical analyst is also able to explore the implications and consequences of particular events and processes or theories and concepts. Above, we read about the fact that more and more children have televisions in their bedrooms. By itself, this fact is not very interesting. It becomes important, though, when we realise its implications: with televisions in their bedrooms, it is easier for children to watch a lot of violent programs without their parents knowing, a situation that previously seldom arose.

Critical analysis and awareness

By now, you are probably beginning to realise that critical analysis is quite a complex phenomenon. There is still, however, another aspect that needs to be explored. All of us have attitudes and values that influence our judgement. Good critical thinkers recognise this and understand the ways in which their judgement is influenced by their own attitudes and values. Good critical thinkers also recognise that the attitudes and values of their culture shape their thinking and understand the effects of this on the judgements that they make. They recognise also that at times they need to suspend judgement in order to arrive at an understanding of a situation.

THINK ABOUT THIS

- Choose one of the modules you are taking and select a single assignment from it. What aspects of critical thinking do you think are called for in this assignment?

Problem-solving

When critical thinking is used to make decisions in practical situations, or to develop solutions to particular problems, it is referred to as *problem-solving*. Problem-solving is particularly important in applied disciplines such as accounting, nursing, engineering and management. It is also important in the sciences and in fields such as physics and chemistry.

While the skills involved in problem-solving are the same as those involved in critical thinking, problem-solving also stresses:

- suggesting and evaluating solutions to problems
- transferring knowledge and understanding to new contexts.

Suggesting and evaluating solutions to problems

Many disciplines ask you to analyse a particular problem, and then to suggest a solution based on one or more of the theories that you have been studying. At times you may be expected to outline several possible solutions and then decide which is the most appropriate. The opposite of evaluation is the automatic application of a formula or a set of procedures without considering whether they are appropriate for the task at hand.

Transferring knowledge and understanding to new contexts

Another problem-solving skill involves applying concepts or theories learned in one context to a new or unfamiliar one. This is something that you gradually learn how to do over the course of your studies. However, as you acquire new knowledge, you need to ask yourself how it can be applied, and actively think about new situations in which it might be useful.

THINK ABOUT THIS

- To what extent do you think your assignments involve problem-solving?
- Which, if any, of your modules involves the most problem-solving?

What is description?

While developing critical thinking and problem-solving is a key aim of most university study, it is not the only skill that you will need to demonstrate. You will also need to be able to define and describe concepts, ideas, theories and so on, without evaluating them. Description focuses on giving information and usually involves:

- defining
- describing
- summarising
- giving examples
- outlining.

Description is very common in introductory textbooks – especially in professionally oriented subjects such as management and accounting – or in sciences such as biology. This is because one of the major purposes of a textbook in these subjects is to introduce students to the basic concepts, theories and methods of a subject. Students need to understand these before they can study the higher levels of the subject.

Text 24 is an example of descriptive writing. It is taken from an introductory textbook on management. The writers are introducing the concept of planning. They give a general definition and then expand the definition by distinguishing two types of planning – informal and formal. Descriptions and examples are used to help make the concept clear.

TEXT 24: THE DEFINITION OF PLANNING

What do we mean by the term planning? As we stated in Chapter 1, planning encompasses defining the organisation's objectives or goals, establishing an overall strategy for achieving these goals, and developing a comprehensive hierarchy of plans to integrate and coordinate activities. It is concerned, then, with ends (what is to be done) as well as with means (how it is to be done).

Planning can be further defined in terms of whether it is informal or formal. All managers engage in planning, but it might be only the informal variety. In informal planning, nothing is written down, and there is little or no sharing of objectives with others in the organisation. This describes the planning that goes on in many small businesses; the owner-manager has a vision of where he or she wants to go and how he or she expects to get there. The planning is general and lacks continuity. ...

When we use the term 'planning' in this book, we are implying formal planning. That is, specific objectives are formulated covering a period of years. These objectives are committed to writing and made available to organisation members.

Robbins, S., Bergman, R., & Stagg, I. (1997). Management. Sydney: Prentice-Hall, p. 219.

Critical analysis or description – which approach is best?

The quick answer to this question is 'neither'. Both analytical and descriptive approaches to knowledge are important, but they are used for different purposes. In fact, most academic texts include both descriptive and analytic writing. For example, a research report usually includes four sections: an introduction, a section describing the methods used to carry out the study, a report of the results and a discussion of the results. The methods and results sections are often descriptive, while the discussion section is generally analytical and critical. The introduction is likely to include both descriptive and analytic sections. As an academic reader, you need to recognise which sections of the texts that you read are descriptive and which are analytic. This is the first step in developing your ability to critically analyse the ideas and concepts involved in the discipline that you are studying.

THINK ABOUT THIS

Think about your own education.

- To what extent were descriptive approaches to knowledge stressed?
- To what extent were analytical approaches to knowledge stressed?
- Was there any difference in approach between primary and secondary school?

Are students expected to write descriptively or analytically?

This time, the quick answer is 'both'! Just as you will find both descriptive and analytical writing in the texts that you read for your studies, you will also find that you are sometimes expected to write descriptively and sometimes analytically.

Questions requiring descriptive answers

Short answer questions and multiple choice questions in tests and examinations often (but not always) need descriptive answers. Look at the 'Examples of descriptive questions' box that lists several examples. The first one merely asks you to list the four functions of a manager.

e.g. EXAMPLES OF DESCRIPTIVE QUESTIONS

Management

What are the four major functions of managers?

Accounting

Define inventory as it relates to a merchandiser.

Computing

Outline the stages of the software life cycle.

Psychology

Define each of the following terms:

   a supervised learning

   b unsupervised learning

   c hybrid learning techniques

Biology

All cells of an earthworm have the following components except:

   a mitochondria

   b nuclei

   c plasma membranes

   d cell walls

History

Which country produced the finest porcelain during the 17th century?

   a China

   b United Kingdom

   c Holland

   d India

There are several question words that usually indicate that a descriptive answer is expected. The most common are:

- **define**   give the exact meaning of a term
- **explain**   describe features so that they can be easily understood
- **illustrate**   explain and give examples
- **outline**   list or describe the most important features
- **state**   describe precisely the content of a law, theory or concept
- **summarise**   briefly present all the main points.

Questions requiring analytical answers

Questions that call for longer answers are likely to require analytical answers involving critical thinking. For example, the economics question in the 'Examples of analytical questions' box asks you to make a judgement. You have to decide whether an economy can maintain both low inflation and high employment at the same time. You have three possible ways of replying to this question:

a) Yes, the employment and inflation objectives of macroeconomic policy management can be met simultaneously.

b) No, the employment and inflation objectives of macroeconomic policy management cannot be met simultaneously.

c) The employment and inflation objectives of macroeconomic policy management can be met simultaneously only to a certain extent.

You have to decide which of these three answers you think is most accurate or appropriate and present evidence to support your answer. If your answer is option c, then you also have to decide how far the two objectives can be met at the same time.

---

e.g. EXAMPLES OF ANALYTICAL QUESTIONS

Economics

Can the employment and inflation objectives of macroeconomic policy management be met simultaneously?

Management

The most effective way of limiting environmental damage to a tourist site is to limit the number of visitors to it.
Discuss the validity of this statement in relation to tourism's impact on a range of different environments and identify its management implications.

Sociology

Compare and contrast Marxist and pluralist conceptions of politics, power and the state.

Information technology

Human efficiency is more important than machine efficiency.
Discuss this statement in relation to commercial software production.

History

Is the rise of a nationalist consciousness among colonised people a product of colonialism? Discuss in relation to the rise of anti-colonial movements in one colonised country or one period of time.

Psychology

Why do older children have better memory abilities than younger children?

There are many question words that indicate an analytical answer is expected. The most common ones are:

- **Analyse:** identify the components of a concept, theory or plan and describe the relationship between them
- **Compare:** identify the similarities and differences between concepts, theories, plans or objects
- **Contrast:** identify the differences between concepts, theories, plans or objects
- **Criticise:** identify the weak points of a concept or theory
- **Discuss:** identify different approaches to a question or problem and decide which is most valid or useful
- **Describe:** identify different approaches to a question or problem
- **Evaluate:** decide whether a concept, theory, plan or action is valid or useful
- **Examine:** identify the strengths and weaknesses of a concept or theory

The difficult term in this list is 'describe', which can be used in both types of question. In order to decide which type of answer is required, you have to consider the topic of the question. For example, if the question asks you to describe the life cycle of an insect, then a descriptive answer is almost always required. This is because the life cycle of most insects is understood, so there is not usually any debate about it. However, if the question asks you to describe different theories of motivation, then you are usually expected to write an analytic answer, because there are several different approaches to this topic. You would be expected to compare and contrast the different theories, identifying the strengths and weaknesses of each.

Questions requiring answers that are both descriptive and analytical

Many questions require both descriptive and analytical answers. Look at the following examination question, taken from an economics paper:

What is a comparative equilibrium? Why is it efficient? Why is it important?

As you can see, this question is actually three questions. The first, 'What is a comparative equilibrium?' requires a descriptive answer. The other two demand analytical answers.

One of the most important things that you need to decide when you are answering questions is whether a descriptive or an analytic answer is required. In general, analytic questions attract more marks than descriptive questions, so if you have an assignment like the one above, you should spend more time and effort answering the second and third questions than the first question.

THINK ABOUT THIS

■ Look at an examination paper for one of your unit. Do the questions demand mainly descriptive or analytical answers, or a mixture of the two?

Problem-solving in assignments

We have already noted that problem-solving involves making decisions in practical situations, or developing solutions to particular problems. This often involves critical analysis, but not always. Just as there is a distinction between critical analysis and description, there is also a distinction between simple problem-solving and analytical problem-solving. Text 25 presents a problem from an economics textbook.

TEXT 25

	1987	1988	1989	1990	1991	1992	1993	1994	1995
US	92.7	96.4	98.8	100.00	99.4	101.7	104.8	109.1	112.7
Japan	85.5	90.8	95.2	100.00	104.0	105.1	105.2	105.7	106.5
Germany	87.9	91.1	94.4	100.00	104.6	105.8	103.8	107.4	108.5
Australia	88.8	92.9	96.3	100.00	99.8	100.7	104.1	108.9	113.7
UK	92.8	97.5	99.6	100.00	98	97.5	99.7	103.5	106.0

The table above shows index numbers for real GDP for various countries (1990 = 100).

a Work out the growth rate for each country for each year from 1990 to 1995.

b Plot the figures in a graph. Describe the pattern that emerges.

Adapted from Sloman, J., & Norris, K. (1999). Economics. Sydney, Prentice Hall, p. 346.

This problem requires you to apply your knowledge in a fairly straightforward manner. Problems like this allow you to practise applying basic concepts and using standard tools. They form part of many courses, but they are usually not as important as *analytical* problem-solving.

e.g. EXAMPLES OF SIMPLE PROBLEM-SOLVING QUESTIONS

EXAMPLE 1 – Accounting

From the following information, determine the profit for the month of July 2016 for the Cleanscene Cleaning Company. Note: Depreciation may be ignored.

Jul. 2 Received cash for:

Services: June	$9000
Services: July	$12000
Services: Aug (in advance)	$3000
Loan:	$5000
8 Performed service in June for which customers have not yet paid:	$3800
15 Paid rent for June, June, Aug:	$560
22 Paid wages for June:	$2300
Paid wages for July:	$5300
23 Unpaid wages July:	$1500
28 Paid for cleaning supplies	$2000

EXAMPLE 2 – Information technology

The table below describes the task dependencies of a project.

a Draw a PERT chart.

b Show the ECT (earliest completion time) for each event.

c Show the LCT (latest completion time) for each event.

d Determine the critical path and mark it clearly.

Task	Duration (weeks)	Predecessors
A	4	–
B	10	A
C	3	–
D	7	A
E	12	B
F	1	B
G	11	F
H	4	B
I	5	C, D, E
J	3	G, H, I

Analytical problem-solving

Analytical problem-solving is a practical activity. It asks you to use the concepts and methods that you have been studying in your course to solve a problem. You may be asked to analyse data, explaining what it shows and developing a reasoned explanation for it. You may be presented with a case study that asks you to explore a specific problem, for example in a company or a workplace, or you may have to identify and evaluate solutions to a local problem such as poor access to a library or traffic congestion in a local shopping centre.

As you can see, analytical problem-solving takes many forms. However, with most problems, there are three general steps that you need to follow:

1. **Identify the problem:**
   - What are the significant features of the problem?
   - What information is given and what needs to be found out?
   - What theories, concepts and methods are relevant to this problem?

2. **Identify solution(s):**
   - How do the theories, concepts and methods you have identified relate to the problem?
   - What solution(s) do they suggest?
   - If you have been given numeric data, how can you use it?

3. **Evaluate solution(s)**
   - Why is your suggested solution an appropriate one?
   - Does the case illustrate or contradict other research?

Most of the problems that you are asked to solve in university courses tend to be analytical problems. Questions that only require you to apply formulae or apply basic concepts in a straightforward way tend to be worth fewer marks in assignments.

---

e.g. EXAMPLES OF ANALYTICAL PROBLEM-SOLVING QUESTIONS

EXAMPLE 1—Accounting

Mr Smith bought a machine on 1 January 2011 for $22 000 that was expected to have a four-year life and a scrap value of $4000. He used it evenly throughout its life and employed straight-line depreciation.

You are Mr Smith's accountant. Write a short report explaining:

a what depreciation is

b why depreciation is not based on the selling price, which was:

Date	Selling price of used asset ($)
31/12/11	9000
31/12/12	11000
31/12/13	5000
31/12/14	4000

c why the machine depreciated so much the first two years.

EXAMPLE 2 — Ethics

William Labov was a famous American linguist who was interested in the ways that people from different socioeconomic backgrounds pronounce certain words. For instance, he was interested in the way people in New York pronounce words like 'thirty' and 'third'. To collect data on this, he would hide a tape recorder in his pocket and then approach people in shops and on the street, asking questions that would involve these words in the answer. For example, in a shop, he would ask where the menswear section was, knowing that it was on the third floor. Each answer was secretly recorded. People giving the answers did not know that they were taking part in an experiment, or that they were being recorded.

   What ethical issues are raised by this case?

THINK ABOUT THIS

Look at the assignments and examination papers in one of your modules.

■ Do they involve problem-solving?

■ If so, are the problems mainly simple?

■ How many involve analytical problem-solving?

A final word

Critical thinking and problem-solving may appear difficult and daunting at first. Don't be put off. You will develop your ability to think critically and apply what you are learning to solving real-world problems throughout your university career. As a first step, focus on how the texts that you read use analysis.

SUMMARY

1. Critical thinking or critical analysis involves:
   - evaluating the reliability of sources of information
   - distinguishing between relevant and irrelevant information
   - comparing and contrasting ideas, concepts, theories
   - making connections between ideas and concepts in different disciplines.

2. You demonstrate critical thinking by:
   - making appropriate generalisations from evidence
   - recognising contradictions
   - evaluating ideas, concepts and theories
   - identifying assumptions and evaluating them
   - exploring implications and consequences.

3. Critical thinkers are also aware of:
   - the ways in which their own attitudes and values influence their judgements
   - the ways in which the attitudes and values of their culture influence their judgement.

4. Problem-solving involves:
   - applying critical thinking to practical situations
   - using critical analysis to develop solutions to particular problems.

5. Problem-solving stresses:
   - suggesting and evaluating solutions to problems
   - transferring knowledge and understanding to new contexts.

6. Description focuses on providing information. It usually involves:
   - defining
   - describing
   - summarising
   - giving examples
   - outlining.

7. Critical analysis involves asking questions and evaluating. When you analyse a theory, position, concept or claim, you may:
   - ask how important it is
   - ask how valid it is
   - compare and contrast it with other theories, positions, concepts or claims
   - identify strong and weak points
   - apply it to the real world.

8. Academic writing involves both description and analysis, but each are used in different situations for different purposes.

9. Question words that usually indicate a descriptive answer is required include 'define', 'explain', 'illustrate', 'outline', 'state' and 'summarise'.

10. Question words that usually indicate that an analytic answer is required include 'analyse', 'compare', 'contrast', 'criticise', 'discuss', 'describe', 'evaluate' and 'examine'.

11. Many assignments include both questions requiring description and questions requiring analysis.

12. Problem-solving is widely used in professional disciplines such as accounting.

   - Descriptive problem-solving requires you to apply basic concepts and methods to solve simple problems.

   - Analytical problem-solving asks you to apply concepts and methods to complex problems.

 SKILLS PRACTICE

Task 1

Here are a number of questions taken from examination papers in various subjects.

   - How many questions are there in each of the following assignments?

   - Identify which sections of the assignment involve a descriptive answer and which an analytical one.

e.g. EXAMPLE:

What is the Balance of Trade? What is a Balance of Trade deficit? Which part of the Balance of Payments includes the Balance of Trade? Is a positive Balance of Trade always desirable?

Answer: 4 questions, the first 3 are descriptive; question 4 is analytical.

a. How and why do governments intervene in markets? What are the effects?

b. What are the three types of unemployment? What types of unemployment exist when the economy is operating at potential? How would the changes in the economy in 2009 (the year of the global financial crisis) change each type of unemployment?

c. In the last 20 years, rates of divorce have risen significantly in Western countries. Critically analyse some of the different explanations given for this phenomenon. In your discussion you should consider what implications these explanations might have for social policy.

d. Describe the factors that contributed to the increase of opium production in the Golden Triangle in the second half of the twentieth century.

e. The Chief Executive Officer of Benstow Corporation has noticed that poor work practices are increasing in the company. For example, employees are often late for

work and are taking long lunch breaks. The CEO recognises that the culture of the company may be contributing to these poor work practices, so he engages a consultant (you) to prepare a report addressing the following topic:
What is an organisation's culture and how can it be managed?

f. Explain how the tilt of the Earth's axis with regard to the ecliptic causes seasons on Earth. What would seasons be like on Earth if the Earth's axis was more tilted with regard to the ecliptic (.23.5°)? What would seasons be like on Earth if the Earth's axis had no tilt? Explain your reasoning in each case.

g. Describe the reproductive cycle of the sporophyte and the gametophyte in plants.

h. What is the difference between a normal good and an inferior good? Describe what happens to the demand for an inferior good when (i) income falls, and (ii) price increases.

i. Discuss the ways in which the late Roman Empire influenced the Byzantine Empire, the early medieval states of Europe and the Islamic caliphate. Consider culture (including religion, art and architecture), trade and language.

j. With specific reference to both income and expenses, explain the differences between the cash basis and accrual basis of accounting for profit.

k. Most of the mistakes that second language learners make are due to interference from their first language. Evaluate the evidence for this statement.

l. Almost every day supervisors must help employees resolve conflicts with other employees. Select one conflict resolution strategy, describe it and explain why it is useful in resolving conflict.

m. *"The primary causal factor influencing the severity of tourism's environmental impact is simply the number of tourists visiting a destination. Limiting the number of tourists is the most effective way of minimising environmental damage."*

Discuss the validity of this statement in relation to tourism's impact on a range of different environments, and highlight any significant management or policy implications which emerge.

n. Is the rise of a nationalist consciousness among colonised people a product of colonialism? Discuss in relation to the rise of anti-colonial movements in colonised countries. You may restrict your examples to one country or one period of time.

Task 2

Texts 26 and 27 are extracts from two essays on the following topic:
Does the use of mobile phones pose a risk to human health?

- Which extract uses an analytic approach and displays critical thinking?
- Which extract uses a descriptive approach?
- Give reasons for your answers

TEXT 26

Identifying links between cancer and the use of mobile phones is difficult because cancer has many causes. Even before the introduction of mobile phones, people developed brain cancer, so before investigating the effects of mobile phones, the change in the number of cases of brain cancer since the introduction of mobile phones needs to be investigated. Then research is needed to discover whether these extra cases are related to the use of mobile phones or whether there are other possible causes.

In order to investigate these questions, a large number of studies have been carried out on both animal and human subjects. In one study, Rothman (1996) reviewed the health records of more than 250 000 mobile phone users and found no evidence for an increase in the rate of cancers. He did, however, find that the longer a person talked on a mobile phone while driving a car, the more likely he or she was to have a car accident.

Smith (1998) assessed mobile phone use by brain tumour patients in comparison to healthy controls. The study found no correlation between use of mobile phones and increased rates of cancer. However, it did find that users of mobile phones who had developed certain types of brain tumours were more likely to report having used the phone on the side of the head with the tumour than on the other side. But the association was weak. It was not statistically significant and might easily have been a result of recall bias. Recall bias is the tendency of subjects to remember exposure to something more readily if they developed a disease. The brain cancer patients in the study knew their diagnosis before they were asked about their use of mobile phones.

TEXT 27

Rothman (1996) reviewed the health records of more than 250 000 mobile phone users and found no evidence for an increase in the rate of cancers. He did however find that the longer a person talked on a mobile phone while driving a car, the more likely he or she was to have a car accident.

Smith (1998) assessed mobile phone use by brain tumour patients in comparison to healthy controls. The study found no correlation between use of mobile phones and increased rates of cancer. However, it did find that users of mobile phones who had developed certain types of brain tumours were more likely to report having used the phone on the side of the head with the tumour than on the other side.

Task 3

Texts 28 and 29 are two short answers written in response to the question 'Are children better than adults in learning a second language?'

- Which text displays a descriptive approach and which a critical one? Underline the sections of the text that allowed you to decide.

- Which text do you think a university lecturer would prefer and why?

TEXT 28

The question of whether children are better than adults in learning a second language has attracted a good deal of attention in recent decades. Snow and Hoefnagel-Hohle (1978) found that adults were better than children in learning Dutch after a year of exposure to the language. Krashen, Long, & Scarcella (1979) reviewed 23 studies of second language learning and concluded that while adults might learn more quickly in the short run, over a longer period of time children outperformed adults. Long (1990) stated that while adults learned more quickly than children in the first year of study, children were better learners overall. Aoyama et al. (2008) also indicated that children learn better than adults in the long term.

TEXT 29

The question of whether children are better than adults in learning a second language has attracted a good deal of attention in recent decades. Snow and Hoefnagel-Hohle (1978) found that adults were better than children in learning Dutch after a year of exposure to the language. This result was challenged, however, in an article by Krashen, Long, & Scarcella (1979) who reviewed 23 studies of second language learning and concluded that while adults might learn more quickly in the short run, over a longer period of time children outperformed adults. Long (1990) carried out a similar review and echoed these findings, stating that the adult advantage disappeared after about one year. More recently, Aoyama et al. (2008) made similar findings.

Task 4

Think about your own education.

- To what extent were descriptive approaches to knowledge stressed?
- To what extent were analytical approaches to knowledge stressed?
- Was the approach the same in primary and secondary school?
- If you have previously studied in a university or college, what approach to knowledge was stressed in that institution?
- What differences do you expect to find between the demands of your previous education and the demands of study in a western university?

Task 5

- What are the advantages of a descriptive approach to knowledge?
- What are the advantages of an analytical approach?

Share your ideas with a partner.

11 SOURCES OF ACADEMIC KNOWLEDGE

 LEARNING OBJECTIVES

When you have finished this chapter, you will be able to:

- identify the different types of texts that you may have to read at university
- understand what makes a text authoritative and reliable
- know how to check whether a text is authoritative and reliable.

 WORD LIST

Do you know the meaning of these words? Many have special meanings in academic culture. You can check their meaning in the glossary at the back of the book.

- ☐ authoritative
- ☐ current
- ☐ objective
- ☐ peer-reviewed
- ☐ reliable
- ☐ transparent

How do we know whether information is reliable?

In today's world, we are surrounded by information. At the click of a mouse, we can access thousands of web pages, many containing what looks like useful information. There are also thousands of books, journals, magazines and other printed sources that present information on every possible subject. Unfortunately, much of that information is not reliable in academic terms. Information that is not reliable cannot be used as evidence in an academic discussion.

To decide whether information is academically reliable, we need to ask five questions:

- Where does the information come from?
- Who is the audience for the information?
- How is the information verified?
- Is the source of the information objective?
- Is the information up-to-date?

Where does the information come from? The authority test

When you are sick, you are likely to see a doctor. You may not have seen this doctor before, so how do you know that he or she is capable of treating you appropriately? Most people trust doctors because they have studied at a university and as a result they have been certified as having the skills and knowledge that allow them to diagnose and treat illness. In other words, one of the major reasons for trusting a doctor is that he or she has a certificate from an authoritative source.

In the same way, to be acceptable in academic terms, information must come from an authoritative source. One of the most common authoritative sources are peer-reviewed journals. In the academic world, a journal is a specialised magazine that is published regularly, usually once every three or six months. It contains articles on specialised academic topics written for an audience of academics and students. Peer-reviewed journals contain articles that have been read by several academics before being accepted for publication. This review ensures that the standard of each article is high, that the argument is clear and that the evidence presented has been collected in ways that are acceptable and appropriate. Every discipline has many peer-reviewed journals. They may be available as hard copies in the university library, or electronically, through databases or the internet.

e.g. EXAMPLES OF PEER-REVIEWED JOURNALS

- *Journal of Business Ethics*
- *Language Learning*
- *American Sociological Review*
- *Journal of International Economics*
- *Australian Journal of Biological Sciences*

There are also many journals and magazines that are not peer-reviewed. These may also be reliable sources if they are published for a professional audience. For example, the *Harvard Business Review* is a magazine that publishes up-to-date information and analysis for a professional business audience.

It is often more difficult to decide whether a web page is authoritative. You need to find out whether it is part of the official site of a university or international organisation – such as the Food and Agriculture Organisation (FAO), the World Bank or United Nations. Pages on the sites of national and local organisations such as the London Stock Exchange or local councils are also generally considered to be reliable. Online journals and magazines such as *Fortune* or *Fortune 500* are also reliable sources as they are aimed at an audience of business men and women.

Sites such as Wikipedia are more problematic. In general, Wikipedia is not considered an appropriate academic site because it can be edited and changed by anybody, regardless of their qualifications and knowledge of the subject. At best, you might use Wikipedia to get a quick overview of a new subject, but you would then have to check the information that you gain from more authoritative academic sources such as journal articles.

If you are using the official site of a registered company, you need to take more care because you will need to distinguish between advertising and reliable information. The annual report of the company is generally a reliable source (because it is produced according to rules established by the government), while claims about the performance of a company's product may not be. This issue will come up again when we explore the third question, 'How is the information verified?'

THINK ABOUT THIS

- Do you think the news website *BuzzFeed* is a reliable academic source? Why or why not?

Who is the audience for the information? The audience test

Different types of publications are written for different audiences. Peer-reviewed journals, for example, are written for academics and students while professional magazines present material of interest to people who work in a specific field. Magazines such as *National Geographic* are written for a broad audience of educated people who are interested in the world around them.

In general, information is reliable in academic terms if it is written for an academic or a professional audience. We have also seen that information on professional websites such as *Fortune* or *Fortune 500* may also be considered reliable. However, it is not usually appropriate to use information written for a popular audience. For example, magazines such as *Time* and *Newsweek* are not usually regarded as authoritative academic sources, although they may deal with serious issues. This is because in order to make complex issues easily understandable, magazines like these focus on individual experience, and tend to report only some aspects of academic discussion. Their aim is to illustrate and explain issues rather than to critically analyse and evaluate them in academic terms. For example, the issue of *Time* for 17 October 2013 contains a long article on human evolution. While the article is interesting, it would not be appropriate to refer to it in an essay on human evolution because it focuses on the experience of individual scientists rather than on a critical analysis of what has been discovered.

THINK ABOUT THIS

- You have already considered whether *BuzzFeed* passes the Authority Test. Does it pass the Audience Test?

How is the information verified? The transparency test

Different disciplines collect information in different ways. In the natural sciences and some of the social sciences, laboratory experiments are important. Surveys, observations and questionnaires are also widely used in the social sciences. Statistics collected by government agencies play a major role in economics, while the study of original documents is important in disciplines such as history.

Each of these methods of collecting information is governed by principles of methodology that attempt to ensure the accuracy of the information presented. A discussion of these principles is beyond the scope of this book, but in general we can say that reliable information is collected and analysed in ways which are transparent – that is, available for all to see. These ways of collecting and analysing also need to be rational and verifiable, meaning that they can be checked by others. Most importantly, they need to be ways that are agreed by most scholars in the field to be appropriate.

If you are using information from web pages, you need to be particularly careful, as the web is unregulated. If someone wants to state that the moon is made of green cheese, there is nothing to stop him or her posting this statement on a website. You need to ask what evidence is provided to support claims, and where that evidence comes from. In other words, you need to use the authority test (above), and the objectivity test, which we will discuss next.

THINK ABOUT THIS

Wellness Mama is a health and lifestyle blog. In one post, the writer states that while table salt is bad for health, real salt is good. Look at the blog-post:

https://wellnessmama.com/13164/eat-more-salt/

- What evidence is presented for the claim that real salt is better than table salt?
- Do you think this site passes the transparency test?

Is the source of the information objective? The objectivity test

Most people today are aware of the link between smoking and lung cancer. This link has been established by many studies carried out by researchers in many different countries. However, there are also studies claiming that there is no link between smoking and lung cancer. Many of these studies have, in fact, been financed by tobacco companies, which do not want people to stop smoking. It is easy to see that these studies are not objective, as tobacco companies have an interest in finding that there is no link between smoking and cancer. Studies that are carried out by people or organisations that have an interest in the result are not considered to be reliable sources of information. Many databases containing peer-reviewed scientific journals indicate if the authors of the article received support for their research and if so, the source of the support. They also indicate if the authors have any connection with companies that might benefit from the research. Here is an example:

Citation: Wu Jinping & Carter, John (2017) Deforestation and Food Security. *Current Biology*. Vol 21 No 3	Details of the article (authors, Title, name of journal etc.)
Funding: This research was supported by the French Research Foundation. The funders had no role in study design, data collection and analysis, decision to publish, or preparation of the manuscript.	Source of funding
Competing interests: The authors have declared that no competing interests exist.	Competing interests

In the same way, it is important to be sure that the information being presented has a scholarly purpose rather than an advertising purpose. In other words, we have to be sure that the information is not being presented in order to encourage us to buy a product.

THINK ABOUT THIS

The question of whether or not to take dietary supplements such as vitamins, minerals and herbs is hotly debated.

Which of the following two sources containing information about dietary supplements passes the Objectivity Test?

- Food supplements summary – Australian Government Department of Health.
- Nutritional Supplements – Nutritional Supplements is committed to producing the most complete line of science-based supplements. Products contain no fillers or flavour enhancers.

Is the information up-to-date? The currency test

Information and ideas change and develop rapidly in some fields. In computing, for example, information that was published five years ago may be out of date now. Similarly, in the fields of business studies and accounting, company reports and similar documents need to be updated annually. In other disciplines, such as philosophy, ideas first put forward two thousand years ago may still contribute to discussion today.

Whether or not information is considered up-to-date depends not only on how quickly change occurs in a particular field, but also on the importance of a particular idea or approach. For example, imagine that you are asked to write an essay on theories of motivation. A major scholar in this field is Maslow, who published his most important work in 1954. Although a great deal of important work has taken place in this field since 1954, Maslow's theory is still current and has had a major influence on studies carried out since. However, if your essay focused on Maslow and on approaches developed in the 1960s and 1970s, and did not examine theories developed in the last decade, this would fail the currency test.

THINK ABOUT THIS

You are writing an essay on growing inequality around the world. Your focus is on access to the internet – referred to as the digital divide. You find the following article:

> Chen, W. & Wellman B. (2004). The global digital divide — within and between countries. *It & Society*, 1(7), 39–45

- Does it pass the Currency Test?

A practical example

We will now examine a number or resources, found with an internet search engine, and see whether they pass the complete five-question test.

Imagine that you have been asked to write the following essay for a course on health and nutrition:

Evaluate the argument that coconut oil contributes to heart disease.

Text 30 lists six of the sites that an online search found on the topic of coconut oil. Let's see which can be used as a source in your essay.

TEXT 30

a. Does coconut oil raise your Cholesterol levels? Lucy Bee
   http://www.lucybee.co/blog/

b. The cholesterol-lowering effect of coconut flakes in humans ...www.ncbi.nlm.nih.gov/...
   National Center for Biotechnology Information
   This study investigated the effect of coconut flakes on serum cholesterol levels of
   humans with moderately raised serum cholesterol in 21 subjects.

c. Cholesterol in Coconut – Coconut Info
   www.**coconut**-info.net/general/**coconut_cholesterol**.php
   If you are wondering about coconut cholesterol, then you should consider reading this
   article, which will increase your knowledge.

d. Barbara Quinn: Cardiologist talks cholesterol, coconut oil
   www.montereyherald.com/.../barbara-quin... The Monterey County Herald
   Barbara Quinn: Cardiologist talks cholesterol, coconut oil. By Barbara Quinn On
   Nutrition. Posted: 07/24/13, 12:01 AM PDT | Updated: on 07/24/2013.

e. Fact Sheet: Coconut Oil and Health – IFIC Foundation – Your ...
   www.foodinsight.org/**Coconut Oil**... International Food Information Council
   Oct 15, 2016 – Other claims are that coconut oil may prevent and even treat cancer, ...
   Coconut oil has been shown to raise both total and HDL cholesterol.

f. Does Coconut Oil Lower Cholesterol? – Linda Carney MD
   www.drcarney.com/blog/entry/does-**coconut-oil**-lower-**cholesterol**
   Sep 16, 2015 – Those who profit from this highly-refined product claim that Consuming
   coconut oil lowers bad LDL cholesterol while at the same time raising good HDL
   cholesterol.

Site a gives a clear and easily understandable explanation of the cholesterol content of coconut oil and its effects, written by a doctor. However, this site is not one that you can cite in your essay. This is because it is a commercial site that aims to sell coconut oil. It fails not only the authority test but also the objectivity test, because it has an interest in the information it presents.

Site b is the official government website of the National Center for Biotechnology Information. The link takes you to PubMed, a public database that allows people to access academic articles from hundreds of different medical and health-related journals. In this case, the article is from the *Journal of Medicinal Food*, a peer-reviewed medical journal. It is therefore a reliable source.

Site c aims to give information about coconuts and their products, but there is no information about who controls the site and few if any links to evidence that supports the claims that the site makes. The site therefore fails the authority test and the objectivity test, and as it is aimed at a popular audience, it also fails the audience test.

Site d takes us to an article from the *Monterey Herald*, a newspaper. Newspaper articles are written for a popular audience rather than an academic one, and so generally fail the audience test. This is so even though the article is written by a doctor.

Site e is interesting. It is the website of the International Food Information Council and presents a fact sheet outlining research evidence for and against the beneficial effects of coconut oil. This is useful, and you might use it to give you a quick overview of some of the research findings about coconut oil. However, there is no information on who or what the International Food Information Council is, so the site fails both the authority and the objectivity test, as we haven't got enough information to determine either.

Site f is another interesting one. It is a site of a doctor who supports and encourages healthy eating and healthy living. She summarises the work of another expert, a pharmacist, regarding coconut oil, and gives links to his publications. However, although Dr Carney and the pharmacist she cites are experts, the site is not an acceptable one because the writer is not attached to a university or other authority. Individual writers by themselves do not usually have authority: authority comes from the institution a person belongs to.

Is reliable information 'true'?

The answer to this is both 'yes' and 'no'. It depends what you mean by 'true'. Reliable information is information that passes the five tests that we have discussed in this chapter. In that sense, it is 'true'. But the world is very complex, and so people will find different answers to the same question because they investigated it in different ways. For example, some studies show that the earlier you start learning a second language, the better you will acquire it. Others show that factors such as motivation, personality and time available may be equally important. All of these studies may be reliable, but that does not mean that they all support the same conclusion. As we pointed out in the first chapter, all theories about the way the world works are partial and incomplete. Ideas, concepts and theories are constantly changing and developing, and in that sense they are not about what is true and fixed but about what describes the real world most accurately.

 **SUMMARY**

Information is reliable if it passes the five tests:

- the authority test: what institution or other authority does this source represent?
- the audience test: who is this source written for?
- the transparency test: how was this data/information collected?
- the objectivity test: why is this information being provided? Is it trying to persuade us to buy something?
- the currency test: is the information up-to-date?

 **SKILLS PRACTICE**

Task 1:

Below is a list of hits from a Google search of the phrase 'climate change'.

- Which of the following would you select to read if you were asked to write a report on projected changes in the world's climate over the next 100 years.

- Why?

a. *Climate change – Wikipedia, the free encyclopedia*
en.wikipedia.org/wiki/Climate_change
Climate change is a significant and lasting change in the statistical distribution of weather patterns over periods ranging from decades to millions of years. It may ...
Global warming – Scientific opinion on climate ... – Climate change denial - Mitigation

b. A pause in *global warming* does not disprove a human role in climate change, report says
Chicago Tribune

c. *Global Warming* – Scientific American
www.scientificamerican.com/topic/global-warming-and-climate-change/
Latest in *Global Warming*. Climatewire ... Warming Arctic Spurs Cyclones and Sea Ice Loss ... Stronger Winds over Pacific Ocean Help Slow *Global Warming*.

d. *Climate Change* – Bureau of Meteorology
www.bom.gov.au/climate/change/
Fact sheets and information on *climate change*, with an *Australian* perspective. Also provides annual statements on *Australia's* climate.

e. Understanding *Climate Change* | CSIRO
www.csiro.au › Home › Climate change and adaption
Climate variability, *climate change* and drought in eastern *Australia. Australia* has a highly variable climate with a naturally occurring cycle of wet and dry periods ...

f. [BOOK] Climate change 1992: the supplementary report to the IPCC scientific assessment
JT Houghton, BA Callander, SK Varney – 1992 – books.google.com
This report is a Supplement to the 1990 Report of the Scientific Assessment Working Group of the Intergovernmental Panel on Climate Change (IPCC). The IPCC was set up jointly by the World Meteorological Organization and the United Nations Environment Programme ...
Cited by 4392 Related articles All 10 versions Cite Save More

g. The Australian Climate Sceptics Blog
theclimatescepticsparty.blogspot.com/
18 hours ago – The Australian Climate Sceptics – Exposing the flaws in the greatest
hoax .... They indirectly equate (1) the *skeptics'* view that *global warming is* ...

h. What is *Climate Change?* – New Gen Coal
www.newgencoal.com.au/climate-change.html
Climate change is a significant and long term change in global weather patterns
over periods ranging from decades to millions of years. It may be a change in ...

Task 2

Imagine you have to write a report on the following topic:

The internet has fundamentally changed both the nature and extent of bullying in schools.
Discuss.

- Which of the sources printed on the following pages would be acceptable sources for
  your report and why? Note only the opening section of each source is given.

- Use the internet to identify three more sources which would be suitable for this report.

SOURCE 1

https://aic.gov.au/publications/rip/rip09

| | About us | Media centre | Contact us |

Australian Government
Australian Institute of Criminology

Research   **Publications**   Library   Events   🔍

PUBLICATIONS

Latest publications

Research Reports

Statistical Bulletins

Statistical Reports

Trends & issues in crime and criminal justice

Publications by series

f Share   🐦 Tweet

Published February 2010
Last modified 3 November 2017
Australian Institute of Criminology

Cite article

2010. *Covert and cyber bullying.*
Research in practice No. 9.
Canberra: Australian Institute of
Criminology.
https://aic.gov.au/publications/rip/
rip09

🏠 > Publications > Research in practice

[**Download PDF**]

Research in practice no. 9

Covert and cyber bullying

ISSN: 1836-9111

The Australian Covert Bullying Prevalence Study (Cross et al. 2009) was commissioned by the Australian Government and conducted by the Child Health Promotion Research Centre at Edith Cowan University. It has highlighted the growing problem of covert and cyber bullying affecting Australian schools and their students. Covert bullying can be understood as any form of aggressive behaviour that is repeated, intended to cause harm, characterised by an imbalance of power and is hidden from, or unacknowledged by, adults. It can include the spreading of rumours or attempts at socially excluding others. Cyber bullying is a form of covert bullying and is carried out through the use of technology; for example, on the internet through emails, blogs and social networking sites, as well as via mobile phones (Cross et al. 2009).

Results from this study identified age trends in the occurrence of covert and cyber bullying. For example, 65 percent of Year 4 students experienced covert bullying, with this number decreasing to 35 percent of Year 9 students. Up to 10 percent of students in Year 4 to Year 9 reported having been cyber bullied in the previous term, with older students in this age category reporting a higher rate of victimisation than younger students. The increase in cyber bullying and subsequent decrease in covert bullying as students get older could be attributed to students maturing and becoming more independent and competent in their use of new technologies. The hidden nature of covert and cyber bullying practices makes them difficult for teachers and school administrators to prevent or stop (Smith et al. 2008) and perhaps, as a consequence, students reported a reluctance to inform teachers of incidents. This is particularly concerning, given the potential ongoing social and psychological issues that can result for both students who have been bullied and those who engage in bullying behaviour (Farrington & Tofi 2009).

SOURCE 2

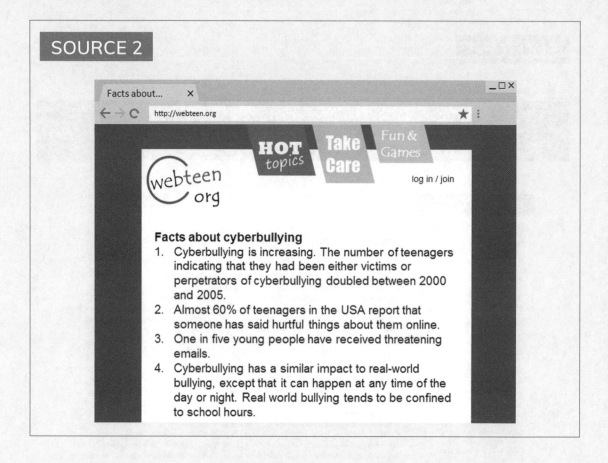

Facts about cyberbullying

1. Cyberbullying is increasing. The number of teenagers indicating that they had been either victims or perpetrators of cyberbullying doubled between 2000 and 2005.
2. Almost 60% of teenagers in the USA report that someone has said hurtful things about them online.
3. One in five young people have received threatening emails.
4. Cyberbullying has a similar impact to real-world bullying, except that it can happen at any time of the day or night. Real world bullying tends to be confined to school hours.

SOURCE 3

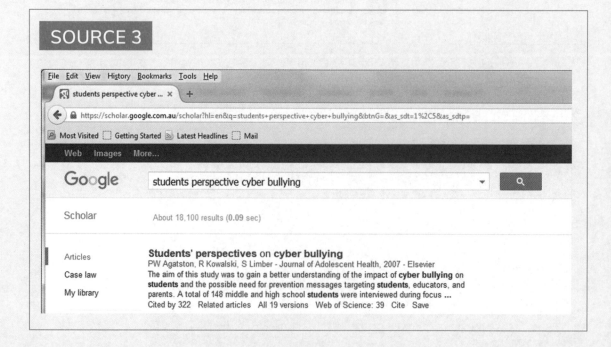

Students' perspectives on cyber bullying

PW Agatston, R Kowalski, S Limber - Journal of Adolescent Health, 2007 - Elsevier

The aim of this study was to gain a better understanding of the impact of **cyber bullying** on **students** and the possible need for prevention messages targeting **students**, educators, and parents. A total of 148 middle and high school **students** were interviewed during focus ...

Cited by 322   Related articles   All 19 versions   Web of Science: 39   Cite   Save

SOURCE 4

Combatting cyberbullying

23 November 2017 | Jane Doe

A local school is taking up the fight against cyberbullying by collecting old mobile phones. Funds raised from the collection will be donated to a national campaign against cyberbullying, which affects up to 40% of teenage children. Matt Sangster, spokesman for the campaign, called on people to check their cupboards. "Cyberbullying is having a really negative effect on an increasing number of children," he said. "It can undermine a child's confidence and destroy their self-esteem at a crucial time in their schooling and their social life." The effects of cyberbullying can be worse that the effects of bullying in real life, as Matt Sangster points out. "In real life, you can escape from bullying outside school hours, but cyberbullying follows children into their homes. There's no escape from it."

Old phones like these are raising funds for a good cause

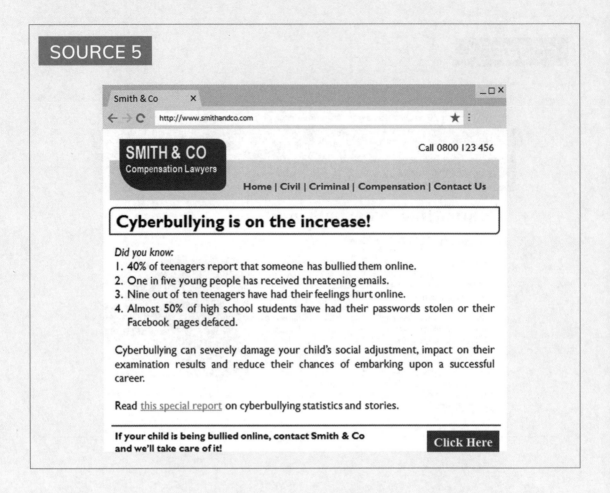

SOURCE 5

Smith & Co ✕

http://www.smithandco.com

SMITH & CO
Compensation Lawyers

Call 0800 123 456

Home | Civil | Criminal | Compensation | Contact Us

Cyberbullying is on the increase!

Did you know:
1. 40% of teenagers report that someone has bullied them online.
2. One in five young people has received threatening emails.
3. Nine out of ten teenagers have had their feelings hurt online.
4. Almost 50% of high school students have had their passwords stolen or their Facebook pages defaced.

Cyberbullying can severely damage your child's social adjustment, impact on their examination results and reduce their chances of embarking upon a successful career.

Read this special report on cyberbullying statistics and stories.

If your child is being bullied online, contact Smith & Co and we'll take care of it!

Click Here

Task 3

Imagine you have to write a report on the following topic:

The internet has fundamentally changed both the nature and extent of bullying in schools. Discuss.

- Which of the sources printed on the following pages would be acceptable sources for your report and why? Note: only the opening section of each source is given.
- Use the internet to identify three more sources that would be suitable for this report.

Part 4

EXPRESSING YOUR VOICE AND REFERRING TO THE VOICES OF OTHERS

12 VOICES IN ACADEMIC TEXTS

LEARNING OBJECTIVES

After completing this chapter, you will be able to:

- explain what voice is
- explain the four types of voice used in academic writing
- identify the different voices in a text
- understand the difference between in-text referencing and footnote/end note referencing
- recognise that different disciplines use different citation systems
- understand how to label different voices.

WORD LIST

Do you know the meaning of these words? Many have special meanings in the academic culture. You can check their meaning in the glossary at the back of the book.

- ☐ citation
- ☐ citation system
- ☐ date of publication
- ☐ direct voice
- ☐ external voice
- ☐ indirect voice

- ☐ family name
- ☐ footnote/end note referencing
- ☐ in-text referencing
- ☐ reference
- ☐ source
- ☐ voice

What is 'voice'?

We know that knowledge develops through discussion and debate. When academics write articles as part of this debate, they not only present their own ideas but also refer to the ideas of other academics. This means that they need a way to distinguish between their own ideas and the ideas of other people. They need to express their own *voice*, and to refer to the voices of others. When an academic refers to the ideas of another person, we call that person a *source*.

Direct voices and indirect voices

Text 31 is a short example of academic writing introducing a discussion on the definition of critical thinking. How many voices can you identify?

TEXT 31

There are several definitions of critical thinking. Halpern (1997) defines it as 'the use of those cognitive skills or strategies that increase the probability of a desirable outcome. It is used to describe thinking that is purposeful, reasoned and goal directed'. Ruggiero (1998) focuses on problem-solving and decision-making.

You probably found that there are three voices taking part in the discussion in Text 31. They are the writer's voice and the voices of two sources. Table 12.1 identifies these separate voices.

The first sentence of Text 31 presents the voice of the writer. In the following sentences, however, we hear the voice of a scholar called Halpern, who gives his definition of critical thinking. In fact, we know that Halpern's exact words are used, because they are

Table 12.1 Identification of voices in Text 31

Text	Voice
There are several definitions of critical thinking.	Voice of the writer
Halpern (1997) defines it as 'the use of those cognitive skills or strategies that increase the probability of a desirable outcome. It is used to describe thinking that is purposeful, reasoned and goal directed'.	Voice of source 1: Halpern
Ruggiero (1998) focuses on problem-solving and decision-making.	Voice of source 2: Ruggiero

enclosed in quotation marks ('...'). Because Halpern's exact words are quoted, we hear Halpern's *direct voice*.

In the fourth sentence, we hear the voice of another scholar called Ruggiero. However, we do not read Ruggiero's own words. Instead we read a summary of his words. We can say that we hear Ruggiero's *indirect voice*.

So, in this short passage, we hear three different types of voices:

- the **voice** of the essay writer
- the **direct voice** of a source (the actual words used by another writer)
- the **indirect voice** of a source (a summary of another writer's ideas).

Referring to other voices

As well as the three types of voices that we have just identified, there is another way of referring to the ideas of other scholars. Text 32 is a section of an article on the effects of television violence on children. In this extract, the writer uses her own voice, and refers to other sources in two different ways. Can you identify those two ways? (Note: Sentences are numbered with superscripted numbers for ease of reference.)

TEXT 32

[1]For over 40 years, academics have been expressing concern about the impact that watching violence on television has on the behaviour of children. [2]Many studies have found that watching television violence is associated with increases in real-world violence in children and adolescents (Street, 1995; Hu & Pickard, 1998). [3]Other studies have demonstrated a steady increase in the number of violent incidents portrayed in popular television shows (Driscoll, 1997; Thompson, 2001). [4]However, as Symonds (1999) points out, television broadcasters continue to claim that there is no link between violent programming and increased aggression.

In sentences 2 and 3, the writer's voice gives us some information, then at the end of the sentence we are told where the information comes from. We do not actually hear the voices of these other sources. We can refer to this type of voice as an *external voice*. Notice that although the second source is written by two people, Hu and Pickard, they have a single voice. Table 12.2 identifies the external voices in Text 32.

Table 12.2 Identification of voices in sentences 2 and 3 of Text 32

[1]Essay writer's voice	External voice of source
[2]Many studies have found that watching television violence is associated with increases in real-world violence in children and adolescents	(Street, 1995; Hu & Pickard, 1998).
[3]Other studies have demonstrated a steady increase in the number of violent incidents portrayed in popular television shows	(Driscoll, 1997; Thompson, 2001).

On the other hand, in sentence 4 we hear the indirect voice of one source, a scholar named Symonds. Symonds's name is included in the sentence, and the date of publication of the article is placed in brackets. Table 12.3 identifies the indirect voice in Text 32.

Table 12.3 Identification of voices in sentence 4 of Text 32

Essay writer's voice	Indirect voice of source
[4]However, as Symonds (1999) points out,	Television broadcasters continue to claim that there is no link between violent programming and increased aggression.

How are voices identified?

In Text 31, we know which voice is Halpern's voice because it is labelled with his name. We also know Ruggiero's voice because it is labelled with his name. In Text 32, we are referred to Street and to Hu and Pickard, although we don't hear their voices. We are also referred to Driscoll and Thompson. Notice that all voices are labelled, except for the voice of the essay (or report) writer. This is very important.

The fact that an unlabelled voice is the writer's voice has important consequences for your writing. When you write an essay or a report (or, in fact, any academic text), you need to remember to label the voices that you use. If you don't do this, readers will think that everything in the essay is your voice. This is a problem, firstly because you may be accused of plagiarism (you will find out more about plagiarism in Chapter 14). Perhaps even more importantly, however, if your voice is the only voice in your text, then the dialogue that drives the development of academic knowledge disappears. All that remains is your single voice presenting unsupported opinions.

THINK ABOUT THIS

Look at one of your own assignments.

■ Is your voice the only voice in the assignment?

■ If not, are you using different types of voices (direct, indirect or external) or are all your voices the same?

Labelling voices

Now that you understand the importance of labelling the different voices in your text, let's look at how to do it. We will use the APA system of labelling, but as you will see in the next section, this is only one way of labelling. There are other systems, depending on the specific discipline.

Labelling indirect voices

Indirect voices give a summary of information given in the source. They are labelled by giving the source's family name and placing only the date of publication in brackets. Page numbers are not necessary when you use an indirect voice.

As Symonds (1999) points out, television broadcasters continue to claim that there is no link between violent programming and increased aggression

Labelling external voices

External voices are used to support the essay or report writer's voice. When you use an external voice, the voice of the source is not heard. Instead, the family name of the source and the date of publication are placed in brackets at the end of the sentence. If more than one source is referred to, each source is separated by a semi-colon.

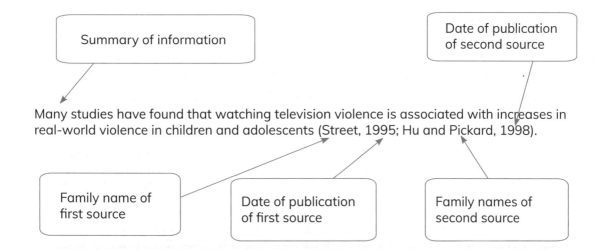

Many studies have found that watching television violence is associated with increases in real-world violence in children and adolescents (Street, 1995; Hu and Pickard, 1998).

Did you notice that the second source was written by two writers, Hu and Pickard?

When you use an external voice in your writing, you need to be especially careful. Look again at the external voices in Text 32. You can very easily see that the external voices of Street and Hu and Pickard support sentence 2. You can also see that the external voices of Driscoll and Thompson support sentence 3.

Text 33 gives another example of an external voice. Can you identify the sentences that it relates to?

TEXT 33

The expectations and behaviour surrounding international business are usually cultur-ally unique. This is especially so in negotiations between people from different cultural backgrounds. Because participants from the two sides think and act differently, com-munication may be impeded. For example, there may be different ideas about who should participate in the negotiation and about how quickly decisions should be reached. Business people from one culture may seek a detailed agreement that covers all possibilities, while those from other cultures may prefer a short and general agree-ment, which leaves room for later change (Johnson & Little, 1991).

You probably found that it is quite difficult to identify which sentences the voice of Johnson and Little relates to. Does their voice support the last sentence? Does it support the whole paragraph? Many academics would consider this use of an external voice as too general. They expect to be able to easily identify which information the external voice supports.

Another problem with placing an external voice at the end of a paragraph is that you make it difficult for the reader to identify your own voice. External voices need to be used with care.

Labelling direct voices

Direct voices use the exact words of the source. They are labelled by giving the source's family name and placing the date of publication in brackets. The page on which the information is located is given at the end of the quotation.

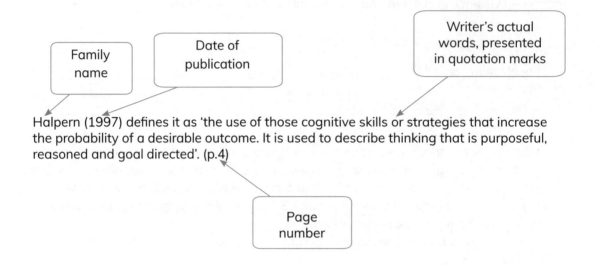

Halpern (1997) defines it as 'the use of those cognitive skills or strategies that increase the probability of a desirable outcome. It is used to describe thinking that is purposeful, reasoned and goal directed'. (p.4)

Alternatively, you can place the author's name and the date of publication after the quotation.

Critical thinking can be defined as 'the use of those cognitive skills or strategies that increase the probability of a desirable outcome. It is used to describe thinking that is purposeful, reasoned and goal directed' (Halpern, 1997, p.4).

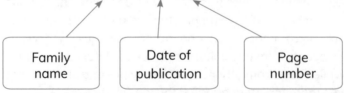

THINK ABOUT THIS

Although, as you will see below, different disciplines use different citation systems, they all require the same type of information, minimally the family name of the author or authors and the date of publication of the text. Look at one of your own assignments.

■ Have you provided this information for each of the voices you use?

NB: Some of your modules may expect you to use footnotes or end notes. If so, you need to read the section below before you answer this question.

Other ways of labelling voices: citation systems

We have just looked at the APA system of labelling voices, but this is not the only way. Ways of labelling are called citation systems, and different disciplines tend to favour different citation systems. For instance, if you are studying history, psychology and physics you are likely to use three different systems. These systems can be divided into two groups, the first involves in-text referencing, the second the use of footnotes or end notes. In-text referencing involves giving details of the author and the date of publication in the text that you are writing or reading. The way of labelling that we have just examined involves one form of in-text referencing, and Texts 31 and 32 are examples of it. The footnote or end note system gives full details of the source either at the foot of the page (footnote) or at the end of the essay, report, chapter or book (end note). We will examine an example of this system below.

While we can divide citation systems into two groups, each group includes different systems. In other words, there are several different systems that use in-text referencing, and similarly different systems using footnotes or end notes.

Table 12.4 lists the most common citation systems; they are ones you are most likely to encounter. The table also tells you which disciplines are most likely to use each system. You will note that the Chicago style has two different versions, one for in-text referencing and one for footnote/end note referencing.

In this book we will not give details of how to use all these systems because such details are easily available: check the website of your university's library or use Google or any other browser to locate a guide to a specific style. However, we have already explored the general principles of in-text referencing using the APA system as an example. We'll now look at an example of a footnote/end note system – the Chicago Notes style.

Table 12.4 Common citation systems

System	Used in ...	System	Used in ...
Modern Languages Association: MLA	Humanities	Chicago Style: Notes system	History, humanities, the arts
American Psychological Association: APA	Psychology, social sciences	Australian Guide to Legal Citation	Law
Chicago Style: In-text parenthetical method	Physical, natural and social sciences	American Chemical Society: ACS	Chemistry
Vancouver System	Sciences, medicine	American Institute of Physics: AIP	Physics

Footnotes and end notes using the Chicago system

Labelling voices using footnotes or end notes is simpler than using in-text referencing. It involves putting a superscript number – that is, a small number raised above the line – at the end of the clause or sentence. Text 34 gives an example.

> ### TEXT 34
>
> The term Silk Roads is used to describe the ancient trade routes linking China, India and the Mediterranean world.[1] David Christian defines them as 'the long and middle distance land routes by which goods, ideas and people were exchanged between major regions of Afro-Eurasia'.[2] William NcNeill has demonstrated their importance, not only in trade but also in the transmission of disease.[3]
>
> [1] Jerry H. Bentley, Old World Encounters: Cross-Cultural Contacts and Exchanges in Pre- Modern Times (New York: Oxford University Press, 1993)
>
> [2] David Christian, 'Silk Roads or Steppe Roads? The Silk Roads in World History', Journal of World History 2, no 1. (Spring 2000): 3
>
> [3] W. H. McNeill, Plagues and Peoples (Oxford: Blackwell, 1977)

The first sentence uses an external voice, as the source (Jerry Bentley) is not actually mentioned in the text. The second sentence uses the direct voice of David Christian, and his exact words are presented in quotation marks. The third sentence uses the indirect voice of William McNeill: his name is given but his ideas are summarised by the writer.

In each case, the full details of each source are given at the bottom of the page. Sources 1 and 3 are books.

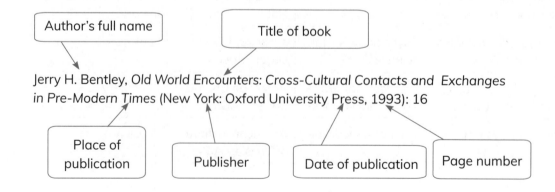

Source 2 is a journal article:

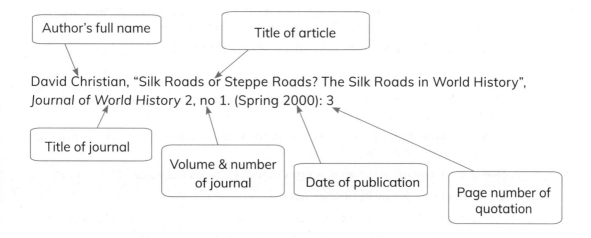

David Christian, "Silk Roads or Steppe Roads? The Silk Roads in World History",
Journal of World History 2, no 1. (Spring 2000): 3

Once you have given full details of the source in a footnote, any further references to the same source can be shortened. For example, if you refer to Bentley again, your footnote would simply give the author's name and the name of the publication:

⁴ Jerry H. Bentley, *Old World Encounters*

Notice also that you can shorten the title of the book by leaving out the subtitle. You can do the same thing with a journal article that you cite more than once:

⁵ David Christian, 'Silk Roads or Steppe Roads?'

THINK ABOUT THIS

Think about the subjects that you are studying and the disciplines they belong to.

- What citation system does each subject expect?
- For each citation system that you are expected to use, is it an in-text referencing system or a footnote/endnote system?

Which voice should you use?

While the actual citation system you use depends largely on the discipline, you are likely to use all three voices, as well as your own, in your writing. The type of voice you use in each particular case depends on the type of information you are presenting. External voices allow you to focus on information, and are they often used to make general points. Indirect voices tend to be used when you are referring to the ideas of particular researchers, while direct voices are often used for emphasis. You will find out more about using different voices in Chapter 15.

SUMMARY

1. When academics discuss issues, they put forward their ideas using their own voice and refer to the voices of others. Other voices are called sources.

2. There are three different ways to refer to the voices of others:

   ■ a direct voice uses the exact words of the source

   ■ an indirect voice summarises the ideas of the source and identifies the source as part of the sentence structure

   ■ an external voice summarises the ideas of the source and identifies the source outside the sentence structure.

3. If a voice is not labelled, the reader interprets that voice as the voice of the writer.

4. The voices of all sources must be labelled:

   ■ A direct voice is labelled using the family name of the source, the date of publication of the source and the page in which the information is found:
   Smith (2004) states that critical thinking is 'the most important skill that students develop in tertiary study' (p. 45).

   ■ An indirect voice is labelled using the family name of the source and the date of publication. The name of the source forms part of the structure of the sentence:
   Smith (2004) believes that the development of critical thinking skills is of central importance for all university students.

   ■ An external voice is labelled using the family name of the source and the date of publication. The name of the source is outside the structure of the sentence:
   Many researchers believe that the development of critical thinking skills is of central importance for all university students (Smith, 2004; Jones, 2005).

5. Different disciplines use different citation systems to label voices. Citation systems can be divided into two groups: in-text referencing and the footnote or end note system.

6. In-text referencing gives details of the author and date of publication in the text, and places full publication details in a bibliography or reference list.

7. The footnote or end note system indicates the citation using a superscript number in the text. Full details of the source are given at the bottom on the page (footnotes) or at the end of the essay, report, chapter and so on. A bibliography may be required as well.

8. Whatever citation system is used, the information given is similar: what changes is the order in which the information is given and the punctuation.

SKILLS PRACTICE

Task 1

For each of the five texts (Texts 35–39), identify which sentences are:

■ the voice of the writer

■ the indirect voice of a source

- the direct voice of a source
- a reference to sources

Each sentence is numbered. You can identify sentences with different voices by the numbers.

TEXT 35

Text	Voice
[1]Cultures differ in the overall amount of touching they prefer. [2]People from high-contact cultures such as those in the Middle East, Latin America, and southern Europe touch each other in social conversations much more than do people from non-contact cultures such as Asia and northern Europe. [3]These cultural differences can lead to difficulties in intercultural communication. [4]Germans, Scandinavians, and Japanese, for example, may be perceived as cold and aloof by Brazilians and Italians, who in turn may be regarded as aggressive, pushy, and overly familiar by northern Europeans. [5]As Edward and Mildred Hall (1990) have noted, 'In northern Europe one does not touch others. [6]Even the brushing of the overcoat sleeve used to elicit an apology.' [7]A comparable difference was observed by Dean Barnlund (1975), who found that American students reported being touched twice as much as did Japanese students.	

Lustig, M. W., & Koester, J. (1999). Intercultural competence: Interpersonal communication across cultures. (3rd ed.). New York: Longman, p 274.

TEXT 36

Text	Voice
[1]Research has shown that in monolingual families (that is, in families where only one language is spoken), the oldest child learns language in a different way from later children (Barton & Tomasello, 1994; Hoff-Ginsberg, 1998; Pine, 1995). [2]This is because parents talk directly to the eldest child, but younger children tend to talk to their parents in the presence of their older brothers and sisters (Pine, 1995). [3]Perhaps as a result, the grammar and vocabulary of firstborn children tend to develop more quickly (Hoff-Ginsberg, 1998). [4]Later-born children tend to produce more personal pronouns (Oshima-Takane et al., 1996) and to develop more advanced conversational skills; they join ongoing conversations between their mothers and elder siblings (Dunn & Shatz, 1989) and use social routines to fulfill their roles in the conversations (Pine, 1995).	

Modified from Shin, S. J. (2002). 'Birth order and the language experience of bilingual children'. TESOL Quarterly, 36 (1), 103–104

155

TEXT 37

Text	Voice

¹Is it possible to persuade consumers in different markets with the same advertising message? ²Or should the advertising message reflect local culture? ³This question is important when planning advertising campaigns in different cultures. ⁴One side in the debate claims that the world can be treated as one large market (Levitt, 1983). ⁵In this view, advertising can be standardised across cultures, and the same values can be used to persuade customers to buy a product. ⁶The opposing side argues that the way in which needs are satisfied differs from culture to culture. ⁷Advertising campaigns should reflect the local habits, lifestyles and economic conditions in order to be effective. ⁸For example, Smith (1989) reports that 'The same product is sold in different countries, but there are important differences in the reasons why consumers in each country purchase it.'

Dahl, S. (2000). Cultural values in beer advertising. Paper presented at the Research Day, Intercultural Research Group, University of Luton. Retrieved January 29, 2006, from http://www.stephweb.com/capstone/beer.shtml

TEXT 38

Text	Voice

¹Though many of the problems of Egyptian education have not been seriously addressed, the government has devoted huge amounts of resources to integrating new technologies in schools. ²This effort is seen as overcoming two great divides, one international, and one domestic. ³At the international level, technology in education is seen as a way to leapfrog ahead and catch up with the West (Bahaa El Din, 1997; Ministry of Education, 1999). ⁴As explained by the Ministry of Education's Technology Development Center (1997):

⁵The whole world is undergoing an overwhelming technological revolution in information, electronics, computers, and communication. ⁶This revolution will widen the gap between the developed and underdeveloped countries. ⁷Those who master science and technology and manage information will survive, those who do not will perish, at least economically. ⁸Egypt must race against time so that it can jump on the wagon of the elite of the developed world before it is too late. (p. 79)

⁹At the domestic level, educational technology is seen as narrowing the gap between the country's elite, almost all of whom live in the principal cities of Cairo and Alexandria, and its poor, who are spread out in urban and rural areas across the nation, especially in more remote communities of Upper (i.e., southern) Egypt. ¹⁰This is to be accomplished through the use of the Internet and satellite television for distance education (Technology Development Center, 1997).

Warschauer, M. (2003). Dissecting the 'digital divide: A case study in Egypt. The Information Society, 19(4) 299.

TEXT 39

Text	Voice
(a) The importance of the Silk Roads rose and fell, partly because of economic and political conditions in the major regions of agrarian civilization. (b) When strong political states dominated large sections of the Silk Roads, merchants could travel more freely.[4] (c) For example, during the seventh and eighth centuries, when China was ruled by the Tang dynasty at one end of the Silk Roads, and the Abbasids dominated what is now the Middle East, traffic along the Silk Roads was heavy. (d) Curtin writes of this period: "The simultaneous power of the Abbassids and the Tang made it comparatively easy for long-distance traders to make the whole journey across Asia and North Africa, in effect from the Atlantic to the Pacific."[5]	

[4] A. French, and B. N. Walters, *World System or World Systems* (New York: Palgrave, 1997)
[5] *Cross-Cultural Trade in World History*. (Cambridge: Cambridge University Press, 1985), p. 105.

Task 2

Write sentences that present the information below using a direct voice, an indirect voice and a reference in APA Style. The first one is done for you as an example.

A	
Information:	In northern Europe one does not touch others. Even the brushing of the overcoat sleeve used to elicit an apology.
Authors:	Edward Hall and Mildred Hall
Date of publication:	1990
Page:	274

Example	
Direct voice:	As Edward and Mildred Hall (1990) have noted, 'In northern Europe one does not touch others. Even the brushing of the overcoat sleeve used to elicit an apology' (p. 274).

Indirect voice:	Hall and Hall (1990) point out that northern Europeans, people rarely touch each other, even casually.
External voice:	Most northern Europeans avoid touching each other, even casually (Hall and Hall, 1990).

B	
Information:	About a third of all adults in the world use tobacco.
Authors:	Ron Carter
Date of publication:	2001
Page:	32

C	
Information:	Cigarettes kill half of all lifetime users. Each cigarette smoked cuts average life expectancy by 7 minutes
Author:	G. Dale
Date of publication:	2003
Page:	78

D	
Information:	Smoking causes 90% of all lung cancers, 75% of chronic bronchitis and emphysema and 25% of blood-related heart disease.
Authors:	H. Wells and T. Price
Date of publication:	2002
Page:	23

Task 3

Select a textbook and a journal article. Examine the way that voices are expressed in each text.

- Are voices used in the same way in each text?
- What do you notice about the way voices are used in the textbook?
- What do you notice about the way that voices are used in journal article?
- Why do you think there might be differences between the two?

Read Chapter 15 of this book and check your ideas against the ideas expressed in the chapter.

13 EXPRESSING YOUR OWN VOICE

✸ LEARNING OBJECTIVES

When you have finished this chapter, you will be able to:
- identify the purpose and audience of an essay
- express your own voice appropriately
- use the voices of others in your writing
- select appropriate reporting verbs.

✓ WORD LIST

Do you know the meaning of these words?

☐ argument   ☐ reporting verbs
☐ logical argument   ☐ supporting voice

What is the purpose of an essay?

Why do lecturers ask their students to write essays? When I ask students this question, many of them say that it allows the lecturer to check that they understand what is being taught. This is true, but it does not go far enough.

💭 THINK ABOUT THIS

- Before you continue reading, take a moment to consider what you think the purpose of an essay is.

The purpose of an essay is to present a clear position and defend it. To defend it, you need evidence to support your position. This evidence is usually supplied by the voices of other scholars. You may also have to present concepts or evidence that do not support your position and show why you do not consider these to be useful or appropriate.

It is important to present and defend a position because by doing this, you are taking part in a discussion with other scholars. Remember that knowledge develops through debate and discussion. Perhaps you feel that you are just a student, and don't know enough to take part in a real academic discussion. It is true that, as a student, you are still developing your knowledge and skills, so when you write an essay, you need to demonstrate that you are developing two things:

- your knowledge of the subject
- your ability to use that knowledge in a debate with others.

Who is the audience of an essay?

THINK ABOUT THIS

- Before you read this section, consider who you think the audience for your essay is.

The audience for your essay is primarily your lecturer. He or she wants to see that you:

- can present a clear position (i.e., that you have a voice)
- can support your position with evidence and/or reasons (i.e., you can develop a logical argument)
- understand the major concepts relevant to the topic you are discussing (i.e., that you understand the positions of other scholars who have discussed the topic)
- can evaluate other scholars' ideas and the evidence they present
- can distinguish both your voice and the voices of your sources and identify each source appropriately.

How are voices used in an essay?

We will use a mini-essay to examine how voices are used in an essay. The essay was written to answer the question:

Analyse the major causes of water shortage in the world today.

Read Text 40 and the analysis of it before you read the comments below. As you read, think about the way the voices are used, then compare your thoughts with the comments.

TEXT 40

[1]During the 20th century, the world's population tripled while water consumption grew sevenfold. [2]As a result, in almost every area of the world today there is a water problem. [3]While the causes of the problem vary, most relate to human activity. [4]Mismanagement and profligate use of available water supplies are a major problem, as are pollution and privatisation of water supplies.

[5]Overuse of water resources is a major problem all over the world. [6]The crisis is particularly acute in relation to groundwater reserves, which lie deep under the surface in aquifers. [7]One-third of the world's population depends on these aquifers, which have taken thousands of years to develop (Brown, 2001). [8]Because the reserves of water they hold are large, they have been used without any thought of the future. [9]Payal Sampat (cited in Brown, 2001) states that worldwide, people use about 200 billion cubic metres more water than can be replaced. [10]In other words, the world's water capital is being steadily used up.

[11]Often, water is used in ways that are wasteful and unproductive. [12]Take California, a dry state which nevertheless has well-watered lawns and 560 000 swimming pools. [13] Barlow and Clark (2002) point out that water from the Colorado River has been used to the limit, and now the region's aquifers are being drained. [14]They predict that by 2020 there will be a water shortfall nearly equivalent to what the state is currently using. [15]Otchet (2002) reports on a huge project in Libya which plans to draw water from an aquifer beneath the Sahara desert and transfer it 3500 kilometres by a network of giant pipelines to irrigate the country. [16] She points out that the cost is estimated at $32 billion and that the water will be so dear – at about $10 000 to irrigate a hectare – that whatever is grown will not be able to cover the cost of supply. [17]The aquifer can never be renewed, as hardly any rain falls in the Sahara and the reserves are estimated to last only between 15 and 50 years. [18]Even more seriously, George (2003) claims the project may result in huge subsidence in the Sahara and the prospect of the Nile seeping into the emptying aquifer, thus plunging Egypt into crisis.

[19]A related problem is the wasteful model of agriculture that has turned food-growing into an industrial process which requires intensive irrigation. [20]Today, farming accounts for 70 per cent of water use with the lion's share taken by irrigation. [21]A UNEP Report (2002) states that irrigation and poor management have led to the salinisation of a full 20 per cent of the world's irrigated land. [22]Postal (1999) suggests that up to 10 per cent of the world's grain is being produced by water that will not be renewed.

[23]Pollution is another major problem (Barlow & Clarke, 2002; Bowch, 2002). [24]Much of Eastern Europe has filthy rivers – in Poland the problem is so bad that the water of the majority of its rivers cannot even be put to industrial use. [25]Even more seriously, aquifers are also being polluted, and the pollution of aquifers is generally irreversible. [26]The WHO report on groundwater (2002) states that groundwater around major cities, near industrial developments or beneath industrial farms inevitably contains contaminants. [27]The report points out that in the US, 60 per cent of liquid industrial waste

is injected straight into deep groundwater. [28]Together, these activities are a deadly form of short-sightedness.

[29]As a solution to the world's water problems, the IMF and World Bank encourage privatisation. [30]They are supported by a number of transnational water companies, such as Suez, which focus on the most profitable sectors, mostly in wealthy areas. [31]Such companies demand tax concessions from governments, raise prices and cut off people unable to pay. [32]The poorer sections of the community are badly disadvantaged by this model. [33]In addition, privatisation contributes greatly to over-exploitation of water resources. [34]As environmental activist Vandana Shiva (2002, p. 23) argues, 'The water crisis is an ecological crisis with commercial causes but no market solutions. [35]Market solutions destroy the earth and aggravate inequality.'

[36]It is clear that the water crisis being experienced around the globe is largely the result of poor water management. [37]Water is wasted on non-essential or poorly planned projects without thought of replacement. [38]At the same time, water sources are being polluted as a result of poor agricultural and industrial management practices. [39]Market solutions to the water crisis favour the rich at the expense of the poor.[40]Immediate measures must be taken to regulate the use of water internationally in order to ensure that everyone has access to a safe and sufficient source of water.

Whose voice is speaking?

Sentences 1–2: Essay writer's voice – essay writer introduces topic

Sentences 3–4: Essay writer's voice – indicates position writer will present

Sentences 5–6: Essay writer's voice – introduces 1st argument: overuse of groundwater reserves

Sentence 7: Essay writer's voice – importance of groundwater: supported by the external voice of Brown

Sentence 8: Essay writer's voice – development of 1st argument: groundwater reserves are being used wastefully

Sentence 9: Indirect source's voice – information from Sampat used to support essay writer's point

Sentence 10: Essay writer's voice – draws conclusion from this section of argument

Sentences 11–12: Essay writer's voice – expansion of 1st argument: example of misuse of groundwater reserves

Sentences 13–14: Indirect source's voice – information from Barlow and Clark used to support essay writer's point

Sentences 15–17: Indirect source's voice – summary of Otchet used to support essay writer's point

Sentence 18: Indirect source's voice – claim from George used to support essay writer's point

Sentences 19–20: Essay writer's voice – 2nd argument: irrigation as a wasteful farming practice

Sentence 21: indirect source's voice – information from UNEP report supports essay writer's point

Sentence 22: Indirect source's voice – information from Postal supports essay writer's point

Sentence 23: Essay writer's voice and reference to other sources – 3rd argument: pollution; external voices of Barlow and Clarke, and of Bowch

Sentences 24–25: Essay writer's voice – essay writer presents examples of pollution
Sentences 26–27: Indirect source's voice – information from WHO report supports essay writer's point

Sentence 28: Essay writer's voice – draws conclusion from this section of argument
Sentence 29: Essay writer's voice – 4th argument: privatisation of water supply **Sentences 30–33**: Essay writer's voice – essay writer outlines problems with IMF/World Bank position

Sentences 34–35: Direct source's voice – source's voice used to support essay writer's position

Sentences 36–40: Essay writer's voice – Essay writer draws conclusions from evidence presented in essay

Based on Dinyar, G. (2003). Precious fluid. New Internationalist, 35, 9.

COMMENTS ON TEXT 40

The essay writer's voice introduces each new point and presents the argument.

You can see this in paragraph 2. Sentence 5 uses the writer's voice to introduce the first argument, which is about overuse of groundwater. Sentences 6 and 7 continue using the writer's voice to point out why groundwater is important. A reference to Brown at the end of sentence 7 supports the point; however, we don't hear Brown's voice. Sentence 8 uses the writer's voice to make another point—that groundwater is being used carelessly. Sampat's voice is brought in to support this point in sentence 9. Finally, the writer's voice in sentence 10 restates the point that groundwater is being overused without thought.

Because the essay writer's voice introduces and presents each argument, it is the dominant voice and the one that controls the argument.

Specific information is usually provided by other voices

While the essay writer's voice presents each argument, other voices are used to support the essay writer's position. They provide evidence—including statistics, examples and so on. Other voices, whether direct or indirect, do not present the argument. They are there to support the writer's voice.

The essay writer's voice is not labelled, while other voices are

Remember that voices that are not labelled are taken to be the essay writer's voice. It is important to remember this for two reasons. Firstly, if the support voices are not named, then it looks as if there is no independent evidence to support the argument. Secondly, remember that academic debate involves a dialogue between many voices. If these voices are not identified, the dialogue disappears and the essay writer appears to be presenting a personal opinion.

There is a third reason why it is important to label supporting voices, and that is plagiarism. We will deal with plagiarism more fully in Chapter 14 but, briefly, plagiarism refers to the use of a scholar's information or ideas without labelling them as belonging to that scholar. Plagiarism is regarded very seriously by universities and university staff, so you need to make sure that you have labelled the sources you use in your essays very carefully.

Indirect voices are used far more frequently than direct voices

You may have noticed that most of the voices used in the essay are indirect voices. In fact, there is only one example of a direct voice. Direct voices are not often used in essays because they are strong. If you use several direct voices, it is easy for your own voice to disappear. This means that the reader may think that you have no position and are just copying what other people say. Therefore, it is usually better to summarise information and use an indirect voice than it is to use the direct voice of a source. For more information on when to use a direct quotation, see Chapter 14 on plagiarism.

THINK ABOUT THIS

Look at the way you have used voices in one of your own assignments.

- Do you introduce each new point in your own voice?
- Do you support your voice with evidence from other voices?
- Can you distinguish between your voice (not labelled) and other voices (which are labelled)?

Labelling voices in an essay

By now you should understand why it is important to label the different voices in your essay. In fact, you often need to label voices more than once.

Look at the two examples below, which come from Text 40.

Otchet (2002) reports on a huge project in Libya which plans to draw water from an aquifer beneath the Sahara desert and transfer it 3500 kilometres by a network of giant pipelines to irrigate the country. She points out that the cost is estimated at $32 billion and that the water will be so dear—at about $10 000 to irrigate a hectare—that whatever is grown will not be able to cover the cost of supply.

The WHO report on groundwater (2002) states that groundwater around major cities, near industrial developments or beneath industrial farms inevitably contains contaminants. The report points out that in the US, 60 per cent of liquid industrial waste is injected straight into deep groundwater.

In each example, the voice of a source is summarised and the summary involves more than one sentence. Notice that we are reminded of whose voice is speaking at the beginning of the second sentence by the use of 'she' in the first example, and 'the report' in the second example.

When you remind the reader in this way, it is important to vary the way that the source is referred to. The paragraph below contains more information taken from the WHO report (not included in Text 40). Notice that the WHO report is named in the first sentence, then referred to as 'the report'. In the third sentence it is referred to as 'it', while the fourth sentence uses 'the report' again.

> The <u>WHO Report on Groundwater</u> (2002) states that groundwater around major cities, near industrial developments or beneath industrial farms inevitably contains contaminants. <u>The report points</u> out that 85 per cent of pesticides don't reach their targets and nitrogen fertilisers readily seep into ground water. <u>It</u> also states that 60 per cent of liquid industrial waste in the US is pumped into the deep ground water. Furthermore, <u>the report</u> claims that coastal aquifers are being drained, allowing seawater to enter and contaminate them with salt.

This variation helps keep the reader interested while at that same time reminding them of whose voice is speaking.

While it is important to remind the reader of whose voice is speaking, it is not usually appropriate to repeat the citation in each sentence of a single paragraph. In other words, a paragraph like this does not sound very good:

> The <u>WHO Report on Groundwater</u> (2002) states that groundwater around major cities, near industrial developments or beneath industrial farms inevitably contains contaminants. <u>The WHO report</u> (2002) points out that 85 per cent of pesticides don't reach their targets and nitrogen fertilisers readily seep into ground water. <u>The WHO report</u> (2002) also states that 60 per cent of liquid industrial waste in the US is pumped into the deep ground water. Furthermore, <u>the Report</u> (2002) claims that coastal aquifers are being drained, allowing seawater to enter and contaminate them with salt.

As we have already stated you need to vary the way you refer to a source.

If, however, you refer to a source using a citation in one paragraph, and then refer to the same source several paragraphs later, you need to repeat the citation form.

THINK ABOUT THIS

Look at the assignment you considered above (p164).
- How might you vary the way you use and refer to voices in your work?

Expressing your voice using reporting verbs

Another way of expressing your own voice is through your choice of reporting verbs. Reporting verbs are the verbs we use when we want to report the ideas of someone else. Some examples of reporting verbs are: 'state', 'claim', 'argue', 'report', 'point out', 'discuss' and 'mention'. There are many reporting verbs, because each one expresses an attitude towards the information that is being reported.

Reporting verbs can be divided them into three major groups: verbs relating to research, verbs relating to discourse and evaluative verbs.

Verbs relating to research

Verbs relating to research include 'study', 'investigate', 'research', 'explore', 'observe' and so on. You use these verbs when you want to indicate the subject or topic of the research without going into specific details.

Bowtch (2002) investigated the extent of water pollution in Eastern Europe. Dalton (2004) studied changes in urban water usage over a five-year period.

Koyama (2004) observed the effects of aquaculture on water quality over a period of ten years.

Verbs such as 'find' and 'report' are used to report the findings of research. Notice that research-related reporting verbs are usually in the past tense because the research that they report is finished.

Al-Khatib (2008) found that aquifers are rapidly being polluted in many parts of the Gulf.

Verbs relating to discourse

Verbs relating to discourse identify what the source is doing with the information. They include verbs such as 'conclude', 'mention' and 'suggest'. When you use a discourse-related reporting verb, you need to make sure that it is appropriate. For example, if you write 'Brown (1997) mentions the role of agriculture in polluting groundwater', you mean that Brown does not spend much time discussing the topic. If, in fact, Brown spends a lot of time discussing the role of agriculture in polluting ground water, then your choice of 'mention' as the reporting verb would be inappropriate.

Table 13.1 presents a list of common discourse-related reporting verbs.

Evaluative reporting verbs

Evaluative reporting verbs reflect your judgement of the source. Verbs such as 'contend', 'assume' and 'assert' are all evaluative, so when you use them make sure that you chose one that accurately reflects your judgement.

Table 13.2 sets out some examples of common evaluative reporting verbs.

As you read academic texts, remember to note the reporting verbs that are used, and make sure that you understand the attitude they express.

Table 13.1 Common discourse-related reporting verbs

Reporting verb	Use	Example
State	To present something as a fact	Payal Sampat (cited in Brown, 2001) states that worldwide, people use about 200 billion cubic metres more water than can be replaced.
Show	To present something as a fact	The WHO's report on the privatisation of water (2008) showed that the poor are the major sufferers.
Explain	To give details of how or why something happens	Otchet (2002) explains how water from underground aquifers will be piped 3500 kilometres across the desert.
Argue	To present someone's position on an issue	Otchet (2002) argues that problems caused by the Libyan irrigation project far outweigh the benefits.
Claim	To indicate that your source has stated something as a fact	George (2003) claims the project may result in huge subsidence in the Sahara, thus plunging Egypt into crisis.
Point out	To present something as a fact	Barlow and Clark (2002) point out that water from the Colorado River has been used to the limit, and now the region's aquifers are being drained.
Reject	To present a position that the source does not support	Shiva (2002) rejects the idea that privatisation will improve water supplies.
Discuss	To indicate the issue or topic that a source examines	Otchet (2002) discusses the problems arising from Libya's proposal to use water piped across long distances for irrigation.
Mention	To indicate that the source deals with an issue very briefly	Brown (1997) mentions the role of agriculture in polluting groundwater.
Note	To indicate that the source deals with an issue very briefly	Thompson (2002) notes that rising sea levels may result in salination of aquifers.
Conclude	To indicate the conclusion the source reaches	Otchet (2002) concluded that the Libyan irrigation project is ecologically destructive.
Suggest	To indicate source thinks something is possibly true	Postal (1999) suggests that up to 10% of the world's grain is being produced by water that will not be renewed.

(continued)

Table 13.1 (continued)

Reporting verb	Use	Example
Propose	To suggest a solution to a particular problem	Brown (2005) proposes a halt to the exploitation of groundwater for industrial purposes.
Emphasise	To indicate the source's most important point	Shiva (2002) emphasises the need for ecologically sustainable use of water resources.
Demonstrate	To show how or why something is the case	In his study of groundwater pollution, Hassan (2001) demonstrated that its effects were felt mainly by the poor.
Describe	To outline a process or the causes and results of a process; to identify something	Li (2002) described a pilot project aimed at irrigating the arid North China plain.

Table 13.2 Common evaluative reporting verbs

Reporting verb	Use	Example
Contend	To indicate that you disagree with your source's position	The World Bank contends that privatisation of resources will reduce corruption and mismanagement.
Assume	To indicate that you think that the source has treated something as factual, but you believe it is not	The World Bank assumes that privatisation will improve the management of water resources.
Reveal	To indicate that the information was previously hidden or not widely known	Bartlett (2003) reveals that some commercial water companies have bribed local officials to obtain permits allowing them to exploit groundwater reserves.
Allege	To indicate that you think a source makes a claim without proof	Cooper and Davy (1999) allege that governments are deliberately understating the extent of water pollution.
Imply	To indicate that the source says something indirectly	Otchet (2002) implies that the Libyan government is mismanaging its water resources.
Exaggerate	To indicate that the source places too much emphasis on something	Jensen (2004) exaggerates the extent to which public water companies are responsible for the water crisis.

THINK ABOUT THIS

- Do you have a 'favourite' reporting verb that you use all the time?
- Choose an assignment in which you have used this verb quite frequently. What other verb might you replace it with?

Disciplinary differences in the use of reporting verbs[2]

As we have just seen, there are many different reporting verbs. However, some are more popular than others, and different disciplines tend to favour different verbs. Ken Hyland investigated the use of reporting verbs in various disciplines and identified seven verbs that are popular in most disciplines. They are:

suggest	find	describe report
argue	show	propose

He also found that there are differences in how often different disciplines use these (and other) reporting verbs. You should make sure that you know the meaning of these verbs, and if you can find which are the most common verbs in the disciplines you are studying, this is also useful. One way to do this is to keep a record of the reporting verbs you see in the articles and books that you read. You will very quickly find which verbs are used most frequently.

Tense in reporting verbs[3]

You can express your voice through your choice of reporting verbs, but you may also express it through the tense that you use. Look at the two sentences below.

Traditional behaviourists believe that language learning is the result of imitation, practice, feedback on success, and habit formation.

Traditional behaviourists believed that language learning is the result of imitation, practice, feedback on success, and habit formation.

In the first example, the present tense shows that you think the behaviourist approach is still relevant and useful. If you use the past tense, however, you show that you believe the behaviourist approach is no longer relevant.

---

[2] The discussion of the use of reporting verbs is based on Hyland, K. (2002). Activity and evaluation: Reporting practices in academic writing. In J. Flowerdew (ed.), *Academic discourse*. Harlow, England: Longman, pp. 115–131.

[3] This discussion is based on Swales, J., & Feak, C. 1994. *Academic writing for graduate students*. Ann Arbor: University of Michigan Press, pp. 183–184.

You can also indicate your attitude to a specific study by varying the tense as the following examples show.

> *Barlow and Clark (2002)* **point out** *that water from the Colorado River has been used to the limit.*

> *Barlow and Clark (2002)* **have pointed out** *that water from the Colorado River has been used to the limit.*

> *Barlow and Clark (2002)* **pointed out** *that water from the Colorado River has been used to the limit.*

By using the present tense, you indicate that you agree with Barlow and Clark's position. Using the present perfect indicates a slight distance between your position and that of Barlow and Clark. A greater degree of distance is indicated by the use of the past tense.

However, the selection of tense in reporting verbs is complex. Your attitude to the source is not the only consideration, and you may find it useful to consult books that deal specifically with the grammar of academic English. You will find some suggestions in Further Reading at the end of this book.

 **SUMMARY**

1 The purpose of an essay is to present a clear position and defend it.
2 The audience of an essay is your lecturer, who wants to see that you can:
   - develop a logical argument
   - understand the ideas of other scholars in the field
   - evaluate the ideas of other scholars
   - distinguish between your own voice and the voices of others by appropriate labelling.
3 Using voices in an essay:
   - The essay writer's voice introduces each new point and presents the argument.
   - Specific information is usually provided by other voices.
   - The essay writer's voice is not labelled, while other voices are.
   - Indirect voices are used far more frequently than direct voices.
4 Labelling voices:
   - If your summary of a source's ideas takes more than two sentences, you need to remind the reader of whose voice is speaking by relabelling.
   - When you relabel, you should use a range of references.

5 Reporting verbs:

- Reporting verbs are used to report the ideas of others.
- They can be divided into three groups: verbs relating to research, verbs relating to discourse and evaluative reporting verbs.
- Your voice is expressed in your choice of reporting verb.
- The tense used in a reporting verb may also reflect your voice.
- Different disciplines tend to favour different reporting verbs.

 SKILLS PRACTICE

Text 41 is a brief description of Maslow's hierarchy of needs.

a) Which sentences are the writer's voice and which are Maslow's?

b) Identify the ways in which the reader is reminded that Maslow's voice is speaking. (Underline the words that show this.)

 TEXT 41

[1]One of the most widely known theories of motivation is Abraham Maslow's (1954) hierarchy of needs. [2]According to Maslow, every person experiences a hierarchy of five basic needs. [3]These are:

- Physiological needs – food, drink, housing, sexual satisfaction and so on
- Safety needs – physical and emotional security and protection
- Social needs – affection, acceptance, friendship
- Esteem needs – self-respect, status, recognition
- Self-actualisation needs – the ability to achieve one's potential.

[4]These needs are arranged in a hierarchy or ladder, with physiological needs as the starting point. [5]Maslow claims that as each need in the hierarchy is largely satisfied, the next need becomes dominant. [6]In order to motivate someone, you need to know where they are on the hierarchy of needs and focus on needs at that level or higher

[7]Maslow went further and divided needs into higher and lower levels. [8]He regarded physiological and safety needs as lower-order needs and social, esteem and self-actualisation needs as higher-order needs. [9]Higher-order needs are satisfied internally and lower-order needs externally.

[10]While Maslow's theory has been extremely influential, it is not based on research, and in fact attempts to validate it have not succeeded.

Task 2

Look at one of your own essays.

- Identify your own voice and the voices of your sources.
- Have you labelled the voices of your sources?
- Which voice presents the argument? Which voice(s) give supporting information?
- How can you improve the way that you use voices in the essay?

Task 3

Text 42 presents three different ways of referring to the voice of a source.

- Evaluate each of the three texts and identify the most appropriate. Give reasons for your choice
- Identify the problems with the other two texts.

TEXT 42

a. One of the major challenges faced by international managers is developing an understanding of the ways in which different value orientations affect the conduct of business. Trompenaaars and Hampden-Turner (1997) claim that one of the key issues on which cultures differ is whether they stress the rights of the individual or the interests of the group. They point out that international managers need to take notice of the preferences of different societies regarding individualism and collectivism, especially with regard to recognising achievement and establishing responsibility. They illustrate this point by examining differing attitudes to pay by performance. Pay by performance tends to be favoured in societies which value individualism, because it assumes that the contribution made by one individual can easily be distinguished from the contributions of others in the group. In contrast, many collectivist cultures tend to favour reward systems which focus on the group, and find pay by performance to be divisive.

b. One of the major challenges faced by international managers is developing an understanding of the ways in which different value orientations affect the conduct of business. Trompenaaars and Hampden-Turner (1997) claim that one of the key issues on which cultures differ is whether they stress the rights of the individual or the interests of the group. They point out that international managers need to take notice of the preferences of different societies regarding individualism and collectivism, especially with regard to recognising achievement and establishing responsibility (Trompenaaars and Hampden-Turner,1997). They illustrate this point by examining differing attitudes to pay by performance (Trompenaaars and Hampden-Turner, 1997). Pay by performance tends to be favoured in societies which value individualism, because it assumes that the contribution made by one individual can easily be distinguished from the contributions of others in the group (Trompenaaars and Hampden-Turner, 1997). In contrast, many collectivist cultures tend to favour reward systems which focus on the group, and find pay by performance to be divisive (Trompenaaars and Hampden-Turner, 1997).

c. One of the major challenges faced by international managers is developing an understanding of the ways in which different value orientations affect the conduct of business. Some researchers claim that one of the key issues on which cultures differ is whether they stress the rights of the individual or the interests of the group. International managers need to take notice of the preferences of different societies regarding individualism and collectivism, especially with regard to recognising achievement and establishing responsibility. For example, pay by performance tends to be favoured in societies which value individualism, because it assumes that the contribution made by one individual can easily be distinguished from the contributions of others in the group. In contrast, many collectivist cultures tend to favour reward systems which focus on the group, and find pay by performance to be divisive (Trompenaaars and Hampden-Turner, 1997).

Task 4

Explain the difference in meaning in the following groups of sentences.

1 a   Postal (1999) states that up to 10 per cent of the world's grain is being produced by water that will not be renewed.
   b   Postal (1999) reveals that up to 10 per cent of the world's grain is being produced by water that will not be renewed.
   c   Postal (1999) contends that up to 10 per cent of the world's grain is being produced by water that will not be renewed.

2 a   Otchet (2002) alleges that the Libyan government is mismanaging its water resources.
   b   Otchet (2002) claims that the Libyan government is mismanaging its water resources.
   c   Otchet (2002) notes that the Libyan government is mismanaging its water resources.

3 a   Bowtch (2002) mentions the extent of water pollution in Eastern Europe.
   b   Bowtch (2002) discusses the extent of water pollution in Eastern Europe.
   c   Bowtch (2002) reports on the extent of water pollution in Eastern Europe.

4 a   Barlow and Clark (2002) argue that water from the Colorado River has been used to the limit.
   b   Barlow and Clark (2002) point out that water from the Colorado River has been used to the limit.
   c   Barlow and Clark (2002) suggest that water from the Colorado River has been used to the limit, and now the region's aquifers are being drained.

5   a   The World Bank states that privatisation of resources will reduce corruption and mismanagement.

     b   The World Bank assumes that privatisation of resources will reduce corruption and mismanagement.

     c   The World Bank argues that privatisation of resources will reduce corruption and mismanagement.

Task 5

Select a chapter from one of your textbooks or a journal article and make a list of the reporting verbs which are used.

- Check that you know the meaning of each verb.
- Compare your list with that of a partner.
- Compile a list of the verbs found by all members of your class and identify the most common five.
- How does your class list compare with that of Hyland?

14 AVOIDING PLAGIARISM

 ## LEARNING OBJECTIVES

After you have completed this chapter, you will be able to:

- understand the meaning of plagiarism
- understand the different types of plagiarism
- identify examples of plagiarism
- understand how to avoid plagiarism
- refer to sources appropriately in essays, reports and other texts
- understand the type of information to record in bibliographies and reference lists.

✓ WORD LIST

Do you know the meaning of these words? Many have special meanings in academic culture. You can check their meaning in the glossary at the back of the book.

- ☐ citation
- ☐ cite
- ☐ dialogue
- ☐ plagiarism
- ☐ patchwork plagiarism
- ☐ summary
- ☐ verbatim

What is plagiarism?

You have probably already heard the word 'plagiarism' many times. It is often talked about in universities because it involves behaviour that is considered to be unacceptable. In fact, plagiarism refers to several different types of behaviour, so we will investigate each in turn.

THINK ABOUT THIS

- Before you continue, take a minute to write down what you think plagiarism is.

Plagiarism and voice: using sources appropriately

Text 43 is a paragraph from the essay that we looked at in the last chapter, but with one important change. What is this change?

TEXT 43

Often, water is used in ways that are wasteful and unproductive. Take California as an example. Water from the Colorado River has been used to the limit, and now the region's aquifers are being drained. By 2020 there will be a water shortfall nearly equivalent to what the state is currently using. A huge project in Libya plans to draw water from an aquifer beneath the Sahara desert and transfer it 3500 kilometres by a network of giant pipelines to irrigate the country. The cost is estimated at $32 billion and the water will be so dear – at about $10 000 to irrigate a hectare – that whatever is grown will not be able to cover the cost of supply. The aquifer can never be renewed as hardly any rain falls in the Sahara and the reserves are estimated to last only between 15 and 50 years. Even more seriously, the project may result in huge subsidence in the Sahara and the prospect of the Nile seeping into the emptying aquifer, thus plunging Egypt into crisis.

You will see that the other voices have disappeared. The paragraph now has only one voice, the voice of the essay writer. The dialogue has gone. This results in two problems. First, we are told that water from the Colorado River has been used to the limit. How do we know that this is true? If there are no other voices to give support, then readers have no way of checking whether the information in the essay is true.

Another problem is that of theft. The information regarding the use of water in California is taken from an article written by two authors, Barlow and Clark. By using their information without identifying the authors, the paragraph writer is stealing their ideas. Remember that, if a statement is not labelled with the names of the writers, it is taken to be the essay writer's voice. By not indicating that Barlow and Clark provided the information, the essay writer is claiming that the information belongs to him or her.

This type of theft is one of the most common forms of plagiarism, and you need to take great care to avoid it.

How can I avoid plagiarism?

Imagine that you have been asked to write a report on the major causes of water shortage in the world today. You find a paragraph in a journal article and want to use the information in your report. The paragraph is reproduced as Text 44, while Table 14.1 presents six different ways of using this information, together with an evaluation of how it has been used. Read each of the six versions and decide which you think are acceptable, then check by reading the comments in the evaluation column.

TEXT 44

Freshwater resources are being wasted due to pollution and the way in which we use water. Some two million tons of waste per day are pumped into rivers and lakes. This includes industrial and agricultural wastes, chemicals, and human waste. Human waste is a special problem, with only about 35 per cent of wastewater being treated in Asia, and about 14 per cent in Latin America. In Africa, the figure is even lower, where only a negligible percentage of treatment has been reported. Even in industrialised countries, sewage is not universally treated.

Hughes, S. (2004). The coming water crisis. Water Conservation. 16(2), 21–25

Table 14.1 Acceptable and unacceptable ways of using a source

1 Freshwater resources are being squandered due to pollution and the way in which we use water. Some two million tons of waste per day are pumped into rivers and lakes. This includes industrial and agricultural wastes, chemicals and human waste. Human waste is a special problem, with only about 35 per cent of wastewater being treated in Asia, and about 14 per cent in Latin America. In Africa, the figure is even lower, where only a negligible percentage of treatment has been reported. Even in industrialised countries, sewage is not universally treated.	This is an exact copy of the original and is unacceptable for two reasons. Firstly, there is no indication of the original source, so it appears to be the report writer's voice. Secondly, even if quotation marks were used, it is still unacceptable, because the words of the source should be summarised unless there is a very good reason to use a direct voice (See pages 155 and 167).

(continued)

Table 14.1 (continued)

2 Hughes (2004) points out that freshwater resources are being squandered due to pollution and the way in which we use water. Some two million tons of waste per day are pumped into rivers and lakes. This includes industrial and agricultural wastes, chemicals, and human waste. Human waste is a special problem, with only about 35 per cent of wastewater being treated in Asia, and about 14 per cent in Latin America. In Africa, the figure is even lower, where only a negligible percentage of treatment has been reported. Even in industrialised countries, sewage is not universally treated.	This is also not acceptable for two reasons. Firstly, Hughes' voice is only labelled once. After 2–3 sentences, the reader cannot tell whether the voice is that of Hughes or that of the essay writer. Secondly, as with 13.1, even if quotation marks were used, it is still unacceptable, because the words of the source should be summarised unless there is a very good reason to use a direct voice (see pages 155 and 167).
3 According to Hughes (2004), freshwater resources are being squandered due to pollution and the way in which we use water. He states that some two million tons of industrial and agricultural wastes, chemicals, and human waste are pumped into rivers and lakes every day. He identifies human waste as a special problem, with only about 35 per cent of wastewater being treated in Asia, and about 14 per cent in Latin America. In Africa, the figure is even lower, where only a negligible percentage of treatment has been reported. Even in industrialised countries, sewage is not universally treated.	Hughes's voice is clearly identified, but this is not acceptable because the essay writer's voice is not heard, and the wording is too close to Hughes's wording.
4 According to Hughes (2004), freshwater resources are being squandered due to pollution. For example, two million tons of waste are pumped into waterways every day. He points out that only about 35 per cent of wastewater is treated in Asia, about 14 per cent in Latin America, and only a negligible proportion in Africa. Even in industrialised countries, sewage is not universally treated.	Information has been omitted in this example, but the words are still Hughes's words. It is not a real summary, as it is too close to the original. Not acceptable.

(continued)

Table 14.1 (continued)

5 Pollution of freshwater sources by industrial and agricultural wastes is a major cause of the water crisis. Even more important is the problem of human waste (Hughes, 2002). In the developing world the amount of wastewater which is treated ranges from 35 per cent in Asia to almost none in Africa. A number of industrialised countries also do not treat their wastewater.	The argument is presented in the essay writer's voice and supported by a reference to Hughes as the source of the specific information. Acceptable.
6 While industrial and agricultural wastes are major sources of freshwater pollution, human waste is of even greater concern. Hughes (2004) states that in the developing world the amount of wastewater that is treated ranges from 35 per cent in Asia to almost none in Africa. He also points out that not all industrialised countries treat their wastewater.	The essay writer's voice introduces the argument and is supported by Hughes's voice. Information summarised appropriately. Acceptable.

The two most important things to keep in mind in order to avoid plagiarism are:

1. **Readers need to 'hear' both the writer's voice and the voices of sources, and the voices of all sources must be clearly labelled.**

   Example 1 is unacceptable because it reproduces Hughes's words without labelling them. We have already noted that when a voice is not labelled, the reader interprets it as the writer's voice. This is a clear example of plagiarism.

   Example 2 is also plagiarism because, while Hughes's voice is labelled at the beginning of the example, the labelling is not repeated, and the words of the source are not summarised. Usually the reader needs to be reminded about whose voice is speaking every two or three sentences. In examples, 3, 4, 5 and 6 each voice is clearly identified.

2. **Information from the source should be summarised.**

   Using a summary of a source's ideas is usually better than quoting the source's exact words. When you quote a source, your reader only hears the voice of the source. So if you use too many quotations, your voice is lost and the voices of your sources dominate. Using summaries, which are indirect voices, allows you to stay in control. Example 3 shows how the writer's voice is lost if the source's words are not summarised. Example 4 is also inappropriate because it uses too many of the source's words. A good summary uses the source's *ideas* but the *words* of the summary writer.

So how can I use other voices?

Examples 5 and 6 in Table 14.1 show two different ways in which the writer can use Hughes's information without losing his or her voice. In example 5, the information is summarised and presented in the writer's voice, and the source of the information is indicated by an external voice. In example 6, the writer's voice is used to present a position that is then supported by Hughes's indirect voice. Both of these examples are acceptable.

THINK ABOUT THIS

- Have any of the lecturers who mark you assignments indicated that you are not citing sources appropriately?
- Have they ever accused you of plagiarism regarding your failure to cite your sources? If so, look at your assignment again:
  - What aspects of your assignment were criticised?
  - What changes would you make to correct the problem?

When can a source's exact words be quoted?

Direct quotations involve the use of the exact words of another voice. If too many direct quotations are used, then the voices of the sources become dominant, and the position that the writer is presenting becomes unclear. Therefore, direct quotations are not often used, and when they are used, it is for a specific reason. Most commonly, a direct quotation is used:

- to underline the importance of a major point that the writer has already made in his or her own words
- when the source is presenting a surprising or controversial view
- when the source's words are particularly well expressed.

If you look at Text 44 again, you will see that while the information the source presents is useful, it is not surprising or controversial; nor is it expressed in a particularly striking manner. (Note that this does not mean that it is badly expressed!) There is therefore no reason to use Hughes's exact words; a summary allows the report writer to maintain control of the argument.

Some scholars use direct quotations to introduce a point that they want to make. This is permissible, but can be dangerous for student writers. This is because it is easy for student writers to lose their voice in the voices of others. In general, it is better to avoid using the words of others to introduce your main points.

For an example of how a direct quotation might be used, let's look again at the essay on the causes of the water crisis that we examined in the last chapter (Chapter 13, Text 40). Here is an extract from that essay:

In addition, privatisation contributes greatly to over-exploitation of water resources. As environmental activist Vandana Shiva (2002, p. 23) argues, 'The water crisis is an ecological crisis with commercial causes but no market solutions. Market solutions destroy the earth and aggravate inequality.'

Notice how the report writer makes a point in the first sentence (privatisation contributes greatly to over-exploitation of water resources), then supports it with a direct quotation from Shiva. Shiva's actual words are used because they state the argument briefly and forcefully.

THINK ABOUT THIS

Some lecturers compare direct quotations to bombs. They can blow up and destroy an assignment.

- Why do you think they make this comparison?
- Do you agree with it?

Patchwork plagiarism

Here is a section taken from another student essay about the causes of the worldwide water shortage. This student wrote:

Barlow and Clark (2002) point out that water is used in ways that are 'unproductive and wasteful' (p. 35). They state, 'Having used the Colorado River to its limit, California is now draining the state's aquifers' (p. 38). A significant percentage of water is used 'for non-productive uses such as watering lawns and filling swimming pools' (p. 37). They further observe that, 'By 2020, the shortfall in water supply will be nearly equivalent to what the state is currently using' (p. 41).

You have probably noticed that this student uses a lot of direct voices. Although each of the direct voices is labelled, many academics will not accept this type of writing. It is called patchwork plagiarism, and it involves stringing together many short quotations from one or more writers in order to stitch together an argument, just as a person might stitch together lots of small pieces of fabric in order to make a garment.

The reason that this type of writing is not acceptable to most academics is that the student writer's voice disappears. Here is the section again, but this time the direct voices have been removed, leaving only the student's voice:

Barlow and Clark (2002) point out that water is used in ways which are … They state … A significant percentage of water is used … They further observe that …

You can see that removing the direct voices has also removed all the important information in this section. The student writer is not saying anything. Lecturers want to see not only that you can use other voices in your writing, but that you can use them appropriately, supporting your voice rather than replacing it.

THINK ABOUT THIS

Look at your own assignments.

■ Are you guilty of patchwork plagiarism?

■ If so, how might you avoid it in future?

Using bibliographies and reference lists

We have now examined how to label the different voices in your text. However, while this is extremely important, it is not enough. You also need to provide details of all your sources in a bibliography or a reference list, which is placed at the end of your assignment, usually on a separate page. This allows your readers to learn more from up the materials you used in your assignment.

Before we identify the details that you need to supply, you need to understand the difference between a bibliography and a reference list.

1 A **bibliography** is a list of all the sources that you consulted in preparing your assignment.

2 A **reference list** is a list of the sources that you have actually referred to in your assignment. In other words, it is a list of the voices that can be heard in your assignment.

If you are using in-text referencing, a bibliography or reference list (not both!) is essential. If you are using footnotes or end notes, a reference list may not be required as you have already given details of your sources in the footnotes or end notes. However, you may be asked to supply a bibliography. Whatever citation system you are using, always check with your lecturer or the unit coordinator to see what is required.

Both bibliographies and reference lists are ordered in the same way. Each source is listed in alphabetical order, using the family name of the first author of the source. Sources are not numbered.

Citing print sources

For each source, you need to supply several pieces of information. Different types of text require you to give different types of information. Whatever citation system you are using, you will need the same information for a specific type of text, but it is arranged in a different order and with different punctuation. Table 14.2 indicates the type of information that you have to give in a bibliography or reference list, depending on the type of source you are citing: books, journal articles or chapters in edited publications.

Before you start reading a chapter, journal article or book, make sure that you note down all the details that you will need to cite it correctly. If you forget, you may find that you can't find the original book or article on the day that your assignment is due, which will cause you a lot of trouble!

Table 14.2 Publication details required for selected print sources

	Printed book	Journal article	Chapter in an edited collection
Name(s) of author(s)	✓	✓	✓
Date of publication	✓	✓	✓
Book/article/chapter title	✓	✓	✓
Publisher	✓		✓
Place of publication	✓		✓
Edition	✓		
Name(s) of editor(s)			✓
Name of journal		✓	
Date of journal		✓	
Journal volume and number		✓	
Page numbers		✓	✓

Here are some examples of citations in a bibliography or reference list using APA style.

Book:

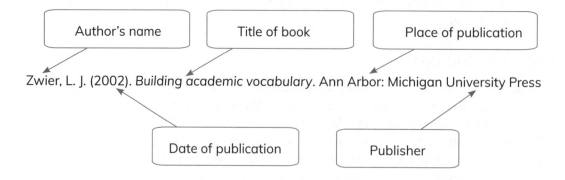

Zwier, L. J. (2002). *Building academic vocabulary*. Ann Arbor: Michigan University Press

Journal article:

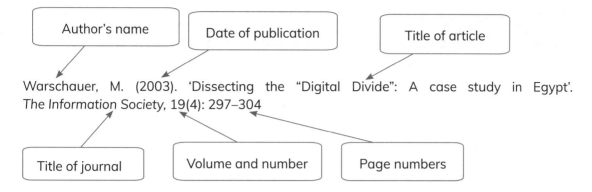

Chapter in an edited publication:

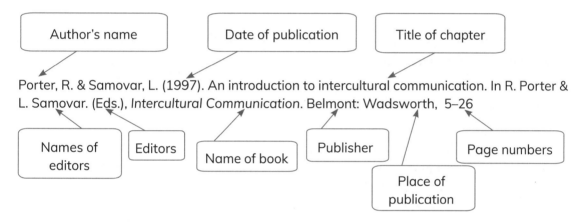

Citing electronic sources

Increasingly, academic texts are accessed online. However, it is usually not necessary to indicate that a book or journal article was accessed electronically unless it is unavailable in print form. In other words, if you access a journal article or a book using a database, you can cite it in the same way as you would if you read it in printed form. However, if the article (or book) is only available in electronic form, you need to indicate this. Although you may sometimes find that not all the information is available, you must conduct a proper search for it before you decide that it is unavailable.

Table 14.3 shows the information that you need to collect about common online sources.

Table 14.3 Publication details required for selected electronic sources

	Online journal article	Non-periodical web document, web page or report
Name(s) of author(s)	✓	✓
Date of publication	✓	✓
Article/document title	✓	✓
Name of journal	✓	
Journal volume and number	✓	
Web page		✓
Internet address	✓	✓

Here are examples of citations in a bibliography or reference list using APA style.

Article in an on-line journal:

Author(s) name(s)	Date of publication	Title of article

Matsuoka, W. & Hirsh, D. (2010). Vocabulary learning through reading: Does an ELT course book provide good opportunities? *Reading in a Foreign Language*, 22 (1). Retrieved from http://nflrc.hawaii.edu/rfl/April2010.

URL		Title of journal	Volume & No.

Non-periodical web document, web page or report:

Author(s) name(s)	Date of publication	Title of article /Title of page

Voiland, A. (2010, November 2). Aerosols: Tiny particles, big impact. *Earth Observatory*, NASA. Retrieved from http://earthobservatory.nasa.gov/Features/Aerosols/

URL

Can students work together on an assignment?

Imagine the following situation. Two friends work together on an assignment, carrying out research, discussing issues and writing it together. Each turns in a copy of the assignment, but the two are almost identical. When they receive their marked assignments back, each has got zero marks. What was the problem?

Lecturers expect all assignments to be completed by individuals mainly working on their own (unless, of course, the assignment specifies group work). This is because your lecturer wants to evaluate:

- how well you understand the content of the course
- whether you have acquired the skills necessary to solve problems and present and evaluate positions.

If two students complete an assignment together, then the lecturer cannot check whether each of them understands the content and has acquired the skills that have been taught.

How much can I discuss an assignment with other students?

Can students ever work together on assignments? Your lecturer may specify certain assignments as group assignments; however, most assignments are intended to be the individual's own work. (We examined group work in Chapter 8.) However, there are several aspects that you can discuss with friends before writing the assignment, such as:

- You can discuss the question with other students to decide what it means and how to answer it.
- You can discuss the position that you want to take and the evidence that supports or opposes your position.
- You can discuss the suggested readings with other students to make sure that you understand them.

However, you must plan and write the essay or report alone. If two students hand in assignments that are very similar or identical, they are each likely to receive no marks because the lecturer cannot identify which student is responsible for the work. The situation is similar if your assignment involves problem-solving. You can discuss different approaches to solving the problem, and you can practise the skills and techniques needed by working together to solve similar problems. However, you must work out the solution to the problems set in the assignment yourself. Again, students who hand in identical solutions are likely to receive no marks.

To sum up: lecturers expect to receive assignments that have been written by individual students. They do not object to students discussing assignments or helping each other to develop the skills needed to complete the assignment. However, students must plan and write the actual assignment alone. Many lecturers regard cases in which two or more students hand in identical assignments as cases of plagiarism.

THINK ABOUT THIS

- Does this description of how to work with other students reflect how you work with others?
- If not, what differences can you identify?
- Do you think your lecturers would approve of how you work with other students?
- If not, how might you change?

Downloading assignments from the internet

You are probably aware that it is possible to download completed essays, reports and other assignments from the internet. It is also possible to ask another person to write an assignment for you, or even to sit an examination. Each of these different types of behaviour involves a student pretending that something is their own work when in fact it is not. These types of behaviour are referred to as 'ghost writing', and ghost writing is regarded very seriously by university authorities. It is considered not just plagiarism, but fraud, and students who commit this type of fraud may face a range of penalties. At best, they are likely to receive no marks for the assignment or they may also be forced to retake the course the following semester. They may even be expelled from the university. In some serious cases, the police have been called in and students have had to face charges in court.

In order to prevent this type of fraud, many universities now require students to hand in assignments in electronic form. This allows lecturers to easily check that students have not handed in identical assignments. It also allows them to compare current assignments with assignments submitted in previous semesters, and to check that assignments have not been downloaded from the internet. Lecturers also pay attention to sudden changes in writing style or accuracy in using English. Major differences in style and language from one assignment to the next usually result in the lecturer interviewing you to check for the possibility of ghost writing. In other words, it is increasingly easy for lecturers to identify students who are committing fraud and to punish them. However, only a very small minority of students deliberately set out to deceive their lecturers by handing in work that they have not completed themselves.

Of course, this does not mean you cannot use the internet at all for information. You can read papers, reports and articles from the internet and then reference any information you use in the same way as you do information from paper-based texts.

 SUMMARY

1. Plagiarism involves failure to label the voices of the sources that you use in the texts you write.

2. If a voice is not labelled, the reader assumes it to be the voice of the writer. If there is only the writer's voice then the academic debate between different voices disappears and the text becomes a personal opinion with no evidence that the reader can check.

3. By using ideas and information from other sources without labelling them, the writer is also stealing them, because he or she is pretending that the ideas and information of others are his (or her) own ideas.

4. Presenting ghost-written assignments (that is, assignments that are written by someone else) or paying someone to sit an examination for you is regarded very seriously, and if caught, you will face major penalties.

5. To avoid plagiarism, writers need to:
    -   label other voices appropriately and remind readers frequently regarding whose voice is speaking
    -   summarise information from sources, using the source's ideas but the writer's words.

6. Direct quotation should be used infrequently:
    -   to underline the importance of a major point that the writer has already made in his or her own words
    -   when the source is presenting a surprising or controversial view
    -   when the source's words are particularly well expressed.

7. Direct quotes may be used to introduce an important point, but this must be done very carefully.

8. Patchwork plagiarism involves stitching together short quotations from one or more sources. It is not acceptable because the writer's voice disappears.

9. A bibliography or reference list is usually included at the end of an essay or report.
    -   A bibliography includes all the sources that you have consulted in writing the essay or report.
    -   A reference list includes only the sources that you have cited in the body of the essay or report.
    -   If you are using in-text referencing, sources are listed in alphabetical order and not numbered.
    -   There are several different styles available for writing bibliographies and reference books. Consult your department to find out which style it requires, and the university library or the internet to find details of each style.
    -   Make sure that you collect all the information needed to cite a source before you start reading the source. This means that you won't be trying to find the necessary information at the last minute.

10. Students can work together on an assignment by:
    -   discussing the question with other students to decide what it means and how to answer it

- discussing the position to take, and the evidence that supports or opposes it
- discussing the suggested readings with other students.

However, you have to plan and write your assignment alone.

11. Downloading completed assignments from the internet is regarded as fraud, and the penalties may be heavy.

SKILLS PRACTICE

Task 1

Imagine that you have to write an essay on the topic:

How has the use of different media impacted the way that young people use their time?

- You want to use the information in Text 45 in your essay. In Table 14.4 are five ways that information could be used. Which are acceptable and which are not? Summarise the reasons for your answers in the evaluation column.

Table 14.4 Acceptable and unacceptable ways of using a source

Version	Evaluation
1 In a national sample of over 2,000 8- to 18-year olds, the Kaiser Family Foundation (Rideout et al. 2010)* found that the average total time that children reported experiencing media in "TV, Music/audio, Computer, Video games, Print, and Movies" rose to 10 hr 45 min (treating simultaneous media use as distinct activities) per day in 2009, up from 8 hr 33 min in 2004 and 7 hr 29 min in 1999 – a 44% increase over a decade. These figures do not include reported hours spent texting, phoning, or using computers for schoolwork. Perhaps most remarkable is that the reported proportion of time spent multitasking – the proportion of media time spent using more than one medium concurrently – increased from 16% in 1999 to 26% in 2004 to 29% in 2009.	

(continued)

Table 14.4 (continued)

Version	Evaluation
2 According to Pea et al. (2012), in a national sample of over 2,000 8- to 18-year olds, the Kaiser Family Foundation (Rideout et al. 2010) found that the average total time that children reported experiencing media in "TV, Music/audio, Computer, Video games, Print, and Movies" rose to 10 hr 45 min (treating simultaneous media use as distinct activities) per day in 2009. This is a 44% increase over a decade. The figures do not include reported hours spent texting, phoning, or using computers for schoolwork. Perhaps most remarkable is that the reported proportion of time spent multitasking – the proportion of media time spent using more than one medium concurrently – increased from 16% in 1999 to 26% in 2004 to 29% in 2009.	
3 According to Pea et al. (2012), the Kaiser Family Foundation's survey of 2,000 8- to 18-year olds, (Rideout et al. 2010) found that the average total time that young people reported experiencing different forms of media was 10 hr 45 min (treating simultaneous media use as distinct activities) per day in 2009, up from 7 hr 29 min in 1999. They point out that this is a 44% increase in ten years. Hours spent texting, phoning, or using computers for schoolwork were not included. They also report that the proportion of time spent multitasking, that is, using more than one medium concurrently, increased from 16% in 1999 to 29% in 2009.	
4 Reporting on a survey of 2000 young people aged between 8 and 18, (Rideout et al. 2010), Pea et al. (2012) point out that total time spent involved with media, excluding time spent on computers for school work, and texting and phoning, rose by 44% in the decade from 1999. They also point to a remarkable rise in the concurrent use of media, from 16% in 1999 to 29% in 2009.	
5 A survey of 2000 young people aged between 8 and 18, (Rideout et al. 2010), found that total time spent involved with media, excluding time spent on computers for school work, and texting and phoning, rose by 44% in the decade from 1999 (Pea et al. 2012). In the same period, they point out that the concurrent use of media rose from 16% to 29%.	

*NB: If you are citing a text that you have not read, but which is cited in the text you are reading, the correct citation form is (Rideout et al. cited in Pea et al, 2012). This is ignored in the present example for the sake of simplicity.

TEXT 45

In a national sample of over 2,000 8- to 18-year olds, the Kaiser Family Foundation (Rideout et al. 2010) found that the average total time that children reported experiencing media in "TV, Music/audio, Computer, Video games, Print, and Movies" rose to 10 hr 45 min (treating simultaneous media use as distinct activities) per day in 2009, up from 8 hr 33 min in 2004 and 7 hr 29 min in 1999 – a 44% increase over a decade. These figures do not include reported hours spent texting, phoning, or using computers for schoolwork. Perhaps most remarkable is that the reported proportion of time spent multitasking – the proportion of media time spent using more than one medium concurrently – increased from 16% in 1999 to 26% in 2004 to 29% in 2009.

Pea, Roy, Nass, Clifford, Meheula, Lyn, Rance, Marcus, Kumar, Aman, Bamford, Holden, Nass, Matthew, Simha, Aneesh, Stillerman, Benjamin, Yang, Steven & Zhou, Michael. (2012). Media Use, Face-to-Face Communication, Media Multitasking, and Social Well-Being Among 8- to 12-Year-Old Girls. Developmental Psychology 48(2), pp. 327–336

Task 2

Look up the plagiarism policies of two different universities (You can find them on the Internet – just go to the web site of each university and use the search function.)

- How does each university define plagiarism? Are there any differences in the definitions?
- Do the plagiarism policies explain what may happen to people who commit plagiarism?
- Are the definitions easy to understand? Can you suggest any ways to make them easier to read?
- Do you think the policies are reasonable? Why or why not?

Task 3

Each of the following activities is considered to be plagiarism.

- Arrange them in order from least serious to most serious.
- When you have finished, compare your list with that of another student.
  1. Material is copied verbatim from a text and the source acknowledged but it is presented as an indirect voice.
  2. Material is summarised from text without acknowledgment of source.
  3. Material is copied from another student's assignment with the knowledge of the other student.
  4. Material is copied verbatim from text without acknowledgment of the source.
  5. The same assignment is submitted more than once for different courses.
  6. The assignment was written by another person, but is presented by a student as his or her own work.
  7. An assignment is copied from another student's assignment or another person's paper without the person's knowledge.

15 VOICES IN DIFFERENT TYPES OF TEXT

LEARNING OBJECTIVES

After completing this chapter, you will understand:

- how the purpose and audience of a text determines how voices are used
- how voices are used in textbooks
- how voices are used in articles in professional magazines.

WORD LIST

Do you know the meaning of these words? Many have special meanings in academic culture. You can check their meaning in the glossary at the back of the book.

- ☐ discipline
- ☐ end notes
- ☐ professional journal

How are voices used in different texts?

You have to read many different types of text while you are at university. Here is a list of some of the most common. Which ones do you use most often? Can you add any to the list?

- Textbooks
- Research reports
- Academic books on specialised topics
- Professional magazines

You may have noticed that different types of texts use voices in different ways. Some texts use only the writer's voice, while others use the voices of many different writers. The way voices are used depends on two factors:

- the purpose of the text
- the audience of the text.

How are voices used in textbooks?

Text 46 is a passage from an introductory textbook on economics. How many voices can you identify in this passage?

TEXT 46

The free-market economy is usually associated with a pure capitalist system, where land and capital are privately owned. All economic decisions are made by households and firms, which are assumed to act in their own self-interest. These assumptions are made:

- Firms seek to maximise profits.
- Consumers seek to get the best value for money from their purchases.
- Workers seek to maximise their wages relative to the human cost of working in a particular job.

It is assumed that individuals are free to make their own economic choices. Consumers are free to decide what to buy with their incomes. Workers are free to choose where and how much to work. Firms are free to choose what to sell and what production method to use.

The resulting supply and demand decisions of firms and households are transmitted to each other through their effect on prices.

Sloman, J., & Norris, K. (1999). *Economics.* Sydney: Prentice-Hall, p. 17.

As you can see, there is only one voice in this text, the voice of the writer. (It is true that there are two authors, Sloman and Norris, but they have only one writer's voice.)

To understand why only one voice is used, we need to think about the purpose and audience of a textbook. It is easy to see that textbooks teach. In other words, they introduce the basic theories, concepts and methods of a subject to students who are new to the subject. Clearly, textbooks do not aim to develop new knowledge. This means that textbook writers are not involved in a dialogue with other scholars. Instead, they are teaching basic information, so they take the role of a teacher and use only one voice.

However, there is something else that we need to notice. If you look again at Text 46, you will see that the information given about the characteristics of a free-market economy is not controversial. Almost all economists agree with this description. When information is generally accepted by most scholars, it is not necessary to label it. Textbooks often present this kind of widely accepted information, so the only voice they use is the writer's voice.

In some textbooks, the writer presents all information in his or her own voice, but uses notes at the end of the chapter or the end of the book to refer to studies that have made the same point.

Text 47 is a paragraph taken from a textbook on management. It explains the meaning of the term 'organisational culture'. In this extract, the writers use their own voice to ask and answer a question about the meaning of organisational culture (sentences 1 and 2). In the following sentences, they give some additional information, and use end notes to refer to two scholars who present this information. However, the voices of these two scholars do not appear in the text itself. They are only referred to in the end notes.

TEXT 47: WHAT IS ORGANISATIONAL CULTURE?

What do we specifically mean by the term organisational culture? We use the term to refer to a system of *shared meaning*. Just as tribal cultures have systems of totems and taboos that dictate how each member will act towards fellow members and outsiders, organisations have cultures that govern how their members should behave. In every organisation there are systems or patterns of values, symbols, rituals, myths and practices that have evolved over time.[10] These shared values determine, in large degree, what employers see and how they respond to their world.[11] When confronted with a problem, the organisational culture restricts what employees can do by suggesting the correct way – 'the way we do things here' – to conceptualise, define, analyse and solve the problem.

End notes

10. Smircich, L. (1983). Concepts of culture and organizational analysis. *Administrative Science Quarterly*, September, p. 339.

11. Sapienza, A. M. (1985). Believing in seeing: How culture influences the decisions top managers make. In Ralph H. Kilmann et al. (Eds.), *Gaining control of the corporate culture* (p. 68). San Francisco: Jossey-Bass.

Robbins, S. P., Bergman, R., & Stagg, I. (1997). Management.
Sydney: Prentice-Hall, pp. 83–84.

Why use end notes?

The choice of whether to use end notes depends on the information the textbook writer is giving. Writers may give information that most scholars think is basic. Everyone who studies the subject needs to understand this basic information because without it they cannot continue to study the subject. In this case, the writer's voice presents the information. We saw this in Text 46, which described the characteristics of a free-market economy

However, writers also need to present information that is important, but is not so basic that everyone agrees on it and needs to understand it. In Text 47, the end notes refer us to articles on how culture influences managerial decisions. There are different ideas about this, so it is not information that is accepted by most scholars. The writer therefore refers us to the articles that present the same point of view.

Sometimes, textbooks need to introduce students more fully to debates and areas of disagreement in the subject. For example, there are several different approaches to understanding how children learn languages. In this case, textbook writers need to identify the voices of the different scholars in the debate. You can see an example of this in Text 48.

TEXT 48

[One] theory of second language acquisition which has had a very great influence on second language teaching practice is the one proposed by Stephen Krashen (1982). ... According to Krashen, there are two ways for adult second language learners to develop knowledge of a second language: 'acquisition' and 'learning'. In his view, we acquire as we are exposed to samples of the second language which we understand. This happens in much the same way that children pick up their first language – with no conscious attention to language form. We learn, on the other hand, via a conscious process of study and attention to form and rule learning.

Lightbown, P. M., & Spada, N. (1999). How languages are learned (Revised Ed.). Oxford: Oxford University Press, p. 38.

Notice how the writers make sure that we know which is Krashen's voice and which is their own voice. In the first sentence, the writers' voice introduces the voice of Krashen. The rest of the extract presents Krashen's indirect voice. Krashen's voice is indirect because the writers summarise his ideas rather than quoting his exact words. Notice also that the writers constantly remind us that we are hearing Krashen's voice by referring to him three times: 'Krashen ...'; 'According to Krashen ...'; 'In his view...'. This means that you can easily tell which voice belongs to the writers of the article and which is Krashen's voice.

THINK ABOUT THIS

- Select a textbook you use in one of your modules. How are voices used in this work?

How are voices used in professional magazines?

Students in disciplines such as business, nursing, accounting and engineering often have to read professional magazines as well as textbooks. The two obviously differ in both purpose and audience, so the way voices are used is also different.

Professional magazines usually contain up-to-date information and discussions on topics of interest to professional people working in specific fields.

Look at Text 49. It is an extract taken from the *Bulletin*, a weekly magazine dealing with current affairs, politics and business, and it outlines some of the ways that companies are improving the interviewing skills of the staff. Can you identify some of the differences in the way that voices are used in this article, compared with a textbook?

TEXT 49: FACE VALUE

[M]any employers are going back to basics as they face the consequences of missing the perfect candidate. Recruitment firms are taking their clients through the professionals' tips on the most crucial point of the process: the interview.

'All of our people are trained in behavioural-based interviewing,' says Nick Adams, regional managing director of Michael Page International. 'And we like to talk through the interview phase with the client before it starts.'

Adams says some clients have trained their people to interview while others leave it to their HR people. Sometimes they have a building filled with smart people who still don't know the basics of interviewing a candidate.

'For some clients we suggest questions and an interview style and we have a chat about what we want to get out of this,' he says. 'The face-to-face interview is an essential part of the process because you get to discover their core competencies. That's what you want to find out and there are ways to conduct an interview so you get that.'

Abernethy, M. (2005, 13 July). Face value. Bulletin.

The first thing you might notice about Text 49 is that the writer frequently uses the direct voice of the source Nick Adams. This approach is used because he is reporting an interview with Adams, not simply reporting on something that Adams has written. Secondly, because he is reporting what Adams said rather than what he wrote, he tells us which firm Adams works for. It is important that the company is mentioned because this gives Adams his authority. Without this authority, we have no reason to take any notice of what Adams says. (Read Chapter 11 to find out more about gaining authority.) Also notice that he uses the present tense 'says'. Doing this helps emphasise the relevance and currency of the information being given.

Professional magazines not only report on developments in different fields, they also discuss important issues. This discussion often involves regular columnists; that is, people who write an article on a topical or controversial topic every week or every issue. The purpose of these regular columns is to present a personal opinion regarding the topic. There is an example of this in Text 50, which argues that Australian business people do not pay enough attention to long-term planning.

TEXT 50

Like all Western societies, Australia is increasingly influenced by short-term decisions, quick-fix solutions to complex problems, and immediate answers to questions. Businesses are increasingly focused on six-monthly profit and loss statements and, if they are listed on the Australian Stock Exchange, on the daily share price. This is both a function of necessity – their masters, the institutional funds, demand companies to constantly lift profits and improve share price performance – and shortening economic cycles and volatile global markets.

The result is companies that do not perform are ditched and their chief executives are shown the door. The average tenure of a chief executive in Australia is 5.6 years, two years shorter than the average in other countries, according to a recent survey by the Business Council of Australia and consultants Booz Allen Hamilton.

Short-term business plans and decisions are a fact of life, but if a company is to prosper in the future, boards need to force management to start developing proper business plans over five and ten years.

Adapted from Ferguson, A. (2004, 16 December). Wasted by time. Business Review Weekly. Retrieved from www.brw.com.au/freearticle.aspx?relId=11358

You can see that the voice of the writer is the most important voice. She presents her opinion with very little support from other voices. In fact, only one other voice is used – when the writer refers to a survey carried out by the Business Council of Australia together with consultants Booz Allen Hamilton. Notice that the date of publication of the survey is not given.

The emphasis in columns like this is on what the writer thinks about an issue. Columnists do not see themselves as involved in a dialogue with others, and so they do not have to relate their ideas to the ideas of other people. Also, they are not writing for an academic audience, so when they do refer to other voices, they can label them informally, as this writer does in sentence 5.

THINK ABOUT THIS

Apart from textbooks and research articles, do you have to read any other type of text in your studies?

- What is the purpose and audience of these texts?
- How are voices used in these texts?

What about voices in my writing?

In this chapter, we have looked at how voices are used in textbooks and in professional magazines. It is likely that you will read many of these types of text during your university studies. However, it is important to remember that the ways that you use voice is determined by your purpose and audience. You are probably not going to have to write a textbook or an article in a professional magazine! This means that the way that you use voices in your own writing will be different from the ways that we have identified in this chapter.

To find out how you should use voices, you need to read Chapters 12, 13 and 14 and the three chapters that look at writing essays, reports and lab reports/research reports.

 SUMMARY

1. Different types of text use voices in different ways, depending on the purpose and audience.

2. The purpose of a textbook is to introduce basic concepts to students. Because these basic concepts are usually accepted as fact by most people in the field, it is not necessary to identify the original sources.

3. When textbook writers refer to ideas and information that are not accepted by most scholars in the field, they often label the ideas and information using end notes. End notes give the reader information about the source of the ideas and information at the end of the chapter or book, so the voice of the source is not heard in the text.

4. Professional magazines contain up-to-date information and discussions on topics of interest to professional people working in specific fields. Professional magazines use voices in different ways:

   - They may use the direct spoken voices of sources by interviewing them. In this case, the company for which the source works is given to establish his or her authority

   - When written sources are used, the name of the source is given, but not the date of publication.

5. As a student, you are writing academic texts for an academic audience, so you need to follow academic practice in labelling your sources.

 SKILLS PRACTICE

Task 1

In each of the extracts below (Texts 51–53), identify:

- the purpose of the text
- the audience of the text
- the number of voices speaking.

TEXT 51: THE PROFIT AND LOSS STATEMENT

The profit is what remains after the expenses of operations have been deducted from the revenue earned.

Revenue represents the amounts earned during a period, usually by selling goods or performing services. The revenue from a retail store comes from the sale of goods. A bus company derives revenue from fares, an accountant from fees charged and a money lender from interest received from clients. The revenue might be received immediately in cash; alternatively, the customer might owe the money so that the revenue is represented initially by an account receivable. ...

Expenses consist of the outflows of resources that were necessary in order to earn the revenue for the period. In a retail store, a major expense is the cost of goods sold during the period. Other expenses include rent, electricity, wages and salaries, and advertising.

Martin, C. (1994). An introduction to accounting (4th ed.) Sydney: McGraw-Hill, p. 14.

TEXT 52: DR KARL'S GREAT MOMENTS IN SCIENCE

How does a python kill its prey?

In the animal world, it's easy to be a top predator. All you need is eyes on the front of your head, sharp eyes and ears to find your next dinner, lots of muscles on your trunk and limbs, and some weaponry such as big teeth, big claws or big talons.

But what if you have no arms or legs, no ears, no eyelids, and no claws or talons?

In that case, you might be a python. Surprisingly, it was only as recently as 2015 that we discovered how they kill their prey.

Karl S. Kruszelnicki, K. (2015). How does a python kill its prey? ABC Science. Retrieved from www.abc.net.au/ science/articles/2015/10/13/4328779.htm

TEXT 53: CULTURE IS NOT INNATE: IT IS LEARNED

From infancy on, members of a culture learn their patterns of behaviour and ways of thinking until they have been internalised. The power and influence of these behaviours and perceptions can be seen in the ways in which we acquire culture. Our culture learning proceeds through interaction, observation and imitation. A little boy in North America whose father tells him to shake hands when he is introduced to a friend of the family is learning culture. The Arab baby who is read the Koran when he or she is one day old is learning culture.

Porter, R., & Samovar, L. (1997). An introduction to intercultural communication. In R. Porter & L. Samovar (Eds.), Intercultural communication. Belmont: Wadsworth, p. 13.

Task 2

Select two of your own textbooks and take one chapter from each. Identify the ways that voices are used in each chapter. Explain to a partner why they have been used in this way.

Task 3

Look back at the last question in Task 3 in Chapter 12. How does the information contained in this chapter help to explain any differences you found in that task?

16 CREATING AN IDENTITY IN DIFFERENT TYPES OF TEXT: PRONOUNS, HEDGES, BOOSTERS, ATTITUDE MARKERS, QUESTIONS AND COMMANDS

LEARNING OBJECTIVES

When you have finished this chapter, you will understand:

- how pronouns, hedges, boosters, and attitude markers create the writer's identity
- the identity writers create in different types of text
- the identity that student writers need to create in their writing
- how to identify common examples of pronouns, hedges, boosters, and attitude markers in texts
- how pronouns are used in different types of text
- the importance of hedges in academic writing
- the dangers of overusing boosters and attitude markers.

WORD LIST

These words all appear in this chapter. Many have special meanings in academic culture. You can check their definitions in the glossary at the back of the book.

- [ ] attitude markers
- [ ] boosters
- [ ] hedges
- [ ] identity

Presenting yourself to readers

We have examined how voice is used in different types of text, and focused on how you express your own voice. However, there is another aspect of expressing your voice that we need to consider. This is the way that you present yourself to your readers.

Look at Text 54.

TEXT 54: THE RELATIONSHIP BETWEEN DEMAND AND PRICE

The headlines announce: 'Major crop failures in Brazil and East Africa: coffee prices soar.' Soon afterwards, you find that coffee prices have doubled in the shops. What do you do? Presumably you cut back on the amount of coffee that you drink. Perhaps you reduce it from say, six cups a day to two. Perhaps you give up drinking coffee altogether. This is simply an illustration of the general relationship between price and consumption: *when the price of a good rises, the quantity demanded will fall.* This relationship is known as the **law of demand**.

Sloman, J., & Norris, K. (1999). Economics. Sydney: Prentice-Hall, p. 42.

The writers of this text are presenting themselves as teachers: they have knowledge that they wish to pass on to students. What is it that tells us this? In order to answer this question, let's look at another text (Text 55).

TEXT 55: ENGLISH: LINGUA FRANCA OR COMMON LANGUAGE?

Today's globalised world increasingly relies on English as a means to enable speakers of different languages to communicate (Crystal 1997, 2003; House 2002). While the number of native speakers of English is estimated to be between 320–380 million, estimates of the number of users of English worldwide range from 1120–1880 million (Crystal 2003: 61). According to Graddol (2006: 14), the number of people learning English is likely to reach around 2 billion in the next 10–15 years. People meeting across cultures and language barriers are thus increasingly likely to communicate in some form of English, making the language a global vehicle of communication in a wide variety of contexts.

Bjørge, A. K. (2007). Power distance in English lingua franca email communication.
International Journal of Applied Linguistics, 17(1), p. 61.

In this text, the writer does not present herself as a teacher. Rather, she is an academic, and she is giving information not to teach students, but to provide a context for the research she is going to present in her article. We can sum up the difference between the two texts by saying that the writers adopt different *identities*. In Text 54, the writers adopt the identity and voice of a teacher. In Text 55, the writer takes on the identity and voice of a researcher and academic. These different identities are created by the different ways the writers use several key language features. In Text 54, the writers address readers as 'you', ask questions to which they already know the answer and comment on the readers' possible behaviours. In Text 55, on the other hand, the writer does not refer to the reader directly, and supports her argument with reference to other voices.

In this chapter, we will examine the aspects of language that create these different voices and identities. In particular, we will look at how pronouns, hedges, attitude markers and boosters are used in different types of text. We will also look at the way that commands, which tell the reader what to do, and rhetorical questions – that is, questions that the writer already knows the answer to – are used to create different identities. Most importantly, we will examine the identity that lecturers expect students to adopt in their academic writing.[4]

Using pronouns

In Chapter 9, we considered the use of 'I' in academic writing, and found that it can be used to take responsibility for an argument or to indicate that the position being expressed is a minority one, one that many other researchers would not agree with. You may also remember that attitudes to the use of 'I' vary between disciplines, and even between different lecturers in the same discipline, so that it is important for you to check with your lecturer before you use it in an assignment.

However, there are two other pronouns that we need to consider; 'you' and 'we'. In Text 54 above, the writers stated,

> The headlines announce: 'Major crop failures in Brazil and East Africa: coffee prices soar.' Soon afterwards, <u>you</u> find that coffee prices have doubled in the shops. What do <u>you</u> do?' (p. 42).

In using 'you', who are the writers referring to? Obviously, they are referring to the student readers. The use of 'you' to refer to readers is very common in textbooks, but rare in other types of academic text.

The use of 'you' to refer to the reader indicates that the writer or writers have power; they know more than the reader, and can therefore direct the reader in different ways. For example, in Text 54 the writers make predictions about the behaviour of readers. In other words, using 'you' indicates that the writer or writers are adopting the identity of teachers, and conversely that they see their readers as students.

What does this mean for you as a student writer? When you are writing, is it appropriate for you to adopt the identity of teacher? Clearly it is not, so generally, you should avoid using 'you' in your writing. (Notice, by the way, that I use 'you' frequently in this book to refer to you, the reader. This book is of course a pedagogic book, that is, a book aimed at teaching, so in this context, the use of 'you' is normal and appropriate.)

---

[4] The argument in this section draws heavily on Hyland, K. (2005). Stance and engagement: a model of interaction in academic discourse. *Discourse Studies*, 7(2), 173–192.

Having considered the use of 'you', we now need to turn to another important pronoun, 'we'. However, before we look at how it is used in academic writing, we need to consider what it refers to. Look at the two examples presented in Text 56. Who does 'we' refer to in the first example and who in the second?

TEXT 56

EXAMPLE 1

(In this paper), <u>we</u> present evidence that captive rooks are able to solve a complex problem by using tools. <u>We</u> presented four captive rooks with a problem: how to raise the level of water in a jar so that a floating worm moved into reach. All four subjects solved the problem with an appreciation of precisely how many stones were needed.

Modified from Bird, C., & Emery, N. (2009). Rooks use stones to raise the water level to reach a floating worm. Current Biology, 19(16), p. 1410.

EXAMPLE 2

As far as consumption is concerned, rational action involves considering the relative costs and benefits to us of the alternatives <u>we</u> could spend our money on. <u>We</u> do this in order to gain the maximum satisfaction possible from our limited incomes.

Sloman, J., & Norris, K. (1999). Economics. Sydney: Prentice-Hall, p. 90.

You probably realised that in example 1, 'we' is the researchers, and that they are using 'we' to take responsibility for their research. 'We' is used rather than 'I' because the research was carried out by two people. It is important to note, however, that this use of 'we' does not include the reader. However, in example 2, 'we' refers to the writers and readers together. Both writers and readers have many ways of spending our money, and we try to get maximum satisfaction from the way that we spend it. In contrast to example 1, this use of 'we' refers to both readers and writers.

This is an important distinction. The way 'we' is used in writing has a major effect on the identity that the writer is presenting. The use of *exclusive* 'we', that is, the 'we' that excludes the reader, allows writers to present themselves as researchers, and to take responsibility for their research. The use of the *inclusive* 'we', where 'we' refers to both writer(s) and readers, is found in textbooks. It allows writers to establish a close relationship with their readers and helps overcome the sense of distance that normally exists between teacher and students.

As a student writer, there are times when you might need to use the exclusive 'we' to take responsibility for research. However, remember that 'we' refers to more than one researcher, so if you are the only writer, you should consider using 'I'. It should be easy to see, however, that you will generally not use the inclusive 'we' for two reasons. First, you are not writing a textbook; you are not trying to teach your readers anything. Consequently, you don't need to overcome any distance between yourself and your reader.

The take-home messages regarding using pronouns in your writing are:

- Use 'I' to take responsibility for your research or your position, but make sure that your lecturer is happy with this before you do.

- If more than one researcher has written the research paper, they will often use 'we' to take responsibility for their research. However, many lecturers do not like their students to do this, so if you are working in a group, check with your lecturer before you refer to yourselves using 'we'.

- Don't use 'you', but remember that you will often see it used in textbooks.

THINK ABOUT THIS

- Do you use 'you' in your assignments?
- Do you use 'we', and if so, is it the exclusive 'we' or inclusive 'we'?
- Evaluate your use of the two pronouns. Is there anything you would change?

Using hedges

Hedges are the terms that modify the positions being put forward. Consider the following statement:

Global warming will cause sea levels to rise by 5 metres over the next century.

This is a categorical statement (see Chapter 9), and one that many scientists would not support even though they believe that sea levels will rise over the next one hundred years. Most scientists would be more likely to endorse one of the following claims:

*Global warming **is likely** to cause sea levels to rise by 5 metres over the next century.*

*Global warming **may** cause sea levels to rise by 5 metres over the next century.*

***It is possible** that global warming **may** cause sea levels to rise by 5 metres over the next century.*

***It is possible** that global warming **may** cause sea levels to rise by **up to** 5 metres over the next century.*

The boldfaced terms 'likely', 'may', 'it is possible' and 'up to' are hedges: that is, they qualify the position of the writer.

Using hedges appropriately is a key feature of academic writing because it allows the writer to present him or herself as a critical and analytical thinker. In other words, the appropriate use of hedges is central in creating the identity and using the voice of a researcher and academic.

Another way to look at hedging is as a form of insurance. When you put forward a position, you know that your readers (and your lecturer!) are going to evaluate it. This means that they may disagree with you. If the evidence for your position is not strong enough, it is easy to point this out and destroy your argument. As a simple example, take the following statement:

> Australians don't study foreign languages at school.

It is easy to disprove this statement: in fact you only need to find one example of a school student who does study a foreign language at school and the argument collapses. You might amend this claim by stating:

> Many Australians don't study a foreign language at school.

This is still relatively easy to attack. What is meant by 'many'? Careful hedging, however, means that readers are likely to accept your argument:

> In some states, as few as 6% of students graduate from high school having studied a foreign language.

While you are a student, your lecturers expect you to adopt the identity and voice of a researcher and academic. Obviously, they don't expect you to write as well as a professional academic does, but they do expect you to use the features of academic language especially with regard to hedging. Hedging allows you to make your position precise and to indicate the degree of reliability of your information. In your essays, reports and so on, you put forward a position and defend it, or analyse a problem and suggest solutions. In both cases, and in other academic texts, you need to make sure that your evidence is strong enough to support your position (or your analysis or solution). Your position needs to be neither too strong nor too weak, but carefully related to the available evidence. Your ability to do this is a key indication of your ability to think critically and analytically; in other words, to adopt an academic identity.

Hedging is not only important in academic writing; you also need to pay careful attention to how academic writers use hedges in the texts that you are reading. It is very easy to ignore the hedges that writers use, especially when you are taking notes. Look at what happened when one student ignored the hedges in a short article on the effects of watching television violence on children's aggression. The original article stated:

> Recent research shows that watching violent television programs could have a long-term negative effect on children. The more children view violent television programs, especially programs in which 'good' characters are violent, the more likely they are to behave aggressively in later years.

Her notes read:

> Violent television programs (esp. violent 'good' characters) cause aggression in later years.

Notice how the hedges in the phrases '**could have** a long-term negative effect' and '**likely** ... to behave aggressively' are ignored, resulting in an inaccurate categorical statement. A better summary would be:

> Violent television programs (esp. violent 'good' characters) are <u>likely</u> to cause aggression in later years.

Table 16.1 Terms used as hedges

about	likely	probable/probably
almost	mainly	relatively
appear to be	may/maybe	seems
approximately	might	unlikely
certain extent	mostly	uncertain
could/couldn't	often	unclear
frequently	perhaps	usually
in general/generally	possible/possibly	would/wouldn't

Many words and phrases can be used as hedges, so it is not possible to give a complete list, but some of the most common are listed in Table 16.1.

To summarise, hedges allow you to:

■ present yourself as a critical and analytical academic student and researcher

■ make your argument precise

■ relate your position carefully and closely to the evidence that you have

■ minimise the chance that your argument will be dismissed.

THINK ABOUT THIS

Look at a research report from one of the units you are enrolled in.

■ Identify the hedges used in Discussion section of this report.

■ Select 5 of the hedges and explain why they are being used.

Using boosters

While hedging helps you to indicate the limits of your position, boosters allow you to express certainty and increase the authority of your voice. They include words such as 'clearly', 'obviously' and 'certainly'. A key aspect of boosters is that they assume that your readers share your perspective; in other words, they agree with you. In the following sentence, there are two boosters. Can you identify them?

> *It is clear that critical thinking is a skill that is both objectively valuable and obviously useful.*

You are right if you selected 'it is clear' and 'obviously'.

While boosters can be useful in establishing your voice as authoritative, and your identity as a confident academic researcher, they need to be treated with a great deal of care. If you overuse them, you may create the impression that you are arrogant and over-confident. If the reader does not in fact share your position, you are likely to alienate him or her, and this is likely to affect his or her final judgement.

Consider this example:

> **As we all know**, *children learn foreign languages more easily than adolescents or adults.*

In fact (another of my boosters!), there is a great deal of argument regarding whether or not children learn foreign languages more easily than adults, so the claim that **we all know** is quite likely to alienate the reader (and undermine your identity as a thoughtful academic because it indicates that you have not read a lot of the literature). Boosters such as 'certain' and 'prove' are particularly dangerous. Especially if you are studying in the social sciences (economics, education, management and so on), very few things are certain, as these subjects deal with people. For the same reason, it is difficult to *prove* something in these fields. People do not behave in standard and predictable ways!

While boosters tend to be avoided in academic texts, they are quite common in articles in professional magazines and journals, so if you read these, you will probably see quite a number. This is because writers in professional journals and magazines are not trying to present themselves as researchers. Rather they tend to want their readers to see them as practical, down-to-earth business people who are interested in results. This means that they often express their positions quite forcefully in order to engage their readers. It is important to remember that you are not usually writing for the same audience as authors of articles in professional journals. Your audience is usually your lecturer, and he or she is likely to expect that you will follow the academic tradition of being cautious in the use of boosters.

As with hedges, there is no definitive list of boosters, but some of the most common ones are listed in Table 16.2.

Table 16.2 Terms used as boosters

actually	definitely	never
always	doubtless	no doubt
apparent	essential	of course
certain that	in fact	obvious(ly)
certainly	indeed	prove
it is clear/clearly	we know	well-known
	must	

Using attitude markers

Attitude markers allow you to indicate how you feel about a particular position or piece of information. They include terms such as 'surprisingly' or 'unfortunately'. As with boosters, you need to be careful how you use them. If you indicate that something is surprising but your readers think it is not, then you risk alienating them. This is especially so if you indicate that something is surprising when it is actually commonly accepted in the discipline. However, attitude markers that refer to the importance of something (including words such as 'importantly' and 'centrally', or 'key' and 'crucial') may contribute to establishing an academic voice when they are used to evaluate academic concepts and evidence from research.

Like boosters, attitude markers are more common in professional journals and magazines than they are in academic journals, so you need to notice when they are used, but not imitate them if you are writing for an academic audience such as your lecturer.

Some of the most commonly used attitude markers are listed in Table 16.3.

Table 16.3 Commonly used attitude markers

amazingly	curiously	interesting(ly)
appropriately	fortunately	surprisingly
correctly	importantly	unfortunately

THINK ABOUT THIS

Go back and look at Text 10 in Chapter 6. This text deals with the process of adapting to a new culture. In this extract, the writer makes several judgements. Can you find them?

Using questions and commands

Finally, a common feature of textbooks is the use of rhetorical questions, which, as we have already seen, are questions to which the writers already know the answers. Questions that ask the reader to apply the knowledge they have just read are also common. The use of questions in a text usually establishes the writer as the person who knows, and the reader as someone who does not know, but is learning. In other words, the use of questions helps establish the identity of the writer as a teacher, and as someone who therefore 'speaks' with the voice of a teacher. If you are writing a textbook, this is appropriate (!), but as a student, you are not usually trying to write with a teacher's voice, so in general it is a good idea to avoid asking questions, especially questions that you are going to answer in the rest of the text.

Commands, where the writer tells the reader what to do (for example, 'Look at Table 6'), are also closely related to the teacher voice and identity, and in general are not appropriate in student writing.

THINK ABOUT THIS

Choose a chapter from one of your textbooks.

■ Does the writer use questions and commands?

■ How are they used and why?

SUMMARY

1. Through your choice of pronouns, hedges, boosters, attitude markers, commands and questions you not only express a voice but you also establish an identity.

2. The appropriate use of hedging is a key aspect of establishing an academic identity and voice. Hedging allows you to modify your position so that it fits available evidence. It:

   a makes your argument precise

   b relates your position carefully and closely to the evidence you present

   c minimises the chance that your argument will be dismissed.

3. In reading academic articles, you need to pay attention to the author's use of hedging so that you do not note down inaccurate categorical statements.

4. Boosters allow the writer to express certainty and increase the authority of their voice. They tend to be used by writers in professional journals and magazines to create an identity that is forceful, authoritative and practical. Student writers need to be careful of boosters to avoid sounding arrogant, and they should only be used when you are sure that your readers do share your position.

5. Attitude markers allow you to express your feelings about a particular position or piece of information. As with boosters, they need to be used very carefully, and only when you are sure that your reader(s) share your position.

SKILLS PRACTICE

Task 1

Texts 57 and 58 both deal with the issue of a carbon tax.

a Identify the type of publication it comes from and its intended audience

b Identify the hedges, boosters and attitude markers that are used

c Compare the use of hedges, boosters and attitude markers in the two articles and suggest reasons for these differences.

TEXT 57

The on-going debate on the benefits and costs of a carbon tax has drawn attention to the hidden taxes, in the form of government charges, on petroleum and petroleum products. Yokoyama et al. (2000) investigated the effects of replacing these charges with a pure carbon tax on CO_2 emissions. They concluded that, under certain circumstances, such a tax could effectively reduce CO_2 emissions without an increase in the total taxes on fossil fuels. They further pointed out that current northern European carbon taxes appeared to have been designed with the aim of maximising public acceptance of the taxes rather than reducing CO_2 emissions, and suggested other considerations that might be taken into account in designing tax regimes that could lead to a reduction in greenhouse gas production.

TEXT 58: CARBON TAX VS. CARBON TRADE

Which would you rather do – trade or be taxed? Perhaps surprisingly, the answer is not clear when applied to carbon emissions. Environmentalists and politicians line up together on both sides of the issue with compelling arguments. Both William Schlesinger (a member of the US National Academy of Sciences and Professor Emeritus of Biogeochemistry at the Nicholas School of the Environmental and Earth Sciences at Duke University in Durham, North Carolina, USA) and Paul Anderson (Chairman of the Board at Spectra Energy Corporation) have come out in support of a carbon tax. On the flip side, Eileen Claussen (President of the Pew Center on Global Climate Change) and James Rogers (Chairman and CEO of Duke Energy) are both in support of a cap-and- trade program. Those in favor of taxes say that taxing is simpler, more transparent, and more easily understood. Those in favor of cap-and-trade counter with the opinion that any accounting system is unlikely to be simple – both would require the setting of limits, monitoring for compliance, and enforcement for noncompliance. ... Carbon tax proponents say that taxes offer less opportunity for manipulation by special interests. And cap-and-trade supporters suggest they should take a good look at the US income and business tax system. But Eileen Claussen may have won in recent rounds of debate with the argument, "...the key difference between a carbon tax and the cap-and-trade approach comes down to the issue of certainty. A tax provides for cost certainty; the cost is fixed because of the tax. Cap-and-trade, on the other hand, provides for environmental certainty. What's fixed is the cap itself – and it is based on an assessment of the level of emissions you need to get to in order to protect the climate."

Modified from Business & the Environment with ISO 14000 Updates;
September 2007. 18 (9), p. 13S.

Task 2

Select a section from an academic article or chapter and analyse how and why the writer has used the following:

- hedges
- boosters
- attitude markers

Task 3

Select a section from a professional or business magazine and analyse how and why the writer has used the following:

- hedges
- boosters
- attitude markers

Compare their use with that in the academic text you used in Task 2. What are the differences? Explain the reason for these differences to a partner.

Task 4

Select a section from a text that you have written and analyse the way you use

- hedges
- boosters
- personal pronouns
- attitude markers

Which is most common in your text?

Do you notice any major difference between the way you use these language features and the way they are used in the text you analysed in Task 1?

Why might this be?

Part 5
WRITING ACADEMIC TEXTS

17 WRITING AT UNIVERSITY

✳ LEARNING OBJECTIVES

When you have finished this chapter, you will be able to:

- explain why writing is important in academic life
- understand the importance of identifying the purpose, audience and structure of the type of text called for in a university assignment
- understand the importance of planning in academic writing
- use an effective writing process when writing assignments.

✓ WORD LIST

Do you know the meaning of these words? Many have special meanings in academic culture. You can check their meaning in the glossary at the back of the book.

- ☐ brainstorming
- ☐ drafting
- ☐ editing
- ☐ proofreading
- ☐ recursive
- ☐ writing process

Why write?

So far in this book, we have considered what the university expects from its students in terms of critical thinking, independent learning and the roles of students and lecturers. We have looked at how lectures and reading contribute to your research, and discussed the use of group work and oral presentations in academic study. Most importantly, perhaps, we have considered how you express an academic identity and voice of your own, and how you relate to the voices of others. All this feeds into the final section of this book, which deals with academic writing.

Academic writing is a central concern for all students because academic knowledge is primarily written knowledge. While oral presentations in tutorials and seminars, and later at conferences, are very important, it is generally when it is written down that this knowledge becomes available for discussion and debate by academics everywhere. In other words, writing is central to the development of knowledge through debate and discussion that we have been talking about throughout this book.

It is for this reason that most assessments at university involves writing. It is true that you will be expected to make oral presentations, but these are likely to form only a small part of the way you are assessed. In other words, your success at university depends largely on your ability to write well.

The key to writing well: the writing process

A short time ago, one of my better students came to see me because she was having difficulties completing an assignment. She explained that she had done all the reading, and was now feeling as if she was drowning in concepts, facts and ideas. 'There's just so much to remember,' she said. 'I get so confused and I can't decide what information is relevant and which to leave out. My report doesn't seem to be going anywhere.'

This is a very common problem, one that many students come to talk to me about. My next question to this student was, 'So tell me what you do when you start to do an assignment. You read the readings; what then?' Her reply was very illuminating. 'Well,' she said, 'I look at the question and start writing my answer'. What she did not say was, 'I make a plan.'

There is a lot of research that shows that the difference between good writers and bad writers comes down to planning. Good writers spend time planning their assignment before they start writing and continually revisit and revise their plan while they are writing. Poor writers, on the other hand, go straight from reading to starting to write, and consequently find, as my student said, that their writing didn't seem to be going anywhere.

Effective planning
Pre-planning: effective note-taking

Effective planning involves several steps, starting with reading and note-taking. We have already considered effective reading in Chapter 6. What about effective note-taking? For many of my students, this is a neglected step. They report that their note-taking strategy involves using a pencil or a highlighter to highlight important sections of the text. Many of these students also report that they find it difficult to remember the main ideas in an article, and may not even remember why they thought a section was important enough to highlight. This is not surprising. The problem with highlighting is that you can do it without actually thinking about the meaning of the text. Efficient note-taking involves actually thinking about the ideas in a text and critically analysing them. So, rather than highlighting, you need to take notes, expressing the ideas in the text in your own words. Using your own words forces you to engage with the text's content, and doing so in turn leads to greater understanding and better recall. This may take longer than merely highlighting, but is quicker in the long run because you remember more. If you still prefer highlighting, then write your own comments in the margins next to the text you have highlighted. Comments might include your evaluation of the idea (good or bad), comparison with ideas in other texts, noting similarities and differences, posing questions and so on.

Once you have read the main readings, and noted their major points, it is time to turn to the actual process of planning your assignment. Assignment planning involves several steps:

- analysing the task
- brainstorming concepts and evidence
- organising content.

You can then move on to:

- drafting
- editing
- proofreading.

Analysing the task

The first step is to analyse the assignment task. What exactly are you asked to do? This involves, for example, deciding how many questions there are, and whether they are descriptive or analytic. It also involves deciding on the type of text you are being asked to write, which can vary depending on the discipline or disciplines you are studying. Nevertheless, the key features you need to keep in mind are:

- What is the purpose of the text?
- What is the (imagined) audience?
- How should the text be structured?
- How will the language I use reflect the answers to these three questions?

In Chapters 19–24, we will examine how these questions are answered for six different types of text: essays (Chapter 19); reports (Chapter 20); research reports (Chapter 21); lab reports (Chapter 22); electronic texts (Chapter 23), reflective texts (Chapter 24) and writing in exams (Chapter 25). At this point, we need to consider two problems many students encounter in trying to determine the type of text they are expected to write.

The first problem relates to what lecturers call the assignments they set. It is quite common for lecturers to call any assignment an 'essay', regardless of the purpose, audience and structure that he or she expects. While you need to note what type of text the assignment specifies, you also need to pay careful attention to the purpose of the assignment. You may find, for example, that while the lecturer has asked for an essay, what he or she actually wants is a report!

The second problem involves the difference between many of the texts you read and the texts you have to write. Especially in your early years of university study, you are likely to read many textbooks. Textbooks are written for a particular purpose and audience; specifically to teach the basic information about a subject to an audience of students. The way they use language (Chapter 16) and the way they relate to the voices of others (Chapter 15) are specific to textbooks and very different from the way that you, as a student, are expected to use language and refer to the voices of others in your assignments. In other words, textbooks are useful sources of information about a subject, but they are very poor models of how to write about that subject. The situation is similar for articles in professional magazines. The purpose and audience, and therefore the structure of these articles and the way they use language, is very different from the purpose and audience of the texts that you write. You will be evaluated in part by how well you can write like an apprentice academic. No one is going to expect you to write as fluently as a professional academic, but you will be expected to refer to the voices of others and to use language in ways that reflect these features in the writing of professional academics.

Having analysed the question and decided on the type of text that is required, you now need to decide on your position, the question you will address or the problem you will analyse. Don't worry if your first answer is not very clear. You are likely to modify it, or even change it completely, as you go through the planning and drafting process. However, having a general answer in place will help you with the next stage, brainstorming.

Brainstorming

Brainstorming allows you to get down all the information that you think will be useful in one place. You don't need to organise it—that's the next stage. Just jot down all the concepts, examples, evidence, technical terms and so on that you think you will use in the assignment. Some students do this on a very large sheet of paper, others use several sheets that they can lay out next to each other. This makes the 'raw material' for the next stage visible and accessible.

Organising

You are now in a position to organise your material. On a separate piece of paper, write down the position you identified in the first stage of your planning process, then use the results of your brainstorming to identify the main points you want to include in your text. Under each main point, note the evidence, examples and so on which support that point. You will end up with a plan that looks something like this:

My position (what I am going to discuss in the assignment)

a Major point 1
- Evidence 1
- Evidence 2
- Example

b Major point 2
- Evidence 1
- Example
- Evidence 2

  c Major point 3

   ■ Evidence 1

 You can then use this plan to guide the next step in the writing process, which is drafting and editing.

Drafting and editing

Drafting and editing are very closely linked. Drafting involves writing out sections of your assignment in full, while editing allows you to evaluate what you have written and make changes for clarity. As you can see from the diagram below, drafting and editing are recursive; that is, drafting leads to editing, which leads to further drafting, and so on.

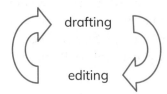

drafting

editing

 During this process, you need to focus on what you are trying to say. Don't worry too much about the grammar: concentrate on establishing the points that you want to make and ensuring that each point is supported by appropriate evidence.

 The drafting and editing process has several important features. The first is that you do not necessarily have to start at the beginning and keep going to the end. If you get stuck on one paragraph, then go on to another and draft that. When you return to the original paragraph, you will often find the difficulty has disappeared. Secondly, drafting and editing is not something that you do only once. A good writer will go through the cycle several times in order to get their ideas as clear and well supported as possible. As part of this process it is quite likely that you will realise at some point that your first answer to the question needs some modification. This is not a problem; it is a strength. Good writers recognise that as they clarify their ideas through drafting and editing, they will probably need to modify their original position. This may result in further brainstorming, and even further reading to locate evidence to support the new position. The organisation of your assignment may change as a result. In other words, the writing process involves moving backwards and forwards, writing your draft, editing, going back to planning and organising, returning to drafting and so on. This means that you should not leave writing your assignment to the night before it is due in!

 Finally, most experienced writers will draft their introduction first, but will rewrite it at least once, at the end of the writing process, because what they want to say will have changed as they write. It is at this stage that many writers will formulate a conclusion by restating their position and drawing together all the main points they mentioned in the body of the assignment text.

Proofreading

The final step in the writing process is proofreading. At this stage, you check your grammar and vocabulary to make sure they are as accurate as possible. Note, however, that this is the last stage of the writing process. Up to this stage, you should focus on clarifying your ideas rather than thinking about the language you use to express them. In this stage, you should also check that you have cited your sources correctly, and that all of them are listed in your reference list. Text 59 is a checklist to guide you through the steps of proofreading stage, from organization to grammar.

TEXT 59: PROOFREADING CHECKLIST

1. **Have I answered the question?**
   a) Is the position I am arguing or the problem I am considering or the question my research is investigating clear?
   b) Do I state it in the introduction?

2. **Is my assignment clearly structured?**

   What type of text am I writing? Essay? Report? Research report? Blog? Reflective text?

3. **Is the structure of my assignment appropriate to the type of text I am writing?**
   a) If an essay: Introduction, body, conclusion?
   b) If a report: Title page, table of contents, executive summary, introduction, body, conclusion, recommendations, bibliography or reference list?
   c) If a research report: Introduction, methods, results, discussion?
   d) If a lab report: Abstract, introduction, materials and methods, results, discussion, references, appendices?
   e) If a reflection: looking back, reasoning and relating, looking forward

4. **Does each paragraph start with a topic sentence?**
   a) Do the topic sentences outline the argument?
   b) Are the topic sentences linked to the introduction by a word chain?
   c) Are paragraphs on the same aspect of the topic linked to each other by a word chain?

5. **Have I labelled all voices?**
   a) Is there a clear distinction between my voice and the voices of others?
   b) Have I formatted the labels correctly?

6. **Have I used appropriate English?**
   a) Have I written complete, grammatically appropriate sentences?
   b) Have I used tenses correctly?
   c) Have I use pronouns, attitude markers, boosters and questions appropriately?
   d) Is my use of hedging appropriate?

7. **Have I proofread my assignment for errors?**

8. **Does my assignment follow any departmental/faculty or university guidelines?**

Now that we have examined the writing process, Chapters 19–25 will consider some of the types of assignment you may need to write, paying particular attention to their purpose, audience and structure.

THINK ABOUT THIS

- To what extent is your own writing process similar to the process described in this chapter?
- Analyse your writing process, identifying its strengths and weaknesses.

SUMMARY

1. Writing plays a central part in the development of academic knowledge, and consequently, the ability to write well is the key to success at university.

2. The key to good writing is the writing process, which centres on good planning.

3. A good process involves several steps:
   - pre-planning: effective note-taking
   - analysing the task
   - brainstorming concepts and evidence
   - organising content
   - drafting
   - editing
   - proofreading.

4. The writing process is not linear – it does not involve starting writing at the beginning and going on to the end. Good writing involves moving backwards and forwards from drafting and editing to brainstorming and organising, returning to drafting and so on.

5. Good writers draft and edit their assignments several times and do not try to complete an assignment the night before it is due.

SKILLS PRACTICE

Task 1

Select an upcoming assignment in your current studies and use the writing process described in this chapter to complete it. After you have finished, evaluate the experience. What did you find useful? Were any steps less useful? How will you use the process in other assignments?

Task 2

Use the internet to identify sites that report on the strategies used by successful writers at university. What strategies did they use? Make a list of strategies that you think will assist you and try them out as you write your next few assignments.

Make sure that the internet sites you identify are reputable academic sites; for example, check that the URL includes .edu or .ac. There are many commercial sites which give poor advice on academic writing.

18 MAKING YOUR ARGUMENT FLOW

✹ LEARNING OBJECTIVES

When you have finished this chapter, you will be able to:

- identify the topic sentence in a paragraph
- understand how topic sentences scaffold an argument
- understand how topic sentences relate to the other sentences in the paragraph
- understand the ways in which topic sentences link paragraphs within a section of an article
- recognise when an argument is unclear
- identify problems caused by placing information in the wrong part of a clause
- use the beginning of clauses to tie clauses together
- use the end of clauses to introduce new information.

✓ WORD LIST

Do you know the meaning of these words? Many have special meanings in the academic culture. You can check their meaning in the glossary at the back of the book.

- ☐ anime
- ☐ data
- ☐ deductive
- ☐ topic sentence
- ☐ word chain
- ☐ hyponym

- ☐ synonym
- ☐ clause
- ☐ clause theme
- ☐ field study
- ☐ given information
- ☐ new information

What makes writing flow?

Students often complain about the difficulty of making their writing flow. Perhaps you have experienced the same thing. You can see very clearly what you are trying to say, but your reader can't. Maybe your lecturer writes comments such as, 'Your argument doesn't hang together' or 'Your argument jumps about' or 'Your poor paragraph structure makes it hard to follow your argument'. They may even say that they can't follow the argument at all. When you get comments like this, one of the first things that you should check are your topic sentences.

THINK ABOUT THIS

- Do you have any comments that regularly get written on your assignments? If so, what are they?
- Why do you think your lecturer makes these comments?

What are topic sentences?

The topic sentence is the sentence in the paragraph that tells the reader what the paragraph is about. In most academic writing, it's the first sentence of the paragraph, but it may come later, especially if the first sentence is used to link a new section of the argument to the preceding section. It may be helpful for you to think about the topic sentence as a signpost for your reader that signals what the rest of the paragraph will be about.

In Text 60, you can see the introduction paragraph and the topic sentences from an essay on the ability of animes to convey the complexities of environmentalism to children. Notice how even though we can't read the whole essay, we can easily recognise that there are four major stages in the argument because the topic sentences outline the argument. We can get a clear idea of the position that the writer is presenting and the evidence he uses to support it by reading the topic sentences alone. So you can see that one important way of making your writing flow is to use clear topic sentences that identify what each paragraph is about.

TEXT 60

1. Animes have the ability to present an understanding of complex issues, which is comparable to more 'adult' forms of media.
2. This essay will begin by presenting two complexities that are involved with environmentalism.
3. The first complexity involves the relationship between humans and the environment.
4. The second complexity will explain how different communities of humans interact differently with the environment.

5. Both the environment and humans have the potential to be impacted by animes.

6. Thus animes and their effectiveness in helping children understand the themes being presented will be discussed in this essay using references to both Hayao Miyazaki's *Princess Mononoke* (1997) and *Nausicaa of the Valley of the Wind* (1984).

7. One of the complexities of environmentalism that is present in Miyazaki's anime films concerns the two-sided power relation between humans and nature.

8. *Nausicaa of the Valley of the Wind* presents the first side of the power relation where humans are inferior to nature.

9. On the other hand, *Princess Mononoke* depicts the other side of this power relation where humans are viewed as superior to nature.

10. Another complexity represented through animes arises from the different interactions of different communities in relation to the environment.

11. In conclusion, animes have the ability to convey the intricacies of environmentalism in comparison to more 'adult' forms of media.

Introduction

→ Identifies topic: animes, like other forms of media, can convey complex understandings.
→ States author's position: Animes can convey complexities of environmentalism to children.

Argument 1

→ Summary of one complexity of environmentalism. Both sides of the power relation explained:

   a. humans are inferior to nature

   b. humans are superior to nature.

Argument 2

→ Summary of second complexity of environmentalism.

Conclusion

→ Animes have the ability to convey complexities of environmentalism.

Modified from an essay by Reyner Sagita

How do topic sentences relate to the introduction?

It is important to link each section of your argument to the position you set out in your introduction. This is usually achieved by linking the topic sentences in the body of your text to the introduction. You can do this by chaining the words you use in your introduction to the words you use in your later topic sentences. By 'chaining the words', we mean using words or phrases that are related to one another in some way. For example, you can simply repeat the same word or phrase exactly, or in a slightly different form, or it may mean that the words or phrases are related in some way to one another, perhaps, for example, as synonyms or hyponyms. Text 61 reproduces the introduction (sentences 1–6) and the major topic sentences from the two main arguments (sentences 7 and 8) in Text 60. You can see that each sentence in the introduction is linked by a word chain to some words in each of the topic sentences. These words and phrases are concerned with 'animes', 'complexity' and the 'environment'.

TEXT 61

1. <u>Animes</u> have the ability to present an understanding of <u>complex issues</u> which is comparable to more 'adult' forms of media.

2. This essay will begin by presenting <u>two complexities</u> that are involved with <u>environmentalism</u>.

3. The <u>first complexity</u> involves the relationship between humans <u>and the environment</u>.

4. The second complexity will explain how different communities of humans would interact differently with <u>the environment</u>.

5. Both <u>the environment</u> and humans have the potential to be impacted by <u>animes</u>.

6. Thus <u>animes</u> and their effectiveness in helping children understand the themes being presented will be discussed in this essay using references to both Hayao Miyazaki's *Princess Mononoke* (1997) and *Nausicaa of the Valley of the Wind* (1984).

7. <u>One of the complexities</u> of <u>environmentalism</u> that was present in Miyazaki's <u>anime films</u> concerns the two-sided power relation between humans and <u>nature</u>.

8. <u>Another complexity</u> represented through <u>animes</u> arises from the different interactions of different communities in relation to <u>the environment</u>.

How do topic sentences relate to each other?

There is another aspect of topic sentences that we need to examine. Some steps in your argument will only need a single paragraph. But some steps may need more than one paragraph, especially if they are the most important points in your argument. Text 62 reproduces the topic sentences from argument 1 in Text 60. Notice how these sentences are linked together by a chain of words and phrases that relate to the specific anime films and to the two different sides of the power relations between humans and the environment. By using a number of different words or phrases, all related to the same thing, the writer has created connections between one topic sentence and the next. This helps to signpost for the reader that the argument is continuing across more than a single paragraph. Why is it important to think about your topic sentences early in the planning stages of your essay? Because, firstly, writing your topic sentences early will help you to sketch out the main steps in your argument. Secondly, having a clear idea of your topic sentences will also make it easier for you to pull together the sentences that will form each paragraph.

In Text 62, you might also notice that there are other chains of words that tie the topic sentences together. For example, there is a chain of words that all refer to the environment. The first sentence refers to 'environmentalism' and 'nature' and the second and third refer to just 'nature'. Can you find other examples in the rest of the topic sentences?

TEXT 62

1. One of the complexities of environmentalism that is present in <u>Miyazaki's anime films</u> concerns the <u>two-sided power relation</u> between humans and nature.

2. <u>*Nausicaa of the Valley of the Wind*</u> presents <u>the first side of the power relation</u> where humans are inferior to nature.

3. On the other hand, <u>*Princess Mononoke*</u> depicts <u>the other side of this power relation</u> where humans are viewed as superior to nature.

To see what happens when chains of related words and phrases do not link topic sentences together, look at Text 63, which is taken from an essay on the topic, 'Discuss the impact of multinational companies on the environment'.

TEXT 63

Over the last 20 years, multinational corporations have had an increasingly negative effect on the world environment. This negative effect involves almost every area of industry and is causing increasingly severe problems.

<u>Multinational companies are responsible for around 50 per cent of all greenhouse gases because they produce half the world's oil and most of its electricity</u>. Burning fossil fuels such as oil produces large amounts of greenhouse gases, which contribute to global warming. Electricity production in many countries depends on burning coal, which also results in the production of greenhouse gases.

<u>Another impact involves agricultural land</u>. Large chemical companies promote the use of pesticides which are both dangerous to human health and contaminate farm lands and water supplies. Multinational corporations force small local farmers off their land and produce cash crops such as bananas and cotton. As a result, the production of food for local consumption declines.

<u>The amount of deforestation has increased too</u>. Commercial timber harvests have increased by 50 per cent between 1965 and 1990.

<u>Commercial fishing has dramatically increased during the last few years</u>. According to United Nations Food and Agriculture Organization (FAO) figures, nearly 70 per cent of the world's conventional fish stocks are either fully exploited, severely overtaxed, declining or recovering. This situation is unsustainable. As well, commercial fishing is destroying the livelihood of traditional fishing communities.

> Multinational corporations have become very strong and powerful. They definitely have a negative impact on the world environment in many areas, including the production of greenhouse gases, agriculture, deforestation and fishing. This is very difficult to control because the strongest have the power and the rights.

In this example, while the topic sentences tell the reader what each paragraph is about, the paragraphs are not linked to each other or to the position that the writer is presenting. The position is stated in the first sentence of the first paragraph, and the topic sentences in paragraphs 2 and 3 are linked to it, although the links are not strong, and the reader is expected to fill in the missing information. For example, he or she has to understand that 'impact' refers to the ways in which multinational companies cause environmental problems in the area of agriculture. Topic sentences 4 and 5 are not linked at all to the position statement, so when readers read the whole article, they are likely to get the impression that this essay has no logical argument.

How do topic sentences relate to the paragraph?

So far we have looked at how topic sentences work together to form the framework for the main arguments in your essay and you have seen why they are important for helping you get your ideas across to your reader. But topic sentences are also important because they help you to organise the detail of your arguments into well-written and logical paragraphs. The topic sentence for each paragraph should be a signpost to your readers that tells them, in general terms, what they can expect you to discuss in the paragraph they are about to read.

A question I am often asked by students is, 'What is a paragraph?' A paragraph is a group of sentences about a single topic and that topic is signalled to the reader in the topic sentence. A well-written and logical paragraph usually begins with a topic sentence as the first sentence and is followed by a series of sentences that are related in some way to this topic sentence, as well as to one another. Sometimes, but not always, your paragraph may end with a sentence that summarises your main point.

If you want to write a well-written paragraph, before you begin to write, it is a good idea to sort out the ideas you want to discuss in your essay and to organise points that are related to one another together in smaller subgroups. When you have written a draft paragraph, one way to check that your ideas are related to the topic sentence and to one another is to check the word chains. Look at Text 64, which is an example of a paragraph from the body of an essay on the topic of anime that we have already looked at. Sentence 1 is the topic sentence. Notice how the word chains of *environment* and *humans* work as a kind of glue to stick each sentence in the paragraph to the topic sentence. We can see that the sentences in this paragraph are related to one another and to the topic sentence because each sentence has something to say that is related to either the environment or humans. There are some other word chains in this paragraph that show more relationships between the sentences. Can you identify them?

TEXT 64

1. One of the complexities of <u>environmentalism</u> that is present in Miyazaki's anime films concerns the two-sided power relation between <u>humans</u> and <u>nature</u>.

2. One such relationship is called the '<u>environmental cost shifting</u>'.

3. This is where 'winners of an <u>environmental outcome</u> are able to inflate their benefits only by inflating the costs to the losers'.

4. In other words, for <u>humans</u> to receive benefits, it is at the sacrifice of <u>nature</u>.

5. For <u>nature</u> to benefit, it is at the sacrifice of <u>humans</u>.

Why is it so important that you use topic sentences to indicate relationships between the major ideas in your argument and the more detailed ones in each paragraph? Firstly, without these signposts, readers get lost. They can't see how each paragraph is linked to the paragraph before. They also can't see how each new section of the argument is linked to the rest of the argument, and how the detail in each paragraph is related to the main topic of the paragraph.

The second reason is related to the deductive way of organising texts that will be discussed in this chapter. In deductive argument, the writer has to show how each new point relates to the preceding points. He or she also has to make it easy for the reader to compare each new point with the position that was stated in the introduction. Word chains linking topic sentences to the position statement in the introduction make this easier to do. In contrast, inductive argument tends to give readers greater responsibility for supplying the links themselves.

The importance of using clear topic sentences that help the reader follow the argument was clearly illustrated when a lecturer asked me to help one of his students. This student was able to explain his ideas very clearly, but when he wrote them down, it was impossible to understand the points he was making. When I looked at his writing, it was obvious that the student did not know how to use topic sentences, and it was a simple task to show him what the problem was. So, as I said at the beginning of the chapter, if your lecturers tell you that they can't understand your argument, check your topic sentences.

THINK ABOUT THIS

Look at a piece of your own writing.

- Do topic sentences start each paragraph?
- Did you use a word chain to link the topic sentences to the introduction and to each other?

Organising ideas in clauses

Sometimes your lecturer may tell you that your argument is illogical or not clear, but you can't find any problem with your topic sentences. What else could be the problem? Well, it might be that you need to look at how you have organised the information in your sentences and clauses. We will use Text 65, a text on television violence, to look at this more closely.

TEXT 65

An important field study was published in 1984. This work involved a study of three neighbouring Canadian towns which differed in the availability of television to each. One community, labelled Multitel, had access to US commercial stations as well as to the single Canadian network, the second (Unitel) had access only to Canadian programming, and the third town (Notel) had no television at all until late 1973. Researchers measured children's aggression in Notel as well as in the other towns, both before and after the regular availability of television in Notel. They found that aggression increased after the introduction of television, and this effect was still observable two years later. Increased aggression involved both boys and girls at all age levels. It included verbal as well as physical aggression.

   Modified from Singer, J., & Singer, D. (1988). Some hazards of growing up in a television environment: Children's aggression and restlessness. In S. Oskamp (Ed.), *Television as a social psychology. Social Psychology Annual 8.* Newbury Park: Sage Publications, p. 186.

Text 65 reports on a field study carried out by a group of researchers. The study compared violence among children in three Canadian towns. One of these towns had no television, one had limited television and one could receive several different television channels. The study found that after television was introduced into the town with no television, children became more violent in their behaviour.

You will find the same text reproduced in Text 66, but this time it is divided into clauses and the first part of each clause, the part before the verb, is underlined. Why underline the first part of each clause? Because, in English, the first part of each clause, known as the clause theme, works as a signpost to indicate to readers and listeners what the rest of the clause will be about. Many writers are unaware of this special significance of clause themes, but once you know and you begin to use it wisely, it is a very useful tool for helping you to write more clearly and logically.

TEXT 66

1. <u>An important field</u> study was published in 1984.

2. <u>This work</u> involved a study of three neighbouring Canadian towns which differed in the availability of television to each.

3. <u>One community, labelled Multitel</u> had access to US commercial stations as well as to the single Canadian network,

4. <u>the second (Unitel)</u> had access only to Canadian programming,

5. <u>and the third town (Notel)</u> had no television at all until late 1973.

6. <u>Researchers</u> measured children's aggression in Notel as well as in the other towns both before and after the regular availability of television in Notel.

7. <u>They</u> found

8. that <u>aggression</u> increased after the introduction of television,

9. and <u>this effect</u> was still observable two years later.

10. <u>Increased aggression</u> involved both boys and girls at all age levels.

11. <u>It</u> included verbal as well as physical aggression.

Linking clauses together

The first thing to notice about Text 66 is that if you only read through all the underlined parts of the clauses, you get a general but clear idea of what the text is about. This is because each clause theme is working as a meaningful signpost that tells the reader what is being talked about in each clause.

The second thing to notice is that it is easy to see that we can divide the clauses into three groups. The first group consists of clauses 1, 2, 6 and 7 and the underlined phrases relate to the study. The second group consists of clauses 3, 4 and 5. The phrases in this group have dashed underlining and refer to a different Canadian town. Finally, in clauses 8, 9, 10 and 11 the phrases with dotted underlining refer to aggression.

You can see how each new sentence or clause is tied to the previous one because they all refer to the same thing, even though the actual words used are different. For example, clause 6 uses the word 'researchers', and we link 'researchers' with the 'study' mentioned in clauses 1 and 2. 'They' in clause 7 links to 'researchers' in clause 6.

Now look at clauses 3, 4 and 5. Here, the highlighted phrases refer to a group of related things. We know that 'the second' means 'the second community', and that 'the third town' is a different way of saying 'the third community'. By using 'one', 'the second' and 'the third' the writer ties the clauses together. But how are these three clauses linked to the first three clauses, which tell us about the study? To answer this question, we have to look at the whole text. Look carefully at clauses 2, 3 and 4 and at clauses 6, 8, 9, 10 and 11 in Text 67.

TEXT 67

1. An important field study was published in 1984.
2. This work involved a study of <u>three neighbouring Canadian towns</u> which differed in the availability of television to each.
3. <u>One community, labelled Multitel,</u> had access to US commercial stations as well as to the single Canadian network,
4. <u>the second (Unitel)</u> had access only to Canadian programming,
5. <u>and the third town (Notel)</u> had no television at all until late 1973.
6. Researchers measured <u>children's aggression</u> in Notel as well as in the other towns, both before and after the regular availability of television in Notel.
7. They found
8. that <u>aggression</u> increased after the introduction of television,
9. and <u>this effect</u> was still observable two years later.
10. <u>Increased aggression</u> involved both boys and girls at all age levels.
11. <u>It</u> included verbal as well as physical aggression.

Introducing unknown information

In clause 2, the writers introduce some new information; that is, they tell us about the three Canadian towns. This new information is introduced after the main verb 'involves'. Then clause 3 refers to one of the Canadian towns, Multitel, at the beginning of the clause. This is because the information about the town is no longer new. We already know about it because it was introduced in clause 2.

You can see the same thing happening in clauses 6–11. In clause 6, the new information refers to measures of children's aggression. It comes after the verb 'measured'. Clause 8 is then able to refer to 'aggression' at the beginning of the clause. The following three clauses use the phrases 'this effect', 'increased aggression' and 'it'. All refer to aggression, which we already know about since it was introduced at the end of clause 6.

The important things to note are:

- new information is introduced after the main verb in a clause
- old information (that is, information we already know about) comes at the beginning of the clause, before the main verb.

We call information that we already know about *given* information. This given information becomes the clause theme and works as a signpost for the reader.

Table 18.1 shows the organisation of given (or old) and new information in sentences 2 and 6 from Text 67.

Table 18.1 Position of given and new information

Given information	Main verb	New information
This work	involved	A study of three neighbouring Canadian towns which differed in the availability of television to each.
Researchers	measured	Children's aggression in Notel as well as in the other towns both before and after the regular availability of television.

Organising information

Text 68 presents two different versions of a text about competency-based training. Both texts contain the same information, but one is easier to understand than the other. Which one do you think is easier to read?

TEXT 68

VERSION A

The impetus for Competency Based Training (CBT) came from two sources. Youth unemployment is related to young people's lack of skills, and Australia's competitiveness in international trade in exports depends on our workers having skills more flexibly available in manufacturing and Human Services. The training reform Agenda was designed to ensure that Australia maintained a skilled workforce and that those skills are directed to the work they have to do and are transferable. All bodies are obliged to implement CBT. Under the terms of the 1988 Wages agreement, each industry in Australia is obliged to implement CBT. The first two major CBT related developments were the Australian Traineeship System and moves towards the competency based training system. The Australian Public Service industry set up the Joint APS Council (JAPSTC) and through a consultative process the APS core competencies were developed.

VERSION B

The impetus for CBT came from two sources. The first of these was youth unemployment, which is related to young people's lack of skills. The second was Australia's competitiveness in international trade. This depends on workers in both manufacturing and human services having flexible skills. CBT, implemented through the training reform agenda, was designed to ensure that Australia maintained a workforce possessing relevant and transferable skills.

Under the terms of the 1988 Wages Agreement, each industry was obliged to implement CBT. One of the first attempts to do so involved the Australian Traineeship System, a competency-based apprenticeship training scheme. Another was the Joint Australian Public Service Council (JAPSTC), which was set up by the Australian Public Service to develop core competencies through a consultative process.

You probably found that Version B was much easier to understand than Version A. Why is this? Let's look at the information that the writer puts before the main verb in each clause. Text 69 presents Version A with the information before the main verb in each clause highlighted. Are these highlighted phrases information that we already know about (old information) or new information?

TEXT 69: VERSION A

1. <u>The impetus for Competency Based Training (CBT)</u> came from two sources.
2. <u>Youth unemployment</u> is related to young people's lack of skills
3. <u>and Australia's competitiveness</u> in international trade in exports depends on our workers having skills more flexibly available in manufacturing and Human Services.
4. <u>The training reform Agenda</u> was designed to ensure that Australia maintained a skilled workforce
5. and that those skills are directed to the work they have to do
6. and are transferable.
7. <u>All bodies</u> are obliged to implement CBT.
8. Under the terms of the 1988 Wages agreement, each industry in Australia is obliged to implement CBT.
9. <u>The first two major CBT related developments were the Australian</u> Traineeship System and moves towards the competency based training system.
10. <u>The Australian Public Service industry</u> set up the Joint APS Council (JAPSTC)
11. <u>and through a consultative process the APS core competencies</u> were developed.

You can see that the beginnings of each clause do not link together. You can also see that new information is being put at the beginning of clauses. For example, the second clause starts with 'youth unemployment', but this has not been mentioned before, so it is difficult for us to see how it fits into the paragraph.

Now let's look at Version B (Text 70). Information in each clause has been underlined or highlighted in different ways to show how new information and given information are linked. Notice how clauses 2 and 3 have been written differently to version A so that they now relate to the end of clause 1. The end of clause 3 introduces Australia's competitiveness in international trade, and this is referred to again at the beginning of clause 4. Clause 5 links back to 'The impetus for CBT' in clause 1.

Clause 6 starts a new paragraph, so the information before the main verb doesn't link back to any specific phrases. This happens quite frequently at the beginning of paragraphs, However, both clause 7 and clause 8 link to the new information introduced at the end of clause 6.

TEXT 70: VERSION B

1. The impetus for CBT came from <u>two sources</u>.
2. <u>The first of these</u> was youth unemployment, which is related to young people's lack of skills.
3. <u>The second</u> was <u>Australia's competitiveness in international trade</u>.
4. <u>This</u> depends on workers in both manufacturing and human services having flexible skills.
5. CBT, implemented through the training reform agenda, was designed to ensure that Australia maintained a workforce possessing relevant and transferable skills.
6. Under the terms of the 1988 Wages Agreement, <u>each industry was obliged to implement CBT</u>.
7. <u>One of the first attempts to do so</u> involved the Australian Traineeship System, a competency-based apprenticeship training scheme.
8. <u>Another</u> was the Joint Australian Public Service Council (JAPSTC), which was set up by the Australian Public Service to develop core competencies through a consultative process.

You can see from these examples that the way that you organise information in your writing is very important. If your lecturer tells you that she cannot follow your argument, you should check your topic sentences and how they relate to other parts of your writing and to the ideas in your paragraphs. You should also check to see that you are linking clauses together and that new and given information is placed appropriately in the clause. Sometimes it can be hard to think about how your clauses are organised as you are writing your early drafts. However, when you have drafted your essay, select one paragraph and check that new information is usually introduced at the end of clauses, and that you are using the part of the clause before the main verb to link your clauses together. You will be surprised at what a difference thinking about organising the main steps in your argument and the detailed ideas in your clauses can make to the clarity of your writing!

THINK ABOUT THIS

Select a paragraph from your own writing and divide each sentence into clauses.

- Are you introducing new points at the end of the clause?
- Are you using the beginning of clauses to link clauses together?

SUMMARY

1. Clear, linked topic sentences outline the writer's argument and make the writing 'flow'.

2. Other sentences in the paragraph are linked to the topic sentence by chains of related words.

3. When several paragraphs all deal with a specific aspect of a topic, the topic sentences of each paragraph are linked together by chains of related words.

4. The topic sentence in a paragraph tells the reader what the paragraph is about. In academic writing, it is usually the first sentence in the paragraph.

5. The clause theme has special significance as a signpost to help organise ideas.

6. New information is introduced after the main verb in a clause.

7. Old information (that is, information we already know about) comes at the beginning of the clause, before the main verb.

8. We call information that we already know about *given* information.

9. Given information is placed in the clause theme position and it helps to link clauses together.

10. After new information has been introduced at the end of a clause, it can be put at the beginning of subsequent clauses as a clause theme.

SKILLS PRACTICE

Task 1

Text 71 contains topic sentences of nine paragraphs taken from a chapter that compares different approaches to education in Asia and Australia. The text is taken from Anthony Milner's book *Comparing Cultures* (1996)[1]

1. Use the topic sentences to answer the following questions:

   a. According to Milner, what belief underlies educational practice in Asia?

   b. What does the author claim a successful student must do?

   c. What does pandai mengapal mean? How does pandai mengapal relate to the previous paragraph?

   d. Does the author believe that students in Asia are encouraged to express their own opinions?

   e. What is the attitude of Asian students to their teachers?

   f. Are Australian attitudes towards education similar to Asian ones?

   g. Does the author believe that Australian education always encourages individualism?

2. Identify the word chains which link the topic sentences to each other.

Which do you think is the most important chain? Why?

TEXT 71

1. Modern classroom practice in Asian countries tends to be based on the traditional belief that human beings are innately good and society is therefore perfectible.

2. The road to educational success begins with the acquisition of factual knowledge.

3. Although the words differ from country to country, classrooms that encourage *pandai mengapal* (clever at learning something by heart) exist throughout Asia.

4. Even in more advanced schooling, or when they are considering something less factual, such as a poem, Asian students tend not to be asked what they think.

5. Private study and the teacher's exposition are thought to provide sufficient knowledge to ensure that, when a teacher asks a question in class, the student called on to answer will be able to do so correctly.

6. To teach is to model; there is no applause here for the stumbler groping towards competence.

7. By definition, the teacher in China, Japan, Thailand and Indonesia is the student's superior in the classroom – an authority figure to whom the student must defer.

8. Students in Asian countries frequently preview what is to be learnt before class.

9. Turning to Australia, we find significant differences to the set of practices outlined above.

Milner, A. (1996). Comparing Cultures. Oxford: Oxford University Press, pp 90–93

Task 2

Text 72 is the first paragraph, in full, of the text introduced in Task 1.

- Identify the word chains which tie the information in the paragraph to the topic sentence.

NB: Each sentence is numbered and started on a new line to facilitate identifying word chains.

TEXT 72

1. Modern classroom practice in Asian countries tends to be based on the traditional belief that human beings are innately good and society is therefore perfectible.

2. Although innately good, humans have to struggle to overcome selfish, undesirable tendencies and let the good flourish.

3. Knowledge is the key to this.

4. It is directly acquired through experience, or vicariously encountered through language.

5. The good in students can only be fostered by encounters with the best of experiences.

6. Thus, not everything from the past is suitable for passing on, and some knowledge is dangerous.

7. The selection of 'good' content is a constant and onerous task in countries such as China and Indonesia, where the central government is concerned to ensure correct development.

8. Indeed, in contrast to the common Western perception of knowledge as open-ended, infinite and theoretically available to anyone, knowledge is viewed in much of Asia as being contained, finite and accessible only by the 'right' people.

9. Deciding what is 'good' content is a risky job for those charged with making the choices.

10. It is a common belief that history, for example, should legitimise the present government and glorify the nation.

11. Humanities subjects must inculcate a sense of right and wrong, and inspire the coming generation to continue along the right path.

12. Harmony is the prime objective; there can be no discordant, opposing views, only the one right view.

Milner, A. (1996). Comparing Cultures. Oxford: Oxford University Press, p 90

Task 3

Text 73 consists of paragraphs 2–8 of the same text used in Tasks 1 and 2.

■ Match the paragraph on the right with the topic sentence on the left. Be ready to explain the reasons for your choice.

TEXT 73

Paragraph	Topic sentence
1. This knowledge is recorded in books and is known by the teacher. A good teacher knows a great deal; the best teacher knows 'everything'. The task of the teacher is to know the content, to organise it systematically and to present it carefully and clearly, in vivid language. Elementary mastery means to have ready, correct recall of factual knowledge from memory. Students imitate a good teacher's display of learning until they have perfected their replication of the teacher's model and they know it by heart. In Indonesia the clever student is described as *pandai*, which in a school context generally means *pandai mengapal* (clever at learning something by heart). Rote learning is the goal of the good teacher and good student alike.	a. Private study and the teacher's exposition are thought to provide sufficient knowledge to ensure that, when a teacher asks a question in class, the student called on to answer will be able to do so correctly.

Paragraph	Topic sentence
2. These classrooms are not places for individual discovery. Asking questions about the content of a text, for instance, is usually considered presumptuous. As one Indonesian student who went to study in Australia put it: *Neither did I know how to read a book, a chapter in a book, or an article. The skill of reading for content only was already very difficult, but it was more difficult for critical reading. I was only taught that the written word was the 'truth'. I had no experience in searching for weaknesses and criticising other people's work.*[36]	b. Students in Asian countries frequently preview what is to be learnt before class.
3. They are not invited to give their opinion of a character in a novel, or of the value of an engineering project. Instead, teachers ask questions that guide students towards the correct answer and correct attitude. They are asked, for instance, to show how the poem is patriotic, how the character is choosing a correct (or incorrect) course of action, or in what way the engineering project will be of great benefit to their country. Exam questions, even in humanities subjects, are often multiple choice, which prevents students from giving their own answers.	c. By definition, the teacher in China, Japan, Thailand and Indonesia is the student's superior in the classroom – an authority figure to whom the student must defer.[38]
4. If a student makes a mistake, it is considered evidence of a lack of diligence or a lack of ability. Instead of enquiring into the source of the error, the teacher will provide the correct answer, modelling it for both the particular student and the whole class, and then continue by asking another question of another student.[37]	d. Although the words differ from country to country, classrooms that encourage *pandai mengapal* exist throughout Asia.
5. Such a student makes a poor model. Only the good student who supplies a model answer to the question is allowed to act as a model for other students. Teachers openly favour those they approve of, and students value and vie for teacher approval. Being favoured will often include real rewards, such as being made privy to 'advanced' knowledge of the latest theories, which go beyond the school curriculum (in Japan), or being given the right to use restricted facilities or material normally in accessible to students (in China). These rewards, pleasant in themselves, often constitute access to a fast track in school, providing potential access to a better university, and to a higher status and better paid job later on. As for the weaker students, they are to be encouraged by teachers. This is achieved through exhortation and by patience and kindness, the cardinal virtues of the good teacher.	e. Even in more advanced schooling, or when they are considering something less factual, such as a poem, Asian students tend not to be asked what they think.

Paragraph	Topic sentence
6. In the classroom – and outside it – the teacher's authority is absolute. A harmonious relationship between teacher and student requires that students do not challenge the teacher. A teacher may interpret even a question as criticism: an indirect suggestion that the teacher has not been clear or lacks knowledge. Questions also waste the time of other students and risk showing the questioner up as lacking diligence or ability.	f. Turning to Australia, we find significant differences to the set of practices outlined above.
7. Then, having observed the knowledge displayed by the teacher in demonstration or explanation during class, they review the material in private. Silence, recitation and copious copying mean that the attributes of a good student are those of the endurance athlete: patience, precision, tenacity, fortitude and regulation of tempo.	g. The road to educational success begins with the acquisition of factual knowledge.
8. In keeping with the cultural emphasis on the individual, students are said to have a right to develop their full capacities, and the curricula and learning styles generally focus on offering children the chance to try many avenues of interest. Rote learning is not valued in itself. Instead, students are invited to explore texts and express personal responses to them. School facilities and relatively small class sizes encourage the teachers to give personal attention and interact with each student as an individual. The student can challenge the teacher, and the 'clever question' is often just as prized as the right answer. Far from being the font of all wisdom, the teacher acts as a spring-board from which the student can pursue knowledge. Through libraries, videos and television, students have access to a great deal of knowledge outside the classroom, independently of their teachers. This allows a variety of opinion and knowledge to enter classroom debates.	h. To teach is to model; there is no applause here for the stumbler groping towards competence.

Milner, A. (1996). *Comparing Cultures*. Oxford: Oxford University Press, pp 90–93

Task 4

Text 74 is a report on a study about smoking and weight reduction. It has been divided into clauses.

- Identify the groups of words and phrases that tie the clauses together.
- Identify places where new information is introduced at the end of a clause, before being placed at the beginning of a subsequent clause.

TEXT 74

1. The tobacco industry names cigarettes 'thins' and 'slims' to attract young weight-conscious women.

2. However, new research shows

3. that smoking does not prevent weight gain in people under 30.

4. A study of almost 4000 young adults aged from 18 to 30 found

5. that smoking has very little effect on body weight.

6. The study examined both continuing smokers and new smokers.

7. Those who smoked, or began smoking, did not lose weight.

8. However, people who stopped smoking gained more weight than people who had never smoked.

Task 5

Select a paragraph of your own writing and identify the clauses.

■ Identify the words and phrases that tie each clause together.

■ Identify places where new information is introduced at the end of a clause, before being placed at the beginning of a subsequent clause.

---

[1] Milner, A. (1996). *Comparing Cultures*. Oxford: Oxford University Press, pp 90–93.

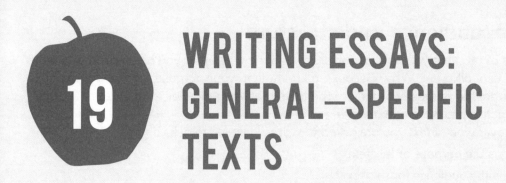

19 WRITING ESSAYS: GENERAL–SPECIFIC TEXTS

LEARNING OBJECTIVES

When you have finished this chapter, you will be able to:

- identify the structure of an essay
- identify the functions of each stage of an essay
- understand the difference between inductive and deductive argument
- understand the role of deductive argument in academic writing
- understand lecturers' expectations regarding deductive argument
- identify the general–specific pattern of an argument
- identify generalisations in a text
- identify specific details that support generalisations.

WORD LIST

Do you know the meaning of these words? Many have special meanings in academic culture. You can check their meaning in the glossary at the back of the book.

- ☐ analytical
- ☐ audience
- ☐ digital divide
- ☐ deductive argument
- ☐ explicit
- ☐ inductive argument
- ☐ implicit
- ☐ infer
- ☐ generalisation
- ☐ general–specific
- ☐ purpose
- ☐ statement of position

Purpose, audience and structure

The types of text that you read at university and the types that you are expected to write are often very different. Why? Because as a student, your purpose for writing is usually different from the purpose of many of the texts that you read. For example, as a student, you are not likely to write a textbook.

Whatever type of text you are asked to write, you need to ask yourself:

- What is the purpose of this text?
- Who is the audience for this text?
- What is the structure of this text?

In this chapter we will examine the features of an essay. We will use Text 75 – the essay on the causes of the worldwide water crisis that we looked at in Chapter 13. The essay argues that the major causes of the crisis are the mismanagement and wasteful use of water, and the pollution of water sources.

What is the purpose and audience of an essay?

In Chapter 13, which was about expressing your own voice, we looked at the purpose and audience of an essay. We saw that the purpose of an essay is to present a clear position to an audience of one or more lecturers. We also saw that the lecturer is looking for evidence that you can take part in a dialogue with other scholars, express your own voice and relate appropriately to the voices of others.

How is an essay structured?

You are probably familiar with the three-stage organisation of an essay:

1. introduction
2. body
3. conclusion.

In this chapter, we will examine the distinctive features of each stage.

What is the function of an essay introduction?

 THINK ABOUT THIS

- Before you continue reading, what do you think the function of an introduction is?
- After you've finished reading the section, compare your answer to the functions it lists.

The introduction to an essay has a number of different functions, which are listed below. Which do you think is the most important?

- to introduce the general topic
- to provide background that puts the topic in a broader context
- to indicate the importance of an issue
- to identify something that we do not know
- to state the position that the author will argue
- to provide an overview of what is to come
- to define important terms used in the essay.

Perhaps the most important function of the introduction is to state the position that the writer will argue. If the essay is very short, for example an essay in an examination, the introduction may only consist of a position statement or, as it is often called, a thesis statement. Introductions to longer essays usually fulfil more of the functions on the list above.

TEXT 75

[1]During the 20th century, the world's population tripled while water consumption grew sevenfold. [2]As a result, in almost every area of the world today there is a water problem. [3]While the causes of the problem vary, most relate to human activity. [4]Mismanagement and profligate use of available water supplies are a major problem, as are pollution and privatisation of water supplies.

In the sample essay from Chapter 13, the introduction (reproduced here as Text 75) consists of four sentences. The first sentence introduces the topic while the second indicates that it is important – almost every part of the world is facing a water crisis. The third sentence states the general position that the essay will argue – that human activity is the major cause of the crisis. The fourth expands on this general position by listing the major types of human activity that will be explored – that is, mismanagement, waste and pollution.

Sometimes it is also necessary to define terms in the introduction. The type of terms that need to be defined include technical terms and terms for which there are several definitions. For example, 'comparative equilibrium' is a technical term taken from economics. Depending on the topic of your assignment, you may need to define this term. On the other hand, a concept such as 'culture' has been defined in many different ways. If you are writing an essay on culture, you may need to define exactly what you mean by this term.

THINK ABOUT THIS

- Look at the introduction to one of your own essays. Which of the following does your introduction do?
  - ☐ introduce the general topic
  - ☐ provide background that puts the topic in a broader context
  - ☐ indicate the importance of an issue
  - ☐ identify something that we do not know
  - ☐ state the position that the author will argue
  - ☐ provide an overview of what is to come
- Which of these functions are not done in your introduction?
- Does your introduction include a clear statement of position?

What is the function of the body of the essay?

The body of the essay develops the position presented in the introduction. It is divided into a number of sections, each section dealing with an argument or part of an argument. Each section is composed of one or more paragraphs and needs to be clearly linked to the overall position. The paragraphs in each section also need to be clearly linked together. Linking each section of the argument to the position, and linking each paragraph in a section together are both usually done by topic sentences. (Re-read Chapter 18 for more information on this process.) An important point to note is that essays do not use headings and subheadings to identify the various stages of the argument.

What is the function of the conclusion to an essay?

The conclusion to an essay generally restates the position that has been presented. However, it may modify the position or even reject it altogether – as long as there is enough evidence in the body of the essay to justify this.

TEXT 76

[36]It is clear that the water crisis being experienced around the globe is largely the result of poor water management. [37]Water is wasted on non-essential or poorly planned projects without thought of replacement. [38]At the same time, water sources are being polluted as a result of poor agricultural and industrial management practices. [39]Market solutions to the water crisis favour the rich at the expense of the poor. [40]Immediate measures must be taken to regulate the use of water internationally in order to ensure that everyone has access to a safe and sufficient source of water.

In the conclusion to the essay on the water crisis (reproduced here as Text 76), sentence 36 confirms the general position presented in sentence 3 of the introduction. Sentences 37 and 39 summarise the major arguments supporting the position, and are clearly related to sentence 4 in the introduction. The final sentence links the essay back to the wider context, just as the first sentence of the introduction indicated the global nature of the problem.

An important point is that the conclusion does not introduce any new material. It is mainly concerned with restating and summarising (very briefly) the position that has been presented in the body of the essay.

THINK ABOUT THIS

Now look at the conclusion to one of your assignments. Having read the section on conclusions above, are there any changes you would make to your conclusion?

Deductive and inductive organisation

By this time, you should be familiar with the idea that the introduction states the position you will argue, the body makes the argument and the conclusion confirms or modifies the position. You might perhaps wonder why so much emphasis is put on this. The answer is that as a language, English favours deductive argument.

When you use a deductive argument, you organise it in three steps. You:

- identify the position that you will present
- present evidence (facts, arguments, reasons, etc.) that supports the position
- reach a conclusion.

Does this sound familiar? Obviously, it is identical with the essay structure that we have just examined.

Deductive argument can be contrasted with inductive argument, which many languages favour. When you use an inductive argument, you use two steps. You:

- present a number of reasons
- come to a conclusion.

Both methods of argument are useful, and can be used in any language. Problems only arise when readers expect one form of organisation but are confronted by the other. To understand why problems arise, let's look at how people follow an argument.

When you read a deductive argument, you can compare the information that is given in the body with the position presented in the introduction. You can ask yourself, 'How does this point support the position?' Your attention moves from the information to the position and back. Finally, you can compare the position stated at the beginning of the text with the conclusion to see if they match. You can see this process illustrated in Figure 19.1.

The process for reading an inductive argument is different. When you read an inductive argument, you let the writer lead you from one reason to the next, until you and the writer reach the conclusion together. As you follow the argument, your attention is on how

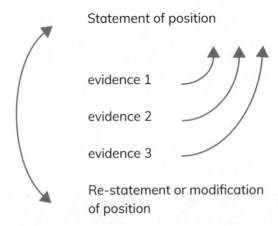

Figure 19.1 Organisation of a deductive argument

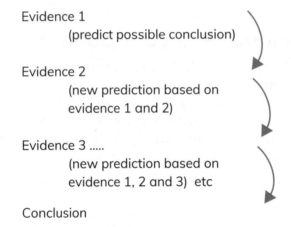

Figure 19.2 Organisation of an inductive argument

one reason links to the next. You ask, 'What conclusion can I reach from this information?' After each new piece of evidence, you can modify your prediction. You can see this process illustrated in Figure 19.2.

When you read a deductive argument, you know what the writer's position is because it is clearly stated at the beginning of the text. We can say that the argument is up-front and explicit. On the other hand, when you read an inductive argument, you have to infer the argument for yourself, which means that the argument is implicit. The writer does not state his or her position until the conclusion.

Most lecturers in English-speaking universities expect students to use a deductive approach in essays and reports. They may not even recognise when inductive reasoning is used. In fact, many lecturers comment that inductively organised texts seem confused and illogical. This is because they do not expect to have to infer the argument. Because they are more familiar with deductive arguments, they expect that it is the writer's job to identify the argument at the outset rather than presenting it as a conclusion.

Without an explicit statement of position in the introduction, lecturers may also feel disoriented because they cannot check how the evidence being presented relates to the writer's position. On the other hand, people who come from cultures that favour inductive organisation tend to find deductive argument repetitive and simplistic. I remember one such student exclaiming in disgust, 'You mean you want me to tell you what I am going to say, then say it, then tell you what I have said? That's ridiculous!' People from cultures that favour inductive organisation may also feel that the explicit nature of the argument forces the reader to a specific conclusion and reduces the possibility of other interpretations. The point to remember is that both types of organisation are good, but that problems arise when a reader expects one type of organisation but gets the other.

Using general-to-specific organisation in essays

Let's now return to our water crisis essay. Text 77 is the fourth paragraph from the water essay. However, one important change has been made. What is that change?

TEXT 77

[20]Today, farming accounts for 70 per cent of water use with the lion's share taken by irrigation. [21]A UNEP Report (2002) states that irrigation and poor management have led to the salinisation of a full 20 per cent of the world's irrigated land. [22]Postal (1999) suggests that up to 10 per cent of the world's grain is being produced by water that will not be renewed.

As you can see, the generalisation has been left out. It originally came at the beginning of the paragraph, and stated:

> A related problem is the wasteful model of agriculture that has turned food-growing into an industrial process which requires intensive irrigation.

Without the generalisation, we are left with a series of facts. You can see the effect of this in Text 78, where two paragraphs from the body of the essay are reproduced with the generalisations omitted.

TEXT 78

[7]One-third of the world's population depends on these aquifers, which have taken thousands of years to develop (Brown, 2001). [8]Because the reserves of water they hold are large, they have been used without any thought of the future. [9]Payal Sampat (cited in Brown, 2001) states that worldwide, people use about 200 billion cubic metres more water than can be replaced. [10]In other words, the world's water capital is being steadily used up.

[12]Take California, a dry state which nevertheless has well-watered lawns and 560 000 swimming pools. [13] Barlow and Clark (2002) point out that water from the Colorado River has been used to the limit, and now the region's aquifers are being drained. [14]They predict that by 2020 there will be a water shortfall nearly equivalent to what the state is currently using. [15]Otchet (2002) reports on a huge project in Libya which plans to draw water from an aquifer beneath the Sahara desert and transfer it 3500 kilometres by a network of giant pipelines to irrigate the country. [16] She points out that the cost is estimated at $32 billion and that the water will be so dear – at about $10 000 to irrigate a hectare – that whatever is grown will not be able to cover the cost of supply. [17]The aquifer can never be renewed, as hardly any rain falls in the Sahara and the reserves are estimated to last only between 15 and 50 years. [18]Even more seriously, George (2003) claims the project may result in huge subsidence in the Sahara and the prospect of the Nile seeping into the emptying aquifer, thus plunging Egypt into crisis.

It is easy to see that without the generalisations, the essay is descriptive rather than analytical. It no longer argues a position. Instead, the reader is expected to provide the link between the facts that are cited and the position that is stated in the introduction.

When you write an essay, it is not enough to present a series of facts. You need to show why the facts are important. As we noted in Chapter 10, generalisations allow you to identify the implications of the facts that you present and to point out their significance. In other words, one of the most important ways that you can demonstrate your analytical skills is through the generalisations that you make from the evidence that you present.

Notice that analysis rests on two legs – generalisation and evidence. Your generalisations must be supported by evidence, just as your evidence needs to form the basis for your generalisations.

Another thing to notice is that the generalisation usually comes before the evidence that supports it. The general–specific pattern is very common in academic writing. A generalisation often forms the topic sentence of a paragraph, but this does not mean that they cannot occur elsewhere in the paragraph. You will see in Text 79, which is an analysis of the water crisis essay, that generalisations may also conclude a paragraph by drawing implications from the evidence that has been presented. However, the overall pattern is that general information precedes specific information.

You may object that many magazine and newspaper articles begin with the stories of specific people and then generalise from the example. However, newspaper and magazine stories are written for a different purpose and audience. Their purpose is to inform or entertain, and their audience is a broad generalist one rather than the specialised audience of experts that characterises academic writing. Articles in newspapers and magazines often attempt to capture the interest of the audience by personalising. In academic writing, however, it is usually the position that is being argued that attracts audience interest. This focuses attention on the generalisations, with the result that they tend to be placed first. In addition, the deductive organisation favoured in academic writing tends to result in a general–specific organisation. Without the generalisations, the essay is descriptive rather than analytical.

Text 79 presents the whole essay again. The column on the right identifies the generalisations that the author makes and the evidence that supports each generalisation.

TEXT 79: ESSAY

Introduction

[1]During the 20th century, the world's population tripled while water consumption grew sevenfold. [2]As a result, in almost every area of the world today there is a water problem. [3]While the causes of the problem vary, most relate to human activity. [4]Mismanagement and profligate use of available water supplies are a major problem, as are pollution and privatisation of water supplies.

[5]Overuse of water resources is a major problem all over the world. [6]The crisis is particularly acute in relation to groundwater reserves, which lie deep under the surface in aquifers. [7]One-third of the world's population depends on these aquifers, which have taken thousands of years to develop (Brown, 2001). [8]Because the reserves of water they hold are large, they have been used without any thought of the future. [9]Payal Sampat (cited in Brown, 2001) states that worldwide, people use about 200 billion cubic metres more water than can be replaced. [10]In other words, the world's water capital is being steadily used up.

[11]Often, water is used in ways that are wasteful and unproductive. [12]Take California, a dry state which nevertheless has well-watered lawns and 560 000 swimming pools. [13] Barlow and Clark (2002) point out that water from the Colorado River has been used to the limit, and now the region's aquifers are being drained. [14]They predict that by 2020 there will be a water shortfall nearly equivalent to what the state is currently using.

[15]Otchet (2002) reports on a huge project in Libya which plans to draw water from an aquifer beneath the Sahara desert and transfer it 3500 kilometres by a network of giant pipelines to irrigate the country. [16] She points out that the cost is estimated at $32 billion and that the water will be so dear – at about $10 000 to irrigate a hectare – that whatever is grown will not be able to cover the cost of supply. [17]The aquifer can never be renewed, as hardly any rain falls in the Sahara and the reserves are estimated to last only between 15 and 50 years. [18]Even more seriously, George (2003) claims the project may result in huge subsidence in the Sahara and the prospect of the Nile seeping into the emptying aquifer, thus plunging Egypt into crisis.

[19]A related problem is the wasteful model of agriculture that has turned food-growing into an industrial process which requires intensive irrigation. [20]Today, farming accounts for 70 per cent of water use with the lion's share taken by irrigation. [21]A

UNEP Report (2002) states that irrigation and poor management have led to the salinisation of a full 20 per cent of the world's irrigated land. [22]Postal (1999) suggests that up to 10 per cent of the world's grain is being produced by water that will not be renewed.

[23]Pollution is another major problem (Barlow & Clarke, 2002; Bowch, 2002). [24]Much of Eastern Europe has filthy rivers – in Poland the problem is so bad that the water of the majority of its rivers cannot even be put to industrial use. [25]Even more seriously, aquifers are also being polluted, and the pollution of aquifers is generally irreversible. [26]A WHO report on groundwater (2002) states that groundwater around major cities, near industrial developments or beneath industrial farms inevitably contains contaminants. [27]The report points out that in the US, 60 per cent of liquid industrial waste is injected straight into deep groundwater. [28]Together, these activities are a deadly form of short-sightedness.

[29]As a solution to the world's water problems, the IMF and World Bank encourage deregulation and privatisation [30]They are supported by a number of transnational water companies, such as Suez, which focus on the most profitable sectors, mostly in wealthy areas. [31]Such companies demand tax concessions from governments, raise prices and cut off people unable to pay. [32]The poorer sections of the community are badly disadvantaged by this model. [33]In addition, privatisation contributes greatly to over-exploitation of water resources. [34]As environmental activist Vandana Shiva (2002, p. 23) argues, 'The water crisis is an ecological crisis with commercial causes but no market solutions. 35Market solutions destroy the earth and aggravate inequality.'

[36]It is clear that the water crisis being experienced around the globe is largely the result of poor water management. [37]Water is wasted on non-essential or poorly planned projects without thought of replacement. [38]At the same time, water sources are being polluted as a result of poor agricultural and industrial management practices. [39]Market solutions to the water crisis favour the rich at the expense of the poor.[40]Immediate measures must be taken to regulate the use of water internationally in order to ensure that everyone has access to a safe and sufficient source of water.

STRUCTURE

Sentences 1–2: Background information – introduces the topic and the problem
Sentences 3–4: Thesis statement – presents writer's position

Body of essay

Sentence 5: Generalisation – introduces problem of overuse of water resources
Sentence 6: Generalisation – overuse of aquifers and explanation of term 'aquifer'
Sentences 7–9: Specific detail supports generalisation – importance of aquifers
Sentence 10: Generalisation – implication of evidence presented in sentences 7–9
Sentence 11: Generalisation – mismanagement of water resources
Sentences 12–14: California example – specific detail to support generalisation
Sentences 15–18: Libya example – specific detail to support generalisation

Sentence 19: Generalisation – mismanagement of water resources in agriculture; irrigation

Sentences 20–22: Specific detail to support generalisation – irrigation

Sentence 23: Generalisation – problem of water pollution

Sentence 24: Specific example to support generalisation – Poland

Sentence 25: Generalisation – pollution of aquifers

Sentences 26–27: Specific detail to support generalisation on pollution of aquifers

Sentence 28: Generalisation – implication of evidence presented in sentences 24–27

Sentence 29: Essay writer's voice – 4th argument: privatisation of water supply

Sentences 30–33: Essay writer's voice– essay writer outlines problems with IMF/World Bank position

Sentences 34–35: Direct source's voice `– source's voice used to support essay writer's position

Conclusion

Sentence 36: Confirms position

Sentences 37–39: Summarises major arguments

Sentence 40: Links essay back to wider context

Based on Dinyar, G. (2003). Precious fluid. New Internationalist 354. March.

 SUMMARY

1. The purpose of an essay is to present and argue a position to an audience of one or more lecturers.

2. An essay is organised in three stages:
   - Introduction
   - Body
   - Conclusion

3. The function of the introduction is to:
   - introduce the general topic of the essay
   - provide background that puts the topic in a broader context
   - indicate the importance of an issue
   - identifies something we do not know
   - state the position the author will argue
   - provide an overview of what is to come
   - define important terms used in the essay

   The most important of these is to state the position that the writer will argue.

4. The function of the body of the essay is to:
   - develop the position presented in the introduction
   - divide the argument into sections which each develop one aspect of the argument. Each section includes one or more paragraphs.

5. The function of the conclusion is to:
   ■ restate or modify the position presented in the introduction
   ■ no new information is presented in the conclusion

6. General-to-Specific organisation
   ■ Generalisations are used to identify implications and point out the significance of facts.
   ■ Specific details provide the evidence that supports generalisations.
   ■ Without generalisations, an essay is descriptive rather than analytical.
   ■ Academic essays are usually organised so that generalisations come before specific detail.

7. Deductive organisation involves
   ■ identifying the position that you will present
   ■ presenting evidence (facts, arguments, reasons, etc.) that supports the position
   ■ reaching a conclusion

8. Inductive organisation involves:
   ■ presenting a number of reasons
   ■ coming to a conclusion

9. Most academics expect essays and reports to be organised deductively rather than inductively.

 SKILLS PRACTICE

Task 1

Texts 80–82 are introductions from student essays. Identify the function of each sentence. (Sentences are numbered to help you.)

 TEXT 80

[1]In recent years, many educational authorities have seen the internet as a way of reducing the cost of education while continuing to enrol greater numbers of students. [2]It is undeniable that the internet presents many new educational opportunities, but whether these are more cost-effective than traditional methods is less clear. [3]This paper will argue that the cost of designing and implementing quality programs using the internet is greater than the cost of similar programs delivered by traditional means.

TEXT 81

[1]While the use of tobacco is declining in many Western countries, it is increasingly common in developing countries. [2]Governments in many of these countries defend the increase because they claim that tobacco production and consumption has economic benefits for the country. [3]However, this claim is questioned by health authorities, which point out the long-term damage to health that is associated with smoking. [4]In fact, the income generated by the production, sale and taxation of tobacco products is far outweighed by the costs of caring for people with tobacco-related diseases.

TEXT 82

[1]In assessing a country's standard of living, it is common practice to use the Gross Domestic Product (GDP) as a measure. [2]The GDP measures incomes that are earned and the goods and services that are produced in the official 'formal' economy. [3]However, this tends not to account for productive activity outside the formal economy. [4]Many activities, such as cleaning, handyman services, babysitting and so on occur in the 'informal' economy. [5]Therefore, they may not be reflected in the GDP. [6]This means that GDP may be an inadequate basis for assessing the standard of living of a country.

[7]Much research on poverty and inequality is based on people's incomes from work in the formal economy. [8]Because activity in the informal economy is not included, some economists argue that the amount of poverty and inequality in a country is overestimated. [9]This essay will demonstrate that the inclusion of data from the informal economy does not change estimates of the level of poverty and inequality in a country.

Task 2

In each of the pairs of sentences below identify the generalisation (G) and the specific information (S).

1. a. Scientists predict that the average temperature may rise by as much as 6 °C by the year 2100.
   b. Global warming is one of the most serious problems facing the world today.

2. a. In 2003, 70 per cent of Internet users were under 30 years of age, compared to less than 30 per cent in the US.
   b. The growth of the Internet is changing the way that business is done on a global scale.

3. a. The management style of managers within multinational corporations is more likely to be influenced by their nationality than by corporate culture.
   b. American managers use colleagues' first names almost immediately, while for German managers it takes a long time to get on a first-name basis.

4. a. Among developed countries the digital divide between those who adopted Internet technology rapidly and those who were reluctant to get involved is narrowing.

b. In 2001, 169 million Americans were online, accounting for about 60 per cent of the country's total population and 29 per cent of the world's Internet population.

Task 3

Text 83 is part of an essay on the following topic:

Discuss the major effects of water shortage in developing countries.

Identify the generalisations (G) and the sentences which present specific information (S).

Note Some sentences, such as the thesis statement in sentence 3, cannot be classified as either G or S.

TEXT 83

¹The water crisis is likely to be one of the great crises facing humanity during the 21st century. ²Lack of access to adequate sources of easily available water has a major impact on the life prospects of large numbers of rural dwellers in developing countries. ³This paper will first establish minimum daily water requirements and then discuss the effects that lack of water has on women and girls, on the maintenance of hygiene and on health.

⁴A huge discrepancy in water consumption exists between those who have easy access to water and those who have to fetch it from a distance. ⁵A joint report by UNICEF and the World Health Organisation (2003) points out that in the developing world, households with multiple taps have an average water consumption of between 100 and 200 litres per person per day. ⁶In rural areas where water has to be collected from up to a kilometre away, this falls to 20 litres per person per day. ⁷If the water source is further than one kilometre away, consumption drops to around five litres per day. ⁸This contrasts with the World Health Organisation (2002) recommendation of 2 to 4.5 litres a day for drinking, and another 4 litres for cooking and food preparation are the absolute minimum limits for survival. ⁹The water needed to raise food is not taken into account in this figure.

¹⁰It is usually women and young girls who are responsible for collecting water from distant sources. ¹¹Not only may this expose them to the possibility of attack in some regions (Dwyer, 2004), but it also reduces time available for other things, such as cooking and agriculture. ¹²Most seriously, it may make it difficult for girls to attend school, thus condemning them to a life of poverty and illiteracy.

¹³In urban areas, the poor are frequently not connected to mains water supply. ¹⁴This means that they are forced to buy water from private suppliers. ¹⁵The World Watch Institute (2001) estimates that they pay an average of 12 times more per litre than those who have access to mains water. ¹⁶In Jakarta, the Institute points out, this

rises to 60 times more, in Karachi, Pakistan, to 83 times more and in Haiti, 100 times more.

[17]When water is scarce, basic hygiene is difficult to maintain. [18]The UN's World Water Development Report (2003) estimates that households with taps use as much as 30 times more water for child hygiene compared with those who have to collect water from a distance.

[19]Lack of water greatly increases the chance of infectious disease, especially diseases such as diarrhoea, typhoid and cholera, which are responsible for 80 per cent of illnesses and deaths in the developing world. [20]Bowden (2002) points out that the simple ability to wash one's hands with soap and water can reduce diarrhoea by 35 per cent.

20 WRITING REPORTS: PROBLEM-SOLUTION TEXTS

LEARNING OBJECTIVES

When you have finished this chapter, you will be able to:

- identify the purpose and audience of a report
- identify the problem–solution structure of a report
- recognise and use the various sections of a report appropriately
- express your voice and refer to the voices of others
- demonstrate your ability to use critical thinking in a report.

WORD LIST

Do you know the meaning of these words? Many have special meanings in academic culture. You can check their meaning in the glossary at the back of the book.

- ☐ appendix
- ☐ bibliography
- ☐ critical thinking
- ☐ discipline

- ☐ executive summary
- ☐ problem–solution text
- ☐ recommendations
- ☐ report

Who writes reports?

In some disciplines, especially those oriented towards the world of work, you are likely to find yourself writing reports more often than you write essays. This is especially so in courses such as business, accounting, engineering and information technology. Professionals working in these areas spend a significant amount of time writing reports, and so the assignments that you complete while studying give you the opportunity to practise report-writing skills. As with an essay, when you write a report you need to ask yourself:

- What is the purpose of this text?
- Who is the audience for this text?
- What is the structure of this text?

THINK ABOUT THIS

- Do any of your modules ask you to write reports?
- How might understanding the purpose, audience and structure of a report be useful in your future career?

What is the purpose and audience of a report?

While essays aim to present and defend a position, the purpose of a report is to examine a problem. As there are several ways of doing this, you may be expected to:

- identify a problem and define its extent; that is, how large or how serious it is, the areas it affects and so on
- identify a problem and justify a solution
- identify several possible solutions to the problem
- evaluate different solutions to the problem
- make recommendations based on your analysis.

The audience for the reports you write is, of course, your lecturers, but while they are not part of the business world, their expectations will reflect many of the same expectations of readers in a professional setting. They will expect you to be able to:

- critically analyse the problem and identify its major features
- suggest logical solutions and explain the reasoning supporting them
- explain the method of investigation or analysis when necessary
- clearly link your recommendations to your analysis of the problem.

What is the structure of a report?

We will examine the structure of reports using a short report on the following topic:

What is culture shock and how is it caused? How likely is it to affect personnel posted overseas? What steps can a company take to minimise the impact of culture shock?

A report contains a number of sections, some of which are necessary and some of which are used only in long reports. The list below identifies the compulsory sections with an asterisk (*):

- title page*
- table of contents
- list of abbreviations and/or glossary
- executive summary
- introduction*
- body*
- conclusion*
- recommendations
- bibliography or reference list*
- appendices.

Title page

The title page must include details of the course for which the report was prepared and the name of the lecturer or tutor, the details of the assignment and the report writer's details. Some university departments will have specific guidelines regarding the contents of the cover page. Check if this is so in your department. A sample cover page for our report topic is presented in Text 84.

 TEXT 84

Report prepared for IB213: International Business Tutor: Dr Mary Shelley	Details of the course for which the report was prepared, together with the tutor/lecturer's name
What is culture shock and how is it caused? How likely is it to affect personnel posted overseas? What steps can a company take to minimise the impact of culture shock?	Details of the purpose of the report
Prepared by Jane Smith Student number XX12345 February 30 2018	Details of the person who prepared the report and date of submission

Table of contents

A table of contents (TOC) is usually required only for longer reports; that is, a report of about ten pages or more. Although the sample report is much shorter than this, we have provided a TOC (Text 85) to illustrate what is necessary.

Number each stage and each substage. For example, Stage 5 has four substages (5.1, 5.2, 5.3 and 5.4). If a substage is further divided, you would number it 5.1.1, and so on. In general you should not need to go beyond this. In other words, you should not need 5.1.1.1! Notice also that the substages are indented in the TOC.

TEXT 85: TABLE OF CONTENTS

1	Introduction	1
2	Definition of culture shock	1
3	Stages of culture shock	1
4	Causes of culture shock	1
5	Managing culture shock	2
	5.1 Pre-departure training	2
	5.2 Settlement support	2
	5.3 Language training	2
	5.4 Development of open and flexible attitudes	2
6	Conclusions	3
7	Recommendations	3
8	Reference list	3

Make sure that your page numbers are accurate. If you have a number of tables and other figures, you may list them separately, giving the title of each figure and the page that it is on.

List of abbreviations and/or glossary

If you have used abbreviations in your report, you should list them on a separate page after the TOC. This may not be necessary in a short report, but in a longer one it is essential.

You may also need to provide a glossary defining technical terms. When you are writing for a professional audience, you may feel that it is unnecessary to define those terms in the body of the report. In that case, you would certainly need to list them in a glossary. This allows the reader to confirm the intended meaning of each term.

Executive summary

The purpose of an executive summary is to give an overview of the whole report. Short reports do not usually include an executive summary, but longer ones in the business world usually do. You may or may not be asked to provide one for the reports you write as part of your course.

As you can see from Text 86, an executive summary summarises each section of the report in one or two sentences. Recommendations are often presented in full as many professionals are most interested in the action that arises from the report.

TEXT 86: EXECUTIVE SUMMARY

Culture shock refers to the stress caused when a person from one cultural background moves to live or work in another culture. It is characterised by a range of physical and psychological symptoms including headaches, disrupted sleeping patterns and feelings of irritation and impatience with host-culture nationals.

Culture shock affects all people living and working in an unfamiliar cultural environment and generally involves a four-stage progression from initial euphoria through crisis and adjustment to full adaptation, a stage that is not reached by everyone.

The causes of culture shock include the cognitive fatigue of having to cope with the unfamiliar, and role shock resulting from different evaluation of roles and responsibilities.

The successful management of culture shock depends both on organisational support, including pre-departure training, settlement support, language training, and on the development of personal qualities of tolerance, adaptability and openness to change.

Recommendations

→ That company personnel assigned to overseas posts undergo pre-departure training to help them to develop a flexible and open attitude when interacting with people of a different cultural background.

→ That a relocation consultant be employed to assist each person relocated overseas with settlement issues including housing, schooling and spousal settlement.

→ That personnel assigned to overseas posts be given language training both prior to their departure and throughout the duration of their assignment.

Introduction

The introduction to a report is similar to the introduction to an essay, but focuses on a problem rather than a position. In general it should:

- introduce the general topic and provide background that puts the topic in a broader context
- indicate the significance of the topic, explaining in general terms why it is a problem
- identify the problem to be investigated
- provide an overview of what is to come
- define important terms used in the report.

In the sample report (Text 87), sentence 1 places culture shock within the context of globalisation and increasing contact between people of different cultural backgrounds. The second sentence indicates the importance of this for business and the third sentence both identifies the problem to be investigated and gives an overview of what will be covered. Notice that the term 'culture shock' is not defined in the introduction because the topic asks for a definition. This means that the definition should be included in the body of the report.

THINK ABOUT THIS

Look at the introduction to one of your reports.

- What functions of an introduction are represented in your introductions?
- In the light of the information about the functions of a report introduction (above), how might you improve your introduction?

Body of the report

The body of the report is divided into sections and subsections. Each section deals with a particular aspect of the topic, which is indicated by a heading. Headings indicate the content of the section, unlike the headings used in research reports, which we will examine in the next chapter. This means that terms such as 'body' or 'body of the report' are never used as headings. A section may also be divided into subsections, as is the case with section 5 of Text 85. Note that the content of each subsection is also indicated in a subheading. All sections and subsections are numbered.

A feature of many reports is the use of figures, tables and diagrams. One type of figure illustrates something such as a process that is described in the report. For example, in the sample report, a figure is used to illustrate the process of adaptation to a new culture. This type of figure is usually accompanied by a description in words. Its function is to support and clarify the description in the text. A second type of figure presents data. We will examine this way of using figures in the next chapter. It is important to label all figures with a figure or table number and to give each a title that indicates what the figure shows. You also need to refer to the figure by name in the text itself, otherwise the reader will not know how it fits into your argument.

Conclusion

The conclusion sums up the major points made in the report. Each conclusion should have been argued in the body of the report, so that no new material is included.

Recommendations

Recommendations are suggestions for future action. Only some reports include recommendations. You need to check with your lecturer regarding the situation with your report.

If you do have recommendations, they must be linked to the analysis included in the body of the report; that is, the reasons that caused you to make these recommendations must be clear. In the sample report, the recommendations are based on the following reasons:

- Culture shock affects people's ability to function in a new environment (sections 2, 3 and 4).
- Culture shock affects all people who live or work in an unfamiliar culture to some extent (sections 2 and 3).
- The effects of culture shock can be minimised in several different ways (section 5).

THINK ABOUT THIS

- Have you included recommendations in any of your reports?
- Are the recommendations clearly linked to the analysis in the report?

Reference list

The reference list should include full details of all the sources you have referred to in the report, arranged in alphabetical order by author's family name. Entries in the reference list should not be numbered.

Appendices

An appendix (plural 'appendices' or 'appendixes') contains material that is too long or too complex to go in the body of the report. For example, if you have used a questionnaire, then it would be placed in an appendix. Large tables and other figures may also be placed in appendices. Each appendix should be numbered and given a title to indicate what it contains. You need to ensure that each appendix is referenced in the body of your report.

TEXT 87: SAMPLE REPORT

1 Introduction

With the increasing mobility and intercultural contact that comes with globalisation, the phenomenon of culture shock is attracting a great deal of attention. Senior management is becoming more aware of the problems that may arise when a person from one cultural background is assigned to work in an unfamiliar culture; for example, when an Australian manager takes up a position in Indonesia. This report will describe the phenomenon of culture shock and its causes and identify steps that can be taken to minimise its impact.

2 Definition of culture shock

Culture shock is the name given to a wide range of symptoms that result when a person is forced to carry out the normal functions of daily life (social interaction, doing business, obtaining daily necessities and so on) in unfamiliar ways (Ting-Toomey, 2001; Brislin, 1981). This is the case when a person from one cultural background moves to live or work in another culture.

Physical symptoms of culture shock may include headaches, constant tiredness, difficulty in sleeping or excessive sleep, and a general feeling of discomfort (Hindmarsh, 1991). Psychologically, culture shock is likely to manifest itself in feelings of irritation and impatience, distrust of host-culture nationals, and the development of negative stereotypes of the host culture (Brislin, 1981). While it is unlikely that anyone suffers all the symptoms of culture shock, Preston (1984) points out that everyone faced with the necessity of interacting in an unfamiliar cultural environment will experience symptoms to some degree.

3 Stages of culture shock

Most analysts identify four stages in the process of adaptation to a new culture (Ferraro, 1990; Kohls, 1984; Preston, 1984). These are:

a **The euphoric stage:** This is the typical experience of people who encounter other cultures on brief business trips or holidays. It is characterised by positive expectations and idealisations about the unfamiliar culture.

b **The crisis stage:** The crisis stage may emerge immediately upon arrival but generally emerges within a few weeks to a month. In this stage, minor issues become major problems and cultural differences become irritating.

c **The adjustment stage:** The third stage involves learning how to adjust effectively to the new cultural environment.

d **The adaptation stage:** The fourth stage involves the development of new ways of behaving and coping that allow the person to operate successfully in the new culture.

While all those exposed to an unfamiliar culture experience some degree of culture shock, many will not experience all four stages. In particular, many will not reach the fourth stage, which involves successful adaptation.

4 Causes of culture shock

While culture shock is a complex phenomenon resulting from a number of factors, two in particular stand out:

→ **Cognitive fatigue:** Guthrie (1975) points out that the unfamiliar culture demands a conscious effort to understand things that are unconsciously processed in a person's own culture. This includes unfamiliar language, behaviours and situations. The effort to understand causes mental tiredness or cognitive fatigue.

→ **Role shock:** Brislin (1981) identifies changes in the ways in which a person's familiar roles are defined as a significant source of culture shock. In particular, role responsibilities in the host culture may differ significantly from those in the home culture.

5 Managing culture shock

The successful management of culture shock depends both on organisational support and on personal qualities of tolerance, adaptability and openness to change.

5.1 Pre-departure training

Pre-departure training can greatly assist in the minimisation of culture shock in the following ways:

→ It prepares managers for the experience of culture shock and so helps normalise unexpected reactions.

→ It provides information regarding the host culture, thus establishing a framework for the interpretation of unfamiliar behaviour.

→ It assists managers in identifying their own attitudes, values and behaviours, and in understanding how these might be perceived by host culture nationals.

→ It facilitates the development of tolerance and openness to change.

5.2 Settlement support

A manager's first 3 months in an overseas position is likely to be the period of peak stress, or culture shock because he or she must adapt to a new working environment with unfamiliar attitudes, values and behaviours. At the same time, he or she has to set up a home, possibly including providing for the needs of spouse and children. Successful adjustment is greatly facilitated by provision of settlement support, including assistance with housing, schooling and spouse support. This allows the employee to focus on familiarising him or herself with the cultural demands of the work environment.

5.3 Language training

Managers who speak the language of the host community with some degree of fluency report more rapid familiarisation with the host culture and higher rates of adaptation (Jones, 1998). The ability to speak the local language is also perceived positively by host country nationals and generally tends to facilitate acceptance.

5.4 Development of open and flexible attitudes

While pre-departure and language training together with settlement support can greatly assist in minimising the severity of the crisis stage of culture shock, successful adaptation depends on the cultivation of openness to new ideas and new ways of doing things. Successful cross-cultural adaptation results in a person becoming bi-cultural, able to respond appropriately in the culture of origin and in the new culture. This requires a willingness to change intellectually, behaviourally and emotionally. Intellectually, it requires an understanding of the attitudes and values which character-ise the new culture; behaviourally, it involves modifying one's own behaviour and understanding the behaviour of others; and emotionally it involves being able to toler-ate the uncertainty that living in a new culture will always involve.

6   Conclusion

Culture shock refers to the stress that results from the loss of familiar ways of thinking and acting when a person moves to live and work in an unfamiliar culture. It is experi-enced to a greater or lesser extent by all those who move from one culture to another.

While some degree of culture shock is inevitable, its effects can be minimised by careful pre-departure training, adequate support during the settling in period and lan-guage training. More important than all of these, however, is the development of atti-tudes that facilitate successful adaptation; that is, an openness to and interest in difference and a toleration of uncertainty.

7   Recommendations

→ That all company personnel assigned to overseas posts undergo pre-departure training to help them to develop a flexible and open attitude when interacting with people of different cultural backgrounds.

→ That a relocation consultant be employed to assist each person relocated over-seas with settlement issues including housing, schooling and spousal settlement.

→ That personnel assigned to overseas posts be given language training both prior to their departure and throughout the duration of their assignment.

8 Reference list

(The reference list is not included in this sample report.)

What is the role of critical thinking in reports?

You demonstrate your critical thinking in reports in several different ways:

- By identifying and analysing the problem. This may involve identifying what the prob-lem is, the extent or seriousness of the problem, and/or what caused it.

- By proposing intelligent, or even original, solutions to the problem. The solutions must be logical and practical. Your lecturer must be able to understand the reasons for your suggested solutions.

- By evaluating different solutions to the problem. In order to evaluate different solutions, you must establish the basis on which you will make your judgement. This could include cost, feasibility, extent to which the problem would be solved, and so on. Your lecturer will check that your choice of measures is appropriate.

- By making practical recommendations where appropriate. Your lecturer will expect that the recommendations that you make are clear, focused and possible to implement.

  Consider the following recommendation:

  Staff should develop a flexible and open attitude when interacting with people of different cultural background.

This recommendation could not be implemented because it is impossible to force people to have certain attitudes. However, the recommendation might read:

All company personnel assigned to overseas posts should undergo pre-departure training to help them to develop a flexible and open attitude when interacting with people of different cultural backgrounds.

This recommendation can be implemented, and so is not only appropriate but shows evidence of analytical thinking.

THINK ABOUT THIS

Look again at the Recommendations in your report.

- Are they do-able?
- How can you make them more do-able?

How do you express your voice in a report?

The way different voices are expressed in a report is very similar to the way they are expressed in an essay. Your own voice is not labelled, but the voices of the different sources that you refer to are all identified.

SUMMARY

1. The purpose of a report is to examine a problem by:
   - identifying a problem and defining its extent
   - identifying a problem and justifying a solution
   - identifying several possible solutions to the problem

- evaluating different solutions to the problem
- making recommendations based on analysis.

2. The audience for a report may be your lecturer at university and/or professional people working in the field. They expect you to:

- critically analyse the problem and identify its major features
- suggest logical solutions and explain the reasoning supporting them
- explain the method of investigation or analysis when necessary
- clearly link your recommendations to your analysis of the problem.

3. A report has the following sections:

- **title page:** gives details of the course, lecturer, assignment, and report writer
- **table of contents:** only necessary for long reports
- **list of abbreviations and/or glossary:** only necessary for long reports
- **executive summary:** gives overview of contents and all recommendations; only necessary for long reports
- **introduction:** The introduction may:
  - □ introduce the general topic and provide background that puts the topic in a broader context
  - □ indicate the significance of the topic, explaining in general terms why it is a problem
  - □ identify the problem to be investigated
  - □ provide an overview of what is to come
  - □ define important terms used in the report.
- **body:** divided into sections, each dealing with a specific aspect of the problem
- **conclusion:** sums up the report, and contains no new information
- **recommendations:** suggestions for future action; closely linked to analysis
- **bibliography or reference list:** in alphabetical order
- **appendices:** material too long or complex to go in the body.

The title page, introduction, body, conclusion and bibliography or reference list are essential.

4. Critical thinking is demonstrated through:

- identifying and analysing the problem
- proposing intelligent, or even original, solutions to the problem
- evaluating different solutions to the problem effectively and efficiently
- making practical recommendations.

SKILLS PRACTICE

Task 1

Look at the way voices are expressed in the sample report on culture shock.

- Which is the dominant voice?
- Are other voices mainly direct, indirect or external? (See Chapter 12 for an explanation of voices.)
- In what sections of the report are other voices heard most often? Why do you think this is?
- In what sections of the report are other voices heard least? Why do you think this is?

Task 2

Text 88 is a report on the global digital divide – the difference between people who can access and use information technology and those who cannot. Read the report and complete the following tasks:

1. Answer the following questions:
   - What problem is this report examining?
   - Does the report focus on describing the problem or identifying solutions?
   - Why are there no recommendations attached to this report?

2. Look at the introduction. Which sentences:
   - introduce the general topic and provide background that puts the topic in a broader context
   - indicate the significance of the topic, explaining in general terms why it is a problem
   - identify the problem to be investigated
   - provide an overview of what is to come
   - define important terms used in the report

   Are any of these functions not present?

3. Look at the way different voices are used in the report.
   - Which is the dominant voice?
   - Are any of the other voices direct, indirect or references?
   - What information is given in small type below Table 20.1?

4. Where would you put the sub-heading Conclusion?

5. Create a Table of Contents for the report.

6. Write a short Executive Summary for the report.

TEXT 88: THE GLOBAL DIGITAL DIVIDE – WITHIN AND BETWEEN COUNTRIES

WENHONG CHEN AND BARRY WELLMAN

The digital divide involves the gap between individuals (and societies) that have the resources to participate in the information era and those that do not. Although there are no reliable data on the size of the world's online population, estimates suggest that the number of Internet users around the globe has surged from 4.4 million in 1991 to 10 million in 1993, to 40 million in 1995, to 117 million in 1997, to 277 million in 1999, to 502 million in 2001, and to more than 600 million in 2002. Thus, the global penetration rate of the Internet has increased from less than 0.1 in 1991 to 2 per cent in 1997, 7 per cent in 2000, to over 10 per cent of the total world population in 2002. Projections for 2004 place the number of global Internet users between 700 million and 945 million, which translates to a global penetration rate between 11 per cent and 15 per cent.

Despite rapid worldwide diffusion of the Internet, a disproportionate number of users are concentrated in more developed countries, especially the United States. In 2001, 169 million Americans were online, accounting for about 60 per cent of the country's total population and 29 per cent of the world's Internet population. There were 172 million users in Europe (28 per cent diffusion), 182 million in Southeast and East Asia, including 145 million in China, Japan, and Korea (23 per cent). South America was home to 29 million users (5 per cent), while there were 11 million in Oceania (2 per cent) and 10 million in Africa (just over 1.5 per cent).

Although there have been many individual–country analyses of the digital divide and some international statistical series (such as those issued by the OECD), there has been little research to compare, synthesize and interpret the worldwide digital divide. In this article, data from national representative surveys – conducted by government agencies, scholarly researchers, and policy reports issued by international organizations – are used to examine the digital divide in terms of access and use of the Internet across eight developed and developing countries: the United States, the United Kingdom, Germany, Italy, Japan, the Republic of Korea, China and Mexico. ...

A narrowing divide between nations

Among developed countries the digital divide between first-movers and latecomers is narrowing. Countries such as the UK, Korea and Japan have caught up to the level of Internet connectivity in the US, as shown in Table 20.1, columns 1 and 2. To some extent, the Internet is expanding in developed countries in similar ways to its expansion in the US, although with a time lag (Bazar and Boalch 1997). For example, the demographic profile of users in developed countries looks roughly similar to that of American Internet users a half-decade earlier: younger, higher-educated males.

On the other hand, different dynamics are influencing the use and the impact of the Internet in different developed countries. Thus, Japan is leading the development of *mobile Internet*; Korea is the world leader of *broadband connections*, while the UK has the highest rate of *digital TV* diffusion in the world. Further, while most countries are

Table 20.1 Percentage (and number) of population online in the eight countries

Country	Month	(1) Per cent of population online in 2002[a] (Millions [M])	(2) Per cent of population online in 2001[b], (Millions [M])	(3) No. of PCs in 2001 (Millions [M])[b]	(4) Per cent of female users in online population[b]
US	April	59% (166M)	50% (143M)	178M	51% (2000)
UK	Sept	57% (34M)	50% (143M)	22M	43% (2001)
S Korea	July	54% (26M)	52% (24M)	12M	45% (2002)
Japan	June	44% (56M)	44% (56M)	44M	41% (2001)
Germany	August	39% (32M	44% (56M)	32M	37% (2001)
Italy	August	33% (19M)	28% (16M)	11M	37% (2001)
China	December	4.8 (58M)	2.5% (34M	25M	39% (2002)
Mexico	NA	NA	3.6% (3.4M)	7M	42% (2002)

Sources: [a]NUA, http://www.nua.ie/surveys/how_many_online/, 2003; [b] ITU, 2002
SOURCE OF DATA FOR EACH COUNTRY – U.S.: NITA 1995, 1998, 2000, 2001; UCLA Internet Report, 2001–2003; Pew Internet and American Life Studies. U.K.: U.K. Online Annual Report, 2002. Germany: ARD/ZDF Online surveys, 1999–2002. Italy: OECD and the World Economic Forum; Supplemented by scholarly research. Japan: Japanese Statistics Bureau, MPHPA (Ministry of Public Management, Home Affairs); World Internet Project Japan, 2002. South Korea: National Computerization Agency, 2002; National Statistical Office; Supplemented by scholarly research. China: CNNIC, 1997–2003. Mexico: World Economic Forum, 2002; OECD, 2002, NUA; Supplemented by scholarly research

lagging behind the U.S. in PC-based Internet use, they are quickly adopting mobile phones.

The digital divide reflects the broader context of international social and economic relations: a center-periphery order marked by American dominance. There are large disparities of Internet access between the affluent nations at the core of the Internet-based global network on the one hand, and the poor countries at the periphery which lack the skills, resources, and infrastructure to log on in the information era on the other. For instance, Italy has the lowest rate of Internet penetration among the developed countries reviewed in the study. Yet, Italy's rate is seven times as high as China's and nine times as high as Mexico's. The average Internet penetration rate in developed countries was 30 per cent in 2001, ten times as high as that in the developing nations (ITU, 2003; International Labor, Office 2001). Therefore, it seems that without intervention, the global digital divide will take a long time to close.

By contrast to the progress in the developed world, the digital divide is widening and deepening within *developing countries*, in spite of efforts at bridging it (see also Kubicek, 2004). It is widening in the sense that few people actively use the Internet, and deepening in the sense that the consequences for not being online may be greater when moving beyond a subsistence level. There is a stark contrast between those who are living in major urban centers with better education, higher income and closer connections to developed countries (both culturally and economically), and those who are even more on the periphery. Only about one-half of the world's Internet users are native English speakers, and only about three-quarters of all websites are in English (World Economic Forum, 2002).

Diverse digital divides within countries

Across the eight countries in Table 20.2, socioeconomic status, gender, life stage, and geographic location significantly affect people's access to and use of the Internet.

1. *Socioeconomic status:* Internet users are more likely to be well-off and better educated than non-users in all eight countries surveyed. In general, the lower the Internet penetration rate in a country, the more elite the online population. While the socioeconomic divide is to some extent declining in the US and Japan, the digital divide elsewhere seems to be increasing along the lines of income and education. This is because, although poorer and less-educated people are accessing the Internet, the rate of increased access is higher among the more affluent and better educated segments of society in developing countries.

2. *Gender:* Men are more likely than women both to access and to use the Internet. With the exception of the US, the share of female Internet users is lower than their share in the general population in each of the countries surveyed. Yet, this gender divide is narrowing, except in Germany and Italy.

3. *Life stage:* In both developed and developing countries, the Internet penetration rate among younger people is substantially higher than that among older people. Students who can get online via school connections make up a big share of Internet users in developing countries. In general, the life-stage divide is declining in most countries, except Korea.

4. *Region:* Geographic location also affects access to and use of the Internet, with more affluent regions having higher Internet penetration rates than poorer ones. Except for Mexico, the overall trend across the eight countries shows a narrowing yet persistent digital divide in terms of geographic location.

   The digital divide has diverse manifestations along these fault lines. For instance, the gender divide is especially wide in Germany and Italy. The proportions of female Internet users in both countries are lower than in all other countries reviewed in this analysis – not only the developed ones, but also in China and Mexico, as shown in Table 20.1. Moreover, the intersection of socioeconomic status, gender, age, language and geographic location tend to increase the digital divide in mutually reinforcing ways within, and between, countries. The largest gap is between better-educated, affluent, younger, English speaking men in developed cities and less-educated, poor, older, non-English speaking women in underdeveloped rural areas.

Table 20.2 Summary of internet access in the eight countries

Country	Socio-economic status	Gender	Life stage	Region
US	Declining yet persistent	No appreciable divide	Declining yet persistent	Declining yet persistent
UK	Increasing	Declining yet persistent	Declining yet persistent	Declining yet persistent
Germany	Increasing	Increasing	Declining yet persistent	Declining
Italy	Large divide based on education.	Increasing	Younger use the Internet more	Northern Italy leads the south
Japan	Declining yet persistent	Declining yet persistent (reversed digital divide in mobile Internet)	Younger use the Internet more	Major cities have higher Internet diffusion than smaller cities
Korea (Rep)	Increasing	Persistent	Increasing	Declining: Seoul is still the most wired area in the country.
China	Huge yet slightly declining	Declining yet persistent	Slightly declining	Huge, yet slightly declining
Mexico	Huge	42 per cent of Internet users are women	Young make up the majority of Internet users	Very uneven. Users are concentrated in the center, Guadalajara, and Monterrey

The diffusion of the internet in international context

The diffusion of the Internet (and its accompanying digital divides) has occurred at the intersection of both international and within-country differences in socioeconomic, technological and linguistic factors. Telecommunications policies, infrastructures and education are prerequisites for marginalised communities to participate in the information age. High costs, English language dominance, the lack of relevant content, and the lack of technological support are barriers for disadvantaged communities using computers and the Internet.

The diffusion of Internet use in developed countries may be slowing and even stalling. Currently, Internet penetration rates are not climbing in several of the developed countries with the most penetration. Compared to the explosive growth of Internet access and use in the past decade, this is a new phenomenon. It is too soon to tell if this is a true leveling-off of the penetration rate, or a short-term fluctuation as Internet use continues its climb to triumphant ubiquity.

With the proliferation of the Internet in developed countries, the digital divide between North American and developed countries elsewhere is narrowing. However, the digital divide remains substantial between developed and developing countries. The divide also remains substantial within almost all countries, developed as well as developing. In some countries, the digital divide is widening even as the number and percentage of Internet users increases. This happens when the newcomers to the Internet are demographically similar to those already online. The diffusion of the Internet is not merely a matter of computer technology, but has profound impacts on the continuation of social inequality. People, social groups and nations on the wrong side of the digital divide may be increasingly excluded from knowledge-based societies and economies.

REFERENCES

Bazar, B., & Boalch, G. 1997. *A Preliminary Model of Internet Diffusion within Developing Countries*. Paper presented at AusWeb97: Third Australian World Wide Web Conference, Lismore.

International Labor Office. 2001. *World Employment Report 2001: Life at Work in the Information Economy*. Geneva.

Kubicek, H. 2004. Fighting a Moving Target. *IT&Society* 1, 6, pp 1–19. World Economic Forum. 2002. *Annual Report of the Global Digital Divide Initiative*. Geneva: World Economic Forum.

Chen, W. & Wellman B. 2004. The Global Digital Divide – Within and Between Countries. *It & Society*, 1, 7, pp 39–45. Retrieved March 25.2006 from http://www.IT

Task 3

1. Evaluate a report that you have written by asking the following questions:

   ■ Does the report focus on investigating a problem or on presenting a solution? Is this indicated in the introduction?

   ■ Are the conclusions and recommendations clearly related to the body of the report?

   ■ Are the sections of the report clearly labelled?

   ■ Is the writer's voice clearly distinguished from the voices of others? Are the voices of others clearly labelled?

2. Select one section of your report and rewrite it in the light of your evaluation.

21 WRITING RESEARCH REPORTS

☀ LEARNING OBJECTIVES

When you have finished this chapter, you will be able to identify the sections of a research report and understand:

- the difference between a research report and a business report
- how to develop a research topic
- the function of each section of a research report
- how voices are expressed in the different sections of a research report
- how critical thinking is reflected in a research report.

✓ WORD LIST

Do you know the meaning of these words? Many have special meanings in academic culture. You can check their meaning in the glossary at the back of the book.

- ☐ analysis
- ☐ field
- ☐ findings
- ☐ focused
- ☐ literature review
- ☐ method
- ☐ variable

What are research reports?

As well as expecting you to write essays and general reports, many courses require you to write research reports. Although both are called reports, general reports and research reports are different types of text with different purposes, audiences and structures.

THINK ABOUT THIS

- Do you have to carry out a research project for any of your modules?
- If so, do you feel confident in carrying it out?
- What difficulties do you anticipate?
- How might you tackle these difficulties?

What is the purpose and audience of a research report?

As you can probably guess from its name, the purpose of a research report is to inform academics and specialists in a particular field about a piece of research and to discuss the results that were obtained. The research is carried out by the writer of the report and usually involves observation and experimentation.

Your lecturer will be looking for evidence that you can:

- identify an appropriate research question
- select an appropriate method to carry out the research
- record the results appropriately
- analyse the results by, for example, identifying major findings, explaining findings, comparing your findings with the findings of others, identifying weaknesses in the research and so on.

How do I identify a research question?

If you are a first- or second-year student, your lecturer will probably give you a research question to investigate. However, in later years you may have to develop your own question. Let's examine how to do this by using a specific example.

Imagine you are a marketing student and that you have been asked to carry out a small research project as part of your course. The first thing you need to do is identify a topic. Your topic should be related to major issues in marketing and should have a research base; that is, it must be related to topics that other researchers have investigated. This is because your research will build on the research that has already been carried out by others. Let's imagine that your topic is 'The relationship between quality of goods and their cost'.

But as a topic, 'The relationship between quality of goods and their cost' is too vague. It gives you no idea about where to start your research, and so it fails the 'do-able' test. The 'do-able' test asks you to think about whether you know exactly what you want to do and whether you have the resources to do it.

In order to pass the 'do-able' test, you need to narrow your topic. You can do this by asking questions, such as:

■ How will I examine the relationship between quality and cost?

■ What type of goods am I interested in?

To answer the first question, you need to know what marketing experts think about how quality and cost are related. This means that you need a research base; that is, you need to read what other people have written about this topic because your research will build on what has already been done.

After you have done some reading, you find that most economists believe that goods of high quality cost more than goods of low quality. However, they also claim that people buy fewer goods if they are expensive.

You decide that you want to test this idea. You want to find out:

■ Do people think that high prices indicate better quality?

■ Are people prepared to pay more to get better quality?

■ If people are prepared to pay more to get better quality, then will they buy more, not less, when goods are expensive?

Now you need to decide what type of goods you will look at. You decide to look at the cost of restaurant meals because this is an area where people are probably prepared to pay more to get better quality. Also, it is easy to gather data because most people have experience in choosing restaurants.

You can now write three clearly focused research questions:

1. Do people believe that high prices at a restaurant indicate better quality?

2. Are people likely to choose expensive restaurants because they believe they offer better quality?

3. Do high prices in restaurants lead to an increase in demand? These questions pass the 'do-ability' test because:

    ■ They are clear and focused – you know exactly what you want to look at.

    ■ They are related to a research base – other researchers have investigated the relationship between price and quality. Your project will test their ideas.

    ■ You have the resources to carry out this piece of research.

THINK ABOUT THIS

■ If you have already completed your research project, what process did you use?

■ In the light of the information above, is there anything you would change for your next alf you have not yet carried out your project, use the process outlined above.

■ Once you have finished, evaluate the process. What aspects helped you and what aspects would you change?

How do I carry out my research project?

Once you have identified your research questions, you need to develop a plan of action to guide you as you carry out your project. This involves:

- developing a timeline, which identifies what you will do and when
- carrying out a brief literature review to find out what other scholars have said about the subject – this builds on the reading that you did to help you decide on your research questions
- designing your research instrument (survey, questionnaire, interview questions and so on)
- collecting and analysing your data
- writing up your research report.

How do I write up my research report?

We will examine what is involved in each section of a report by using a sample research report. This report has been condensed and simplified from a published report (Parikh & Weseley, 2004). It presents findings on the research questions we identified above.

A research report is normally divided into six stages:

- introduction
- literature review
- method
- results
- discussion
- references.

Introduction

The introduction to a research report does several different things. It has to:

- introduce the general topic
- describe what we already know about the topic
- establish a gap in the field; that is, something that we do not know
- identify the research question and show that it will help to fill the gap in our knowledge
- show why the research is interesting and/or important.

Text 89 is the introduction to the research report on the relationship between price and quality in restaurant meals. An analysis of each stage of the introduction is presented in the column on the right.

TEXT 89: INTRODUCTION

[1]When deciding whether or not to buy a product, one of the first things a person typically sees is the price of the item. [2]Because the price is often the only obvious difference between one brand of an item and another, it can affect people's perceptions of the quality and value of an item. [3]Quality and value can influence whether the item is purchased. [4]Research has suggested that people may believe high prices indicate high quality (Dodds, Monroe, & Grewal, 1991). [5]As a result, under some circumstances high prices may lead to an increase in demand (Lambert, 1970; Cialdini, 1993). [6]However, research has not consistently demonstrated this effect.

[7]The price of restaurant meals is one area in which it is likely that high prices are seen as a guarantee of high quality, resulting in an increase in demand. [8]This study was designed to test this hypothesis and to shed light on the extent to which price affects consumers' perceptions of the quality of a restaurant. [9]Specifically, it sought to investigate whether consumers would assume that a high-priced restaurant would offer better quality and whether, consequently, they would be more likely to try such an establishment.

Sentences 1–3: Introduce general topic
Sentences 4-5: Identify what we already know
Sentence 6: Identifies a gap
Sentences 7–8: Identify general research question
Sentence 9: Identifies specific research question

Modified from Parikh, A., & Weseley, A. (2004). The effect of price level on perceptions of a restaurant. *Journal of Research for Consumers*, Issue 7. Retrieved from http://www.jrconsumers.com.

Notice how the topic area is introduced in the first three sentences, which explain the general relationship between quality, price and demand. Sentences 4 and 5 tell us more about this relationship by referring to the writings of other scholars. Then in sentence 6 we are told that the research on the relationship between quality, price and demand is not clear. Some studies show that there is a high demand for quality goods even though the price is high, while other studies do not show this. This indicates a gap in our knowledge: something that we need to investigate further. Sentences 7 and 8 then identify the research questions. Answers to these questions will help to fill the gap identified in sentence 6.

The section of the introduction that explains why the research is interesting or important is optional and is not included in Text 89.

You might also notice that the writers' voice is the dominant voice in the introduction. There is only one section where other voices are introduced – the section in which the writers identify what we already know about the topic. References to other voices and the indirect or external voices of others could both be used in this section, but it is less common to use direct voices. In this introduction, sentences 4 and 5 use the external voices of other writers, but we do not actually hear their voices. In all other sections we hear only the voice of the writers of the report.

We have already seen that writers do not usually label their own voice, but there is one section of the introduction where it can be done. When writers identify their research question and explain what they are going to do they may identify themselves by using 'I', or 'we' if there is more than one author. This is because they may want to take responsibility for the research by saying 'This is **my** study; this is what **I** am doing'. Text 90 demonstrates the two different ways of identifying the research question. The column on the left does not label the writer's voice, while the column on the right does.

TEXT 90

WRITER'S VOICE NOT LABELLED

[7]The price of restaurant meals is one area in which it is likely that high prices are seen as a guarantee of high quality, resulting in an increase in demand. [8]This study was designed to test this hypothesis and to shed light on the extent to which price affects consumers' perceptions of the quality of a restaurant. [9]Specifically, it sought to investigate whether consumers would assume that a high-priced restaurant would offer better quality and whether, consequently, they would be more likely to try such an establishment.

WRITER'S VOICE LABELLED

[7]The price of restaurant meals is one area in which it is likely that high prices are seen as a guarantee of high quality, resulting in an increase in demand. [8]We designed this study to test this hypothesis and to shed light on the extent to which consumers' perceptions of a restaurant are impacted by price level. [9]Specifically, we sought to investigate whether consumers would assume that a high-priced restaurant would offer better quality and whether, consequently, they would be more likely to try such an establishment.

The literature review

The word 'literature' refers to all the books, articles and so on that have been written about a particular subject. We can talk, for example, about the marketing literature, meaning everything that has been written about marketing, or the literature on motivation or on corporate fraud.

A literature review involves reporting on what scholars have written about a particular research topic. Of course, it is not possible to report on everything that has ever been written, so you need to select the studies that are most relevant to your particular research questions. The literature review is important because it helps your readers understand how your study relates to the work of other people in the field.

Text 91 is the literature review from our sample research report. You can see that the voices of other scholars are prominent. However, just as in an essay the writer's voice presents a point that is then supported by another voices, so in a literature review a similar thing happens. The writer's voice presents points, makes comments, compares different studies and so on. Other sources are used to support or illustrate the writer's voice. For example, in sentence 1 the writers' voice makes the point that the relationship between quality and price is not clear. Sentences 2 and 3 illustrate this using the indirect voice of Alpert, Wilson and Elliot. These researchers found that consumers did not think high prices for moisturisers indicated high quality. However, they found that if an expensive moisturiser was packed beautifully and advertised widely, then consumers did expect that the high price was an indication of high quality.

Similarly, in sentence 6, the writers' voice compares the study by Dodds et al. (discussed in sentence 5) with the traditional view of the relationship between price and demand. The writers use the external voice of Kreul to inform the reader where to find the traditional view, but Kreul's voice is not heard. In sentence 7, we hear Rachman's voice, but notice that the word 'conversely' is the writers' voice. This voice tells us that Rachman's findings do not agree with those of Dodds et al. and Kreul. The writers' voice in sentence 8 suggests a possible explanation for the disagreement. Lambert's indirect voice is used to support this suggestion.

 TEXT 91: LITERATURE REVIEW

[1]The relationship between price and perceptions of quality is not clear. [2]Alpert, Wilson, and Elliot (1993) observed that higher price alone did not create impressions of a higher quality facial moisturiser. [3]However, they found that a higher price, coupled with quality signals such as premium packaging and advertising did indicate higher quality to consumers.

[4]High price has been shown to have varied effects on the likelihood of trying a product as well. [5]Dodds et al. (1991) demonstrated that high prices reduced reported willingness to buy products. [6]This finding is consonant with the traditional notions of the demand curve, which suggest that price and demand are inversely proportional (Kreul, 1982). [7]Conversely, Rachman (1999) pointed out that high prices often increase demand for wine, another case in which consumers may equate high prices with high quality. [8]This phenomenon suggests that the impact of a high price on demand is affected by the type of product. [9]Lambert (1970) showed that high priced products were preferred when different brands of the product varied greatly in quality and when the product was socially significant, both of which seem to be the case with wine.

> **Sentence 1:** Writer's voice – introduces topic 1: relationship between price and quality
> **Sentences 2–3:** Indirect voice of source – the findings of Alpert, Wilson, and Elliot on perceptions of quality and price with reference to moisturiser
> **Sentence 4:** Writer's voice – introduces topic 2: relationship between price and likelihood of buying a product

Sentence 5: Indirect voice of source – the findings of Dodds et al: high prices reduced demand
Sentence 6: Writers voice – comment: writer points out that the study by Dodds et al. supports the traditional concept of the demand curve
Sentence 7: Indirect voice of source – writer points out that Rachman's study contradicts the study of Dodds et al.
Sentence 8: Writer's voice – writer identifies a possible implication of Rachman's study **Sentence 9:** Indirect voice of source – Lambert's voice supports the implication identified in sentence 8

The literature review gives you the opportunity to show that you can identify other research that is relevant to your research questions. Secondly, it shows that you can analyse sources, by comparing, contrasting and commenting on them. It also shows that you refer appropriately to this research, using your own writer's voice to make points and supporting them with other voices. In other words, it is crucial in establishing your identity as an academic and a researcher.

Method

The method section of a research report explains how you carried out your research. It is sometimes regarded as the easiest to write up because it is descriptive rather than analytical. This is true if you are using standard or commonly accepted methods, in which case you do not have to explain them in detail or justify them. However, if you are using unfamiliar methods, you may have to describe them more fully, and even to justify them by explaining why they are appropriate.

In general, methods sections in the natural and applied sciences (physics, biology, engineering and so on) tend to be short and descriptive because many researchers use standard methods. However, in the social sciences (economics, psychology, education and so on) and in professional fields such as business, marketing and management, methods sections tend to be longer and to describe what was done in detail. They may also justify the methods that were used. This is because methodology is less standardised in the social sciences, and there is a great deal of debate about different methods. The result is that methods sections in the social sciences and professional fields may involve analysis as well as description.

The sample research report is from the field of marketing and the methods section describes exactly what procedures were used to test the research questions. This allows the writer to establish that the methods were appropriate and reliable. The method section is divided into two parts (see Text 92). The first outlines who took part in the study (the participants) and the second describes how the survey was carried out (the materials). The section on participants tells us:

- how many people participated in the study
- how they were chosen
- the characteristics of the participants (age, sex, etc.).

The materials section describes:

- what materials were used
- how the materials were used.

TEXT 92: METHOD

Participants

The sample for this study was 95 adults entering a local library in an upper-middle class neighbourhood in New York, United States. The participants' mean age was 52 years; the youngest participant was 18 years old, and the oldest was 86 years old. There were 41 males, 52 females, and two people who neglected to report their gender. No incentive was given for participation, and approximately 50 per cent of the people who were approached agreed to participate. Participants were randomly assigned to view one of the four restaurant menus described below.

Materials

Two versions of a menu were created. They were intended to represent a typical Italian restaurant menu. With the exception of the prices, every version was identical. The menus were printed on white paper, no descriptions were provided for any of the menu items, and no name was given to the restaurant. The menus were plain in order to ensure that the participants would be influenced, as much as possible, only by the prices of the menu items. Price was the only aspect of the menus that varied. One version contained inexpensive prices that ranged from $2.99 to $13.00. Prices on the other version ranged from $5.99 to $26.00.

Attached to each menu was a survey that tested perceptions of the restaurant based solely on the menu. Three items dealt with quality-image, three with value-image, and three with likelihood of trying the restaurant. All nine items were answered on a seven-point scale. The final three items on the survey asked about participants' age and gender, and how often they ate out.

Notice also that this section is written impersonally. The focus is on what was done, rather than on who did it. We are told, for example, that 'Participants were randomly *assigned* to view one of the four restaurant menus', rather than 'The authors *assigned* participants randomly to view one of four menus'.

Results

The most important function of the results section is to describe the results of the research. However, writing up the results section is not a simple exercise in description. Many of your results will be presented in the form of figures; mainly tables and graphs. In the last chapter, we saw that there are two main types of figures. One type is generally used to illustrate processes, and is accompanied by a description in words. The second type focuses on presenting data, and only the most significant results are described in words. If you spend time describing all results in detail, you lead the reader to believe that you are unable to distinguish between major and minor findings; in other words, you create the impression that you cannot critically analyse your data.

All tables, graphs, diagrams and other figures must be labelled (Figure 1, Figure 2, etc.) and given a caption that indicates what the figure is about.

TEXT 93: RESULTS

The three items that dealt with quality were averaged to create a Quality Scale that yielded a reliability coefficient of $a = .95$ using Cronbach's alpha. The three questions that dealt with people's likelihood of trying the restaurant were averaged to create a Likelihood Scale with a reliability of $a = .90$.

The survey included a question about how often the participants ate out. This question was intended to ensure that the sample was familiar with restaurants. When the data were analysed, there was no statistical difference between the results when those who reported they ate out once a month or less (7.4 per cent) were included and when they were omitted. Therefore, all participants were included in the final data analysis. Some participants, however, chose not to answer one or more survey questions. Consequently, the final sample consisted of only 88 participants, as only those participants that provided a response for every question could be included in the final analyses.

Because the dependent variables were intercorrelated, the data were analysed using a multivariate analysis of variance. See Table 21.1 for the means of each of the

Table 21.1 Perceptions of menu quality and likelihood of restaurant choice

	Price level	Mean	Standard deviation	N (No of subjects)
Quality	Low	4.31	1.13	24
	High	4.86	1.10	21
	Total	4.56	1.14	45
Likelihood of choice	Low	4.58	1.29	21
	High	3.73	1.58	24
	Total	4.19	1.48	45

groups. A significant multivariate effect was found for price level, $F(3, 82) = 18.01$, $p < .001$.

The effect of price level on perceptions of quality

A significant univariate main effect for price level on perceptions of quality was found. Participants rated the higher priced restaurant as better in quality than the lower priced restaurant, $F(1, 84) = 10.00$, $p < .01$.

The effect of price level on the likelihood of trying the restaurant

A final univariate ANOVA revealed that the effect of price level on the likelihood of trying the restaurant was significant, $F(1, 84) = 10.40$, $p < .05$.

If you use statistics to analyse your data, you usually need to explain what statistical tools you used. You can see an example of this in Text 93. A table is used to present the results in full, and the two most important findings are summarised at the end of the section.

The results section in this research report only present results. However, some results sections may also include discussion about the results. This indicates that the division between the results section and the discussion section is sometimes blurred. In general, however, the discussion included in the results section tends to relate very closely to the results, while the discussion section tends to take a broader view, and explores the wider implications of the results.

Discussion

The discussion section of a research report may also be referred to as the conclusion. It discusses the implications of the findings. It is in this section that you demonstrate your capacity for critical analysis most strongly. You can do this by:

- identifying your findings
- explaining your findings
- comparing your findings with the findings of others
- discussing the significance of your findings
- identifying weaknesses or limitations in the research
- identifying topics for further research.

The discussion section of the sample research report (Text 94) is divided into two parts, each relating to one of the research questions. The first part answers the question 'Do people believe that high prices at a restaurant indicate better quality?' The second part answers the questions, 'Are people likely to choose expensive restaurants because they believe they offer better quality?' and 'Do high prices in restaurants lead to an increase in demand?'

In sentences 1 and 2, the writers' voice confirms the finding that higher priced menus created an impression of higher quality. Sentence 3 explains this finding and supports the explanation with an external voice, while sentence 4 compares the finding with the findings of other studies, pointing out that some studies support the finding, but others do not. In the following five sentences, the writers' voice presents an explanation for the differences between the various findings. The final sentence in the paragraph draws a conclusion from this part of the discussion.

In the following paragraph (sentences 11–16), another way of explaining the writers' finding is presented. The explanation is supported by the external voice of Cooper and Fazio, and this part of the discussion concludes with the identification of a possible subject for further research.

The first sentence in the second part (sentence 17) identifies the second major finding. The writers' voice points out that the second finding supports the economic theory of the demand curve. Sentences 19–21 explain the finding. However, in sentence 22 the writers point to research that does not support the finding. Sentences 23 and 24 identify two possible explanations for this difference and sentence 25 concludes by identifying another possible topic for research.

You can see that the discussion section of a report involves a great deal of critical analysis. In fact, it is probably the section where you can display your analytical skills most clearly. However, critical thinking and analysis are important in all stages of a research report. It is needed when you identify a 'do-able' research question, and show how this question will assist in filling a gap in our knowledge. You need it again as you develop an appropriate method to investigate the question, and when you identify your major findings in the results section. The discussion section involves you in explaining your findings, comparing and contrasting them with other studies, identifying their implications and drawing conclusions. This sounds like a heavy responsibility, but you will find that the more research reports you read, the more you understand how to write them yourself.

 TEXT 94: DISCUSSION[1]

The effect of price level on perceptions of quality

[1]This experiment confirms the association between price and quality. [2]Despite the lack of any other signals of high quality, a higher priced menu created the impression of a higher quality restaurant. [3]The most likely explanation for this effect is that price is generally seen as an indicator of quality (Dodds et al., 1991). [4]The finding conflicts with the observations of Alpert et al. (1993), but supports those made by Dodds et al. (1991) and Venkataraman (1981). [5]This may be because the relationship between high price and high quality may be product specific. [6]That is, it may be true of a restaurant but not of some other goods. [7]In the study by Alpert et al., quality evaluations were made by participants who also knew the store and brand name, whereas the strongest price–quality relationship in Dodds et al. was seen when no brand or store name was

included. [8]The design of this study did not involve brand or store name. [9]Therefore, the price–quality relationship may be stronger when product information is limited to price, and weaker when buyers have knowledge of brand and store name. [10]When little is known about an item besides its price, consumers should be particularly cautious about assuming that higher prices are necessarily indicative of higher quality.

[11]Another possible explanation for the perception that higher priced restaurants are higher in quality is that participants may have been attempting to minimise cognitive dissonance. [12]Cognitive dissonance can occur when people's actions conflict with their beliefs. [13]In such situations, people seek to reduce mental tension by bringing their attitudes into concordance with their behaviour (Cooper & Fazio, 1984). [14]Since the experiment was conducted in an upper-middle class community, many participants may be used to buying high priced goods. [15]In order to justify this behaviour, they may believe that higher price means higher quality and may have accordingly rated the higher priced restaurant as offering a higher quality product. [16]This finding raises the question of whether a less pronounced price–quality relationship might be observed in a lower income area.

The effect of price level on the likelihood of trying the restaurant

[17]People reported that they were more likely to try the low priced restaurant than the high priced restaurant. [18]This finding is consistent with the demand curve (Kreul, 1982). [19]The obvious explanation for this finding is a greater willingness to try the restaurant that posed a lesser risk. [20]Consumers knew nothing about the restaurant except for the items on the menu and their prices. [21]They may have been more prepared to try the restaurant in which they would lose less if they did not have a good experience.

[22]Interestingly, this finding seems to contradict research that shows high priced brands are favoured when dealing with socially significant products (Lambert, 1970; Rachman, 1999). [23]This discrepancy implies that the value of the restaurant may have been more important to consumers than its social significance. [24]On the other hand, it is possible that the restaurant's social significance was minimised by the exclusion of signals such as a familiar name or prestigious address. [25]Further research is needed about how such signals influence people's decisions to try or not to try a restaurant.

THINK ABOUT THIS

- Which of the functions of the Discussion section outlined above appear in your research report?

- In the light of reading this section, is there anything you would change in the way you wrote the section?

- If you haven't written a research report, think about the functions of a Discussion section with regards to a research report on the reading list for one of your modules.

 SUMMARY

1. Research reports inform academics and specialists in a field about particular research projects and discuss the results they obtained.

2. Research questions need to be:
   - related to other research
   - focused
   - do-able with the resources (including time) that you have available.

3. A research project is guided by a plan of action that includes:
   - specifying a time line
   - carrying out a literature review
   - collecting and analysing data
   - writing up the report.

4. A research report is divided into six stages:
   - introduction
   - literature review
   - method
   - results
   - discussion
   - references.

 SKILLS PRACTICE

Task 1

Text 95 is the introduction to a research report on the effect of the internet on peoples' interaction with their families. Read it and answer the following:

(a) Summarise the topic of the research report in your own words.

(b) Which sentence(s) identify the general topic of the report?

(c) Which sentence(s) present the research questions?

(d) How many research questions are there?

(e) Whose voice is dominant in each stage of the introduction?

(f) What are other voices used for?

TEXT 95

INTRODUCTION

[1]Whether the internet plays a positive or a negative role in peoples' social lives is a topic of ongoing debate. [2]Several scholars report negative effects, ranging from an increased rate of depression (Kraut et al., 1998) to a reduction in the amount of time spent with family and friends (Nie, 2000). [3]However, other scholars have found that the internet enhances social life by developing new ways of connecting with family and friends (Rainie, 2000). [4]Lenhart (2001), for example, found that teenagers in particular use the internet to maintain their social connections, while Fox (2001) reported that the elderly are more likely than any other age group to go online every day.

[5]One reason for these different findings regarding the social impact of the internet is that surveys have been conducted at different points in the internet's development. [6]Patterns of usage that prevailed in the late 1990s do not correspond to patterns of usage in the middle of the first decade of the new millennium. [7]One way of measuring the internet's impact on social life more accurately is to track changes in the use of email by users over a period of time. [8]This study reports on the use of email by a group of users in a large Australian city over a period of five years. [9]The study examined changes in the extent to which email was used to maintain contact with family members, and compared this to users' self-reports of the extent to which they felt connected to family members.

Task 2

Read Text 96, a research report about friendship between black children and white children in Zimbabwe in the 1980s, and answer the following questions:

1. Identify the introduction to the report.
   - Which sentence(s) identify the general background to the report?
   - Which sentence(s) indicate why the research is important?
   - Which sentence(s) indicate a gap in our knowledge?
   - Which sentence(s) present the research questions?
   - How many research questions are there?
   - Whose voice is dominant in each stage of the introduction?
   - What are other voices used for?
2. Identify the literature review.
   - What type of voices are used in the literature review?
3. Identify the Methods section in the report.
   - In your own words, describe the methods used.

- Is the Method section descriptive or analytical?
  - How do you know?
  - Why do you think this is?
- Whose voice dominates the section?
- Look at the verbs used to describe the method.
  - What is the most common tense?
  - Are most of the verbs active or passive? Why?

4. Identify the Results section.
   - Summarise the main findings of the study in your own words
   - How are the results analysed?
   - How many voices do you hear in the results section?

5. Identify the Discussion section.
   - Summarise the writers' conclusions in your own words.
   - Which of the following does the section do:
     - identify the findings
     - compare the findings with the findings of others
     - discuss the significance of the findings

TEXT 96: INTERRACIAL FRIENDSHIP IN A ZIMBABWEAN PUBLIC SCHOOL

David Wilson
Susu Lavelle

Department of Psychology
University of Zimbabawe

[1]In 1980, following a protracted war fought largely on racial lines, White-minority-ruled Rhodesia became the independent Black-governed nation of Zimbabwe (Meredith, 1980). [2]Schools, hospitals, and residential areas became racially integrated (Caute, 1983). [3]Zimbabwe is widely regarded as a model of racial reconciliation and an example to the racially divided societies of Namibia and South Africa. [4]Murphree (1986) noted, however, that although White Zimbabweans have generally modified their public behavior, racial insularity is still evident in the attitudes and private social lives of many. [5]The study of interracial friendship among Zimbabwean children may contribute to an understanding of the psychology of racial integration in Zimbabwe. [6]Most pupils in government schools in Zimbabwe are Black, but a handful of primary schools in middle-class suburbs in Harare, the capital city, enroll an approximately equal number of Black and White pupils. [7]One such school was selected for this study.

[8]The literature on interethnic and interreligious friendships in the United Kingdom suggests that in-group friendship preferences become increasingly pronounced as children move from the choice of classroom companions to playmates at school to playmates outside school (Davey & Mullin, 1982; Davies & Turner, 1984). [9]We sought to determine what the interracial friendship patterns would be among schoolchildren in Zimbabwe.

[10]The sample consisted of 94 Black and 110 White children between 7 and 14 years old from eight classes in a primary school in a middle-class suburb of Harare. [11]The children were asked to indicate the child in their class they would choose to (a) sit beside in class, (b) play with in school, (c) play with outside school, (d) invite to spend a night at their house, and (e) visit for a night.

[12]Chi-square tests were used to examine how far children's preferences for friends from the same racial group departed from those expected on the basis of chance. [13]Tests were performed separately for each of the eight classes. [14]Among Black respondents, 2 of a possible 40 (eight classes, five situations) chi-square tests were significant (dfs = 1, ps < .05). [15]One concerned the choice of a friend to sit beside in class, and the other concerned the choice of a friend to play with in school. [16]Among White participants, 9 of a possible 40 chi-square tests reached significance. [17]One concerned the choice of a friend to sit beside in class, one concerned the choice of a friend to invite to visit for a night, two concerned the choice of a friend to play with in school, two concerned the choice of a friend to visit for a night, and three concerned the choice of a friend to play with outside school.

[18]The results, unlike those obtained in the United Kingdom (Davey & Mullin, 1982; Davies & Turner, 1984), did not show a gradation of in-group friendship preferences as children moved from classroom companions to playmates in school to playmates outside school. [19]Some evidence of in-group friendship preference was observed. [20]These preferences appeared more marked among White than among Black children, which accords with sociological observations that racial insularity tends to be more common among White than among Black Zimbabweans (Murphree, 1986). [21]It is perhaps more noteworthy, however, that among Black and White children alike, the majority of chi-square comparisons failed to reveal significant in-group friendship preferences. [22]In light of Zimbabwe's recent history of racial polarization, this is a promising finding.

REFERENCES

Caute, D. 1983. *Under the Skin: The Death of White Rhodesia*. Harmondsworth: Penguin.

Davey, A. G., & Mullin, P. N. 1982. Inter-ethnic Friendship in British Primary Schools. *Educational Research*, 24, 83–92.

Davies, J., & Turner, I. F. 1984. Friendship Choices in an Integrated Primary School in Northern Ireland. *British Journal of Social Psychology*, 23, 185–186.

Meredith, M. 1980. *The Past is Another Country: Rhodesia UDI to Zimbabwe*. London: Pan.

Murphree, M. W. 1986. 'Odds on Zimbabwe'. *Leadership*, 5, 24–28.

Wilson, D. and Lavelle, S. 1990. Interracial Friendship in a Zimbabwean Public School. *Journal of Social Psychology*, 130, 1, 111–113.

Task 3

Select a research report in your own area of study and answer the questions presented in Task 1.

22 WRITING LAB REPORTS

LEARNING OBJECTIVES

When you have finished this chapter, you will be able to understand:

- the purpose and function of a lab report
- the structure of a lab report
- the use of personal pronouns in a lab report

WORD LIST

Do you know the meaning of these words? Many have special meanings in academic culture. You can check their meaning in the glossary at the back of the book.

- ☐ abstract
- ☐ laboratory (lab) report
- ☐ materials
- ☐ methods

As a science student, you will certainly have to write laboratory reports, or lab reports for short. A lab report asks you to record what you did in an experiment, what you learned from it, and why the results matter. A lab report has a very clearly defined structure, so we will go through each section, starting with the title. In your early years of study, you will probably be given the title of your report. If you need to choose your own, remember that the title should reflect the nature and purpose of your experiment. It should also be short, in general no more than 10 or 11 words.

THINK ABOUT THIS

- Do any of your subjects involve lab reports?
- If so, which ones?
- How often do you have to write them?

Structure of lab report

A lab report is normally divided into seven stages:

- Abstract
- Introduction
- Materials and Methods
- Results
- Discussion
- References
- Appendices

Abstract

The abstract is the first section of your report, but while it comes first, it should actually be the last thing that you write. This is because the abstract gives a total overview of your whole project – the purpose of your experiment, what you did, your major results and a brief indication of why you think the results might be important or useful. You need to do all this in not more that 250 or 300 words. Many of your readers will only read your abstract, so you need to make sure that it is both clear and comprehensive. Text 97 presents an example of an abstract.

TEXT 97: ABSTRACT

Flies use receptors on their tarsi (feet) to test sugars before eating. This study reports on the ability of blowflies (*Sarcophaga bullata*) to taste different sugars. To do this, flies were attached to the ends of sticks and their tarsi lowered into solutions with different concentrations of sugars. A positive response was recorded when the fly lowered its probiscus to feed. Results showed that the flies responded to lower concentrations of sucrose than of glucose, and they did not respond to saccharin at all. This is probably because the sodium salt of saccharin was used, and the flies reject salt solutions. Overall, results showed that blowflies distinguish large sugar molecules more easily than small ones, and that they are able to reject potentially dangerous foods.

THINK ABOUT THIS

Select a published lab or research report and read the abstract.

- What is the report about?
- How was the experiment carried out?
- What was the result?
- Why was it important?

Introduction

The introduction to your report should situate your experiment in the wider field of what we already know about the field. You may have to explain or define the specialised terms you use. Having done this, you can narrow your focus to the specific topic that you are investigating. and why it is important. You may need to explain the significance of the particular question you are exploring. A brief literature review is also useful here, summarising the results of the most important studies relevant to your topic. Finally, indicate exactly what the topic of your experiment is; the hypothesis you are testing or the specific questions you are trying to answer. Text 98 gives you an example.

TEXT 98: INTRODUCTION

All animals rely on the senses of taste and smell to find food that is safe for them Humans, for example have receptors on their tongue and in their nose (Campbell, 2008). Studies of sensory physiology have often used insects as experimental subjects because they are easy to manipulate and because their sensory-response system is relatively simple (M. Carter, personal communication). By virtue of the receptors in their tarsi, flies are able to taste food by walking on it (Dethier, 1963), and their receptor neurons can distinguish between water, salts and sugars, and between different sugars (Dethier, 1976).

In this experiment, the ability of the blowfly *Sarcophaga bullata* to taste different sugars and the sugar substitute, saccharin, was tested. Because sucrose is so sweet to people, it was expected that flies would be able to taste lower concentrations of sucrose than they would of maltose and glucose, which are less sweet to people. Because saccharin is also sweet tasting to people, I expected the flies to respond positively and feed on it as well.

THINK ABOUT THIS

Read the introduction to the report you have chosen:
■ What information does it give you?

Materials and methods

In the next section, you indicate as clearly as possible the exact steps that you took to investigate your question. A stranger reading your report should be able to carry out your experiment exactly, based only on reading this section. Be careful, however, that you don't overwhelm the reader with trivial detail. If you use a particular piece of equipment that would not normally be used in an experiment, this needs to be described, and the heading will be Materials and Methods. Otherwise, the heading will simply be Methods, and equipment will not be described. Text 99 gives you the materials and Methods section of the lab report on flies. Why is it headed Materials and Methods?

TEXT 99: MATERIALS AND METHODS

Flies were stuck on icy pole sticks by pushing their wings into a sticky wax rubbed on the sticks. A dilution series of glucose, maltose, and sucrose in one-half log molar steps (0.003M, 0.01M, 0.03M, 0.1M, 0.3M, and 1M) was made. The flies' sensory perception was tested by giving each fly the chance to feed from each sugar, starting with the lowest concentration and working up. Flies were 'rinsed' between tests by swishing their feet in distilled water. A positive response was counted whenever a fly lowered its proboscis. To ensure that positive responses were to sugars and not to water, we let them drink distilled water before each test.

THINK ABOUT THIS

Read the Materials and Methods section of the report you have chosen:

- Is it called Materials and Methods?
- If not, what is it called?
- Why do you think it has this title?

Results

Finally, in this section, you describe the results of your study. Focus on your major findings, and as far as possible, use tables and graphs to present total findings. Tables and graphs can in general show clearly what you might struggle to say in words. Remember that you need to number each table or graph and clearly state exactly what it shows. If you are presenting graphs, you can call each a Figure, abbreviated to Fig. Tables are referred to as Tables. Also remember to make sure that each axis on your graphs and each column in your tables are labelled. All tables and graphs also need to be mentioned in the Results section. Do not include a graph and then not mention it in your Results. See Text 100.

TEXT 100: RESULTS

Flies responded to high concentrations (1M) of sugar by lowering their proboscises and feeding. The threshold concentration required to elicit a positive response from at least 50% of the flies was lowest for sucrose, while the threshold concentration was highest for glucose. Hardly any flies responded to saccharin. Based on the results from all the lab groups together, there was a major difference in the response of flies to the sugars and to saccharin (Table 22.1). When all the sugars were considered together, this difference was significant ($t = 10.46$, $df = 8$, $p < .05$). Also, the response of two flies to saccharin was not statistically different from zero ($t = 1.12$, $df = 8$, n.s.).

Table 22.1 The average number of flies in each lab group that fed from 0.3M concentrations of each chemical tested. The mean +− standard deviation is shown

Chemical tested	Number of 10 flies responding
Glucose	3.2 + 1.5
Maltose	7.8 + 2.3
Sucrose	8.6 + 2.1
Saccharin	0.2 + 0.5

THINK ABOUT THIS

- What extra information about the results is included in this section, but not in the abstract?
- Why?

Discussion

In the Discussion section of your paper, you need to discuss the importance of your findings. You may also indicate whether your findings agree or disagree with the findings of others, and you may indicate areas or issues where further research is called for. What information does the Discussion section of the lab report on flies (Text 101) give you?

TEXT 101: DISCUSSION

The results supported the first hypothesis that sucrose would be the most easily detectable sugar by the flies. Flies show a selectivity of response to sugars based on molecular size and structure. Glucose, the smallest of the three sugars, is a monosaccharide. A higher concentration of this small sugar was needed to elicit a positive response.

Maltose and sucrose are both disaccharides with differing molecular weights.

It has been shown that flies respond better to alpha-glucosidase derivatives than to beta-glucosidase derivatives (Dethier, 1975). Because sucrose is an alpha glucosidase derivative, it makes sense that the threshold value for sucrose occurs at a lower concentration than that for maltose.

The second hypothesis was not supported, however, because the flies did not respond positively to saccharin. The sweetener people use is actually the sodium salt of saccharic acid (Budavari, 1989). Even though it tastes 300 to 500 times as sweet as sucrose to people (Budavari, 1989), flies taste the sodium and so reject saccharin as a salt.

Flies accept sugars and reject salts, a selectivity that is a valuable asset to a fly because it helps the fly recognize potentially toxic substances as well as valuable nutrients, (Dixon, 1982). Substances such as alcohols and salts could dehydrate the fly and have other harmful effects on its homeostasis (Dethier, 1976). Thus, flies are well adapted to finding food for their own survival.

THINK ABOUT THIS

■ In the report you have read, describe what the Discussion section of it does

References

Finally, list all the references that you have read in preparing for the study in the References section, making sure that you include all relevant details (see Chapter 14).

Appendices

In the later years of your studies, you may also want to include tables and graphs that show the minor findings of your study, tables and graphs that you did not consider important enough to include in the Results section. Place these in a section headed Appendices.

Personal pronouns

You have probably noticed that the sample lab report makes no mention of the person or persons carrying out the study. In general, many lecturers do not like any indication of the personal in lab reports. However, this is an area that is rapidly changing, and some lecturers, particularly the younger ones, welcome the use of *I, me, my, we, us* and *our*. You need to check with your lecturer to find out his or her preferences. If you do use personal pronouns, make sure that you only use pronouns referring to you individually if the work is in fact your own individual work. Many studies are carried out by teams of people, and your use of pronouns needs to reflect this.

SUMMARY

- Lab reports are commonly required in science subjects
- A lab report asks you to record the topic of your report, what you did, what you learned and why the results matter.
- Lab reports have a very clearly defined structure.
- Lab reports involve an abstract, an introduction; a materials and methods section, a results section and a discussion.

SKILLS PRACTICE

Select a lab report that you have previously written and give it to a partner.

- How does your partner judge your report? Does it adequately explain what you wanted to do, how you did it, and what you found?
- What information did you discuss in the Discussion section?
- How might you improve the report?

23 WRITING ELECTRONIC TEXTS: DISCUSSION FORUM POSTS, BLOGS, AND E-PORTFOLIOS

 LEARNING OBJECTIVES

When you have finished this chapter, you will be able to:

- understand the role the audience plays in creating electronic texts
- identify the correct way to address your audience in different types of electronic texts
- understand the purpose and structure of electronic texts

✓ **WORD LIST**

Do you know the meaning of these words in this chapter?. Many have special meanings in the academic culture. You can check their meaning in the glossary at the back of the book.

- ☐ email
- ☐ e-portfolio
- ☐ discussion forum
- ☐ blog
- ☐ learning management system (LMS)
- ☐ post
- ☐ spam filter

Do electronic texts matter in academic culture?

Knowing how to create and communicate through electronic texts is an important part of contributing to modern academic culture. Nearly all communication and teaching in Australian universities has an electronic component to it. For example, all students and academic staff at a university will have an official email address. In addition, a large proportion of teaching and learning materials is now in electronic form.

You should also understand that the most common way of connecting students and staff involved in a course is though a series of websites that provide access to materials related to that course. This collection of websites is organised by a learning management system, or an LMS. By using an LMS, everyone involved in the unit or course can interact on forums, submit and retrieve marked assignments, and access electronic versions of lectures notes and digital recordings of lectures. Different universities use different LMSs: two common ones are Blackboard and iLearn. One of the first things to do when you start your university study is to find out which system your university uses and how to access it.

Of course, by making these electronic resources available, universities assume that students have the skills to engage in these online situations. Your lecturers will expect that you know how communicate effectively using electronic texts. They will also expect that you can interact in shared online spaces, such as on discussion forums. This means that you are aware of your online audience and can interact with them appropriately.

What types of electronic texts are used?

Now you understand why students are expected to create and communicate through electronic texts, we can look at three common types of electronic texts students create. These are discussion forum posts, blogs, and e-Portfolios. In each case, you will see that you need to understand both the audience and purpose of your text in order to create an appropriately structured electronic text.

The style of writing in electronic texts ranges between the two extremes of informal spoken conversation and highly formal written academic text. Remember that for spoken conversation, the purpose is to engage or chat in a social setting, with an audience you can see and are familiar with. The structure of informal chat is not fixed and shifts based on the needs of the conversationalists. In formal academic writing, the purpose is to communicate information, and the type of audience is assumed but unseen. The structure of a formal academic text is usually fixed and conveys a sense of unchanging certainty.

When you create electronic texts for an academic audience, you need to be aware of the need to meet the expectations of your audience while managing the requirements of the type of text you are creating.

THINK ABOUT THIS

■ What type of electronic texts do you use in your studies?

Discussion forums

Discussion forums are the electronic equivalent of a real world notice board. However instead of pinning a paper note to a cork board, you post your message to the electronic discussion forum. The word 'post' is also used to describe the text that you create on the forum.

An electronic discussion forum is a place to share information. Forums are usually intended for short, quick communication, although they permit longer posts. In an academic setting, you would usually have access to a specific unit's electronic discussion forum on that unit's webpage via the LMS.

Text 102 shows an example of a short discussion between students on a university discussion forum. As you can see, each post has a time stamp on it to indicate when the reply was posted. This gives readers of the forum information about when the question

TEXT 102 ECON123 ECONOMICS IN AUSTRALIA: DISCUSSION FORUM

Survey for research report
By: Harada Smith – 23 June 2020, 3:30 PM
Does anyone know how many people we can survey for our research reports?
Thanks, H

EDIT REPLY

> **RE: Survey data for research report**
> By: Kim Lee – 23 June 2020, 3:42 PM
>
> Dr Jones didn't say in last week's lecture. But I think my tutor said that it was up to our groups to decide... but you would have to think that you'd need at least 30 to have any decent stats...
>
> REPLY

>> **RE: Survey data for research report**
>> By: Harada Smith – 23 June 2020, 3:55 PM
>>
>> Thanks Kim. Ok. I guess I'd better print more surveys!
>>
>> EDIT REPLY

was posted and allows them to determine whether an answer is still required. The fact that the post was answered and the writer responded within 25 minutes is an indication of the speed of discussion forum interactions.

Who is the audience of your discussion forum post?

Discussion forums are designed to be available to a large audience. In fact, it is usual for the audience of a discussion forum post to be everyone associated with a course. This means that everybody can read what you post. It also means that you cannot specify who sees your post. Because you have such a large audience, you should be careful not to respond to posts on the forum without careful thought about what and how you write. You should also take care not to post personal information. Instead, leave private material to emails.

What is the purpose of your discussion forum post?

Discussion forums are used to discuss matters relating to your course with as large an audience as possible. This means that information related to the course is available to everyone involved. Topics could be to do with lecture material, readings or assessments. You will usually find that your lecturer expects you to ask any questions or observations you have about your course on the discussion forum rather than by email. This is because everyone can see the answer on a forum, while only you can see an email response.

Posting to a discussion forum

Posting to a forum is a straightforward process. You can post new topics to a forum, or you can reply to an existing post. To post a new topic to a forum, you would most often click on a button that says something like 'Add a new topic'. Once you click on that button, you will go to a new webpage where you will be asked to type in a title for your post. The title you choose should give a short summary about the topic of your post. In Text 102, Harada has chosen a short title that clearly states his topic.

You will also be asked to type in the content of your post in a separate area. Once you have typed in your post, you should click 'Post' or "Enter'. To reply to an existing post, you would simply click on 'Reply'. Remember that Learning Management Systems will vary, and you will need to work out how your specific system works. As you can see in Text 102, it is quite normal for several people to reply to a post. It is also quite normal for each reply to add a little more information to the previous one.

Discussion forums tend to be a place where writers use less formal language. For example, in Text 102, the writers include words such as 'Ok' and 'stats' instead of 'statistics', as well as using exclamation marks '!' to add emphasis. As a result, most discussion forum posts are often written in a 'spoken' style, rather than in a written one. This is due to the informal and speedy nature of forum posts. However, you should choose your words carefully. Remember that your reader cannot see your face, and does not have the additional information that a smile or a shrug supplies in face-to-face situations.

Given the informal style of discussion forum posts, you do not need to include some of the information you are required to provide in other types of electronic text, such as a formal email (see Chapter 3). As you can see in Text 102, user information is automatically displayed in the layout of the forum. In particular, your forum username – which on university discussion forums is usually your full name – will be displayed above your posts. This means that there is no need to for you to sign off formally at the end of your post.

THINK ABOUT THIS

■ Evaluate your own posts in the light of this discussion.

Blogs

A second type of electronic text that students are often asked to write is a Blog. The word blog is a multipurpose one that can be used to describe both the electronic text and the action of creating that text. A 'blogger' is someone who writes blogs, and the act of writing a blog is called 'blogging'. Individual entries on a blog can be called 'blogs' or 'posts', or sometimes 'blog posts'.

As a university student, you may be asked to write blogs for a range of purposes. It is likely that you will be asked to write a blog as part of your participation in online tutorials and seminars. It is also likely that you will be asked to write a blog about a specific topic or in answer to a question as a part of your unit's assessment. Most often, you will post your blog in a special section of the LMS.

Blogs are a poorly defined text type. A quick search of the Internet will show you that they can be about any topic, they can be written in any style, and they can be any length! However, as a student, you will be given instructions from your lecturer, which should clarify requirements for the topic, length and writing style.

Who is the audience of your blog?

Bloggers generally write with a specific audience in mind. Because they are aware of that audience, they choose their language accordingly. In a very general sense, the audience of a blog has an influence on what you choose to include in your blog. Knowing who you are writing for also helps you to decide what needs to be explained and what can be treated as assumed knowledge. The amount of technical language used can be increased, and the use of colloquial or slang language is also more common.

Writing a blog for a university assessment is only slightly different to writing one for an Internet audience. As a university student, your lecturer will most likely give you a specific question or topic. On top of this, you will be writing your blog to be read by your lecturer and possibly your classmates. Both of these things will help you to identify your audience and the purpose for writing your blog.

Blogging is slightly different to traditional academic writing because the audience of the text has the opportunity to respond immediately to what you write. The potential for immediate feedback is often evident in the written style of blogs. The audience can be directly addressed and the author will often refer to themselves directly. This is a very different style from formal academic writing, and is often interpreted as a more personal form of writing.

What is the purpose of your blog?

As a student, you will probably be given a specific topic to write about, or question to answer. Part of the purpose of a blog is to share ideas in a way that is accessible to your specific audience. Remember that because bloggers know who their audience is, they moderate their language to address that audience.

Blog structure

There are no set rules for blog structure. However, because you will be writing for an academic assignment, some approaches will work better than others. The title of a blog in an academic context has a slightly different function to a blog that appears in a more general context. The title of a general-purpose blog is usually written to grab the attention of a reader. However, in an academic context, your audience is expecting to see a blog related to a specific topic, so your title should be more finely structured. Make sure the title of your blog indicates how it will answer the question, and that it sets out the purpose of the post.

Just like a mini-essay, blogs usually begin with an introduction that sets the scene for your post. Blogs also have more impact when the first line of each paragraph in your blog functions as a topic sentence. These will help set the scene for your response and indicate to your marker how you intend to answer the question or approach the topic. Text 103

TEXT 103

The task:

ECON123 Short Answer Task 1: Write a short blog (250 to 300 words) for your fellow ECON123 classmates describing how you think a group project can be completed successfully.

The student blog:

How to Survive a Group Project in Three Easy Steps.

Blog post by Harada Smith 01-06-2020 10:30 AM

You've just seen the ECON123 unit outline, and there's a group presentation due in the last week of classes!! Maybe you run screaming from the classroom. Or maybe you just withdraw from the unit, and decide to ditch Economics and study Linguistics instead. (Until you see that they have to do group projects too- LOL!).

Fear not my fellow ECON123 students, there is any easy way to survive a group project, and I can explain it in 3 easy steps.

1. Make a signed agreement before you begin. That way everyone knows what everyone else has agreed to do, and what the consequences are if they don't do it. Signing the agreement should make everyone realise how serious the project is and encourage everyone to stick to what they say they will do.

2. Meet regularly. A group project is not a mushroom and it will not survive neglected in the dark. You have to talk about things, sort out any problems and keep the momentum up. Don't let anyone hide!

3. Have fun! Seriously, you will be working with a group of people you may never have met otherwise, and you get to share in the creation of something that could be quite cool. (Well, maybe not cool, but it might get you higher marks than anything you could create on your own.) Best of all, it will only be for a semester- if you don't want to, you will never have to work with them again!

What do you think? Have you any other tips? What about stories about your previous experience (good or bad) working on group projects? Leave a comment below :) H.

shows both the task set by a lecturer and the blog written by a student in response to the task.

As you can see in Text 103, Harada has created a blog that begins with an introduction presenting a humourous description of the common student reaction to the prospect of a group task. He then offers a solution of "3 easy steps" before listing those steps. The language used in the blog is often informal e.g. 'decide to ditch ECON123'. Harada also uses acronyms such as 'LOL' (laugh out loud) and an emoticon e.g. :) which are common features in online communication.

Harada's blog also shows the direct connection that exists between blog writers and their audience. He addresses his readers directly e.g. 'You have to talk about things', and highlights his relationship with them e.g. 'my fellow ECON123 students'. He also asks them direct questions, e.g. 'What do you think?' which encourages them to respond to his post.

While Text 103 shows a blog written in response to an open question, what you include in your blog is dependent on what you lecturer has asked you to do. Depending on the assessment questions or topic, you may write an overview of an area, or a detailed analysis of one aspect of a topic. Or, you may argue for (or against) a particular position. You may even present an overview of different positions on an issue, or present a solution to a problem.

THINK ABOUT THIS

Have you ever written a blog post?

- How would you describe the title? After reading the section above, how would you change it?
- What is the structure of your post?
- Look at a blog post written that you find interesting, and analyse it. What are the features of the post that make it effective?

Eportfolios

The eportfolio is an electronically stored collection of examples of your university work. This work can include text, images and other media such as videos, and each text can be either formal or informal, depending on what your lecturer has asked you to do. Eportfolios use a variety of technologies ranging from simple blog platforms to dedicated eportfolio software and apps. If you are asked to construct an eportfolio, your lecturer or tutor will instruct you on what they want you to use and how to use it.

The eportfolio is becoming more and more popular as your lecturers become interested in awarding you marks not just for the essays, exams and other assessment texts your produce (often called learning products), but also look for ways to give you marks for how your learning develops over the session (often called learning process). An eportfolio does this because your collection of texts lets you and your lecturer track your learning over a period of time, usually a single session. As you, as a student, reflect on this learning, evidence suggests you then begin to set your own learning goals to work toward. An added bonus is that your eportfolio can also be used as a way of showcasing for future employers both your skills and what you know.

SUMMARY

1. Modern universities expect their students to have the ability to create a range of electronic texts. They also expect their students to know how to behave appropriately in online environments.

2. Three common types of electronic texts created in an academic setting are emails, discussion forum posts, and blogs. All vary on their audience, purpose and structure.

3. Emails:

- The audience of an email is limited to the person or people the message is sent to
- The purpose of an email in an academic setting is usually to discuss some aspect of an academic course.
- Emails have a predictable structure, with a subject line, a greeting, am email body, and a sign-off.
- The writing style of emails is formal.

4. Discussion forum posts:

- The audience of a discussion forum post is large, and not selected by the person posting to the forum. This means that discussion forum posts are public.
- The purpose of discussion forum posts is to share information with as many people as possible, as quickly as possible.
- The structure of discussion forum posts is predictable with a subject and body usually entered into specific sections if a forum web page.
- The writing style of discussion forum posts is informal.

5. Blogs:

- In an academic context, the audience of a blog is likely to be staff and students from specific course. This means that blog posts are public.
- In an academic context, the purpose of blogs is usually to answer an assignment question or to write to a set topic.
- Blogs are a free-form type of text and have no fixed structure. However, lecturers will clarify requirements for the topic, length and writing style.

 SKILLS PRACTICE

Task 1

Text 6 (on p. 30) and Text 102 (on p. 304) both present questions about the same topic, but in different types of electronic text.

- Identify differences in the way the sender addresses their audience.
- How does the style of language used in the email differ from the style of language used in the discussion forum? Can you give examples?
- What information has to be given explicitly in the email that is implicit in the discussion forum?
- How do the sign-offs differ between the email and discussion forum post?

Task 2

Text 104 is an example of an email sent to a lecturer.

- What changes would you make to the email?
- Justify each of the changes you suggest.

TEXT 104

H-S <h-s-email@email.com >   23:30 (11 hours ago)
to Dr Josh Jones <josh.jones@ youruniversity.edu.au>

Hey- Jonzie

so look im gunna b up front with u. ive got work things going on & i'll be away for a bit. i get back the day U want the report and TBH I live quite far from uni, submitting my assignment on time wld mean taking 2 buses and a train out to uni- thats a total travel time round trip equalling over 3 hrs solely to put a piece of paper in a box. :(

Reckon I could send just a submit it a day late?

Cheers H

Task 3

Read Text 105 below. It is the opening section of a post taken from the blog The Thesis Whisperer (http://thesiswhisperer.com/)

- What features of this post set it apart form normal academic writing?
- How many examples of person pronouns can you find? What is the writer trying to achieve by including personal pronouns?
- Are there examples of informal language? List them.
- Can you rewrite Text 105 so that it resembles a piece of academic writing? List the changes you had to make.

TEXT 105

Are you a piler or a filer?
June 28, 2012 · by Thesis Whisperer

Every month a plastic wrapped wad of paper, sometimes 300 sheets thick, used to land on my desk. This was contained the ethics committee paperwork, usually around 20 applications and supporting documents, for me to review.

　　This pile of paper drove me nuts. Not only was there so damn much of it, it was hard to manage. Ethics committee is your classic 'baking powder' job; generating an increased workload with no corresponding time compensation. Consequently I read ethics committee paperwork on the train, tram, in cafes, queues and on the couch at home – almost never at my desk. I was always losing sheets, spilling coffee on it or tearing corners as I stuffed the wad in my bag. By the time the meeting rolled around it looked like a truck had driven over it.

Source: http://thesiswhisperer.com/2012/06/28/
is-becoming-paperless-a-bit-like-giving-up-smoking/)

24 WRITING REFLECTIVE TEXTS

✳ LEARNING OBJECTIVES

When you have finished this chapter, you will be able to:

- explain the purpose of reflection
- understand what your lecturer expects you to write about in a reflection
- describe the structure and language features that are used in reflections
- write a reflection

What is reflection?

Reflection is an active process that involves you thinking about your learning. Consciously making time to think about what you have been reading, hearing and doing helps you to deepen your understanding of important ideas. Ultimately, reflecting also helps you to make links between what you are learning at university and your experiences outside of university.

THINK ABOUT THIS

- Do any of your units ask you to write a reflective text?
- What do you think a reflective text involves?

What is a reflective text?

A reflective text is one where you express in writing, or sometimes through video, your thoughts and reactions to some aspect of your learning. Of course, thinking about your learning is always helpful. But, the process of writing or otherwise representing your reflection helps you to sift through your ideas, thoughts and reactions to focus on a specific aspect of your learning. Through this, you begin to see more clearly what you have learnt, where you might have gaps in your learning and how what you have learnt might be applied in your future career.

You are particularly likely to be asked to write a reflective text if you are studying a professional course such as nursing, social work, or occupational therapy. This usually involves you thinking about a placement you have completed, and identifying the ways in which it has helped you to become an effective professional in that area, and the problems you encountered. Often, you will be expected to identify a way or ways in which you might cope with the problem. However, even if you are not undertaking a professional degree, you may be expected to write a reflective text thinking about your learning process or reacting to an article or an idea in your discipline.

Learning to write good reflective texts gives you the opportunity to take charge of your own learning and, at the same time, provides you with a bridge between what you are learning at university and how you might use that learning in your future profession.

Because lecturers want you to be active and involved in your own learning, reflections as a form of university assessment are becoming more and more common. So, it is important you understand what is expected of you when you create a reflective text. You should also understand what makes a text reflective, how you organise a reflective text and the sort of language you should be using in a reflective text.

What do lecturers expect?

When your lecturers ask you to write a reflection, they are usually expecting you to write about your thoughts and reactions to something you have been learning about in your unit. Sometimes your lecturer will guide you to a topic and sometimes you will need to choose your own topic. Your assignment question will make this clear for you. Whatever your reflection topic, it is important you do not just write a description. This is because your lecturer is looking for evidence that you are thinking deeply about the process of your learning and how this topic relates to other aspects of your learning and future careers. They want to see evidence that you are an active learner and a critical thinker.

What makes a text reflective?

This is a question we are often asked by students, and writing a good reflective text can be a challenge, especially when writing one for the first time. Firstly, reflections require you to include personal thoughts. It can seem strange to put personal thoughts into a university text, when for most university assignments, you are being told to be objective and impersonal. This can be confusing for students, and the result is that when asked to write a reflection, many simply write a description of the topic or idea. This leads to negative feedback because a simple descriptive text does not give the reader (and marker) any evidence that you are engaging actively or critically with the subject area.

So how can you make your description into a reflection? Let's look at Texts 106 and 107 below where a student has been asked to reflect on their first tutorial of the semester.

TEXT 106

This is my very first week at university and on Wednesday I had to go to my first tutorial class. It was hard to find but I got there on time.

Everyone sat down and the tutor called the class roll.

The tutor then told us that we had to introduce ourselves to the other students in the class and gave us about 10 minutes to prepare our short presentations. Then we each took turns standing up to talk to the class. After the tutorial finished, I went to the café.

You can see that Text 106 describes the first tutorial, but it doesn't give us any insights into the student writer's thoughts, reactions or understandings about the tutorial experience. Simply describing the event is not enough. Text 106 is an example of the sort of text many inexperienced students produce when asked to write a reflection – but it is not a reflection.

Now read Text 107. It also describes the first tutorial, but it does a lot more besides. Text 107 is clearly a reflection.

TEXT 107

I am writing this because I've been asked to reflect on my first tutorial at university and to think about the experience and how I can relate it to my ongoing approach to my studies. I guess the first week at university will set me up for the rest of my degree, so it's pretty important. Honestly, there were times through my last year at school when I wondered if I would even get into uni!

I was worried about turning up late so I made sure I downloaded a campus map and gave myself plenty of time. It was tricky finding the room (the university campus is like a maze with very strange building names! I wonder if all universities are like this?). I was about 10 minutes early and had to wait for the earlier class to finish. I wasn't alone – two students were already standing outside the door and I wondered if they were in my class.

The tutor arrived just after I sat down. She introduced herself and seemed nice. I feel she will be approachable and supportive so that should help me to do my best this coming semester. When I think back, a good relationship with my teacher has always been an important aspect of my learning process. When everyone had found a seat, the tutor called the class roll. That seemed funny to me at first – it was like being back at school. But now I can understand why she did this, because it helps the tutor get to know our names, and in this unit, you do get a small mark for participation, so I guess checking tutorial attendance helps the tutor to work out this mark at the end of semester.

The tutor then explained that the main activity we needed to cover in this tutorial was to introduce ourselves to the class. I felt nervous about this because I didn't know anyone and I was concerned I would say the wrong thing and make myself look silly. I've never liked public speaking! But then I reminded myself that most of the students would be in just the same position as me and anyway, if I want to improve speaking skills in front of a group so I can get better marks later on, then this would be a good opportunity to practice. The tutor gave us 10 minutes to prepare our short presentations. I was wondering what I could tell the class, so I was pleased that she gave us a list of suggestions of points about ourselves that we might want to share. Actually, now I think about it, I realise that there was so much I could say about myself and the hard part was cutting it down to just 2 minutes! When it came to my turn, I was nervous. But everyone was very supportive and I felt so good when it was over. In fact, I felt like doing it again! So I'm going to remember that for the future when I have to do tute presentations etc. – so long as I'm well prepared, I now realise that public speaking can be quite fun!

The introduction process was really successful I think! After the tute, a few of us went for a coffee together and now I feel as if I've made not only new friends, but some potential new study buddies. Even though we didn't do much 'work' in the first tutorial, there were some surprises and challenges. Thinking and writing about these has made me see that I did learn quite a lot about others in my tute as well as about myself. I feel as if I've learnt about how to approach my public speaking (which I've always dreaded) differently in the future and I also feel I'm starting to build a peer support network in the tutorial. Knowing that I have others I know in the class to discuss the subject matter with is going to be really useful over this coming semester. I'm sure quite a few others in the class would feel the same way.

How is a reflective text organised?

Reflections, as with many other academic texts you will be asked to write, need to be structured as a sequence of paragraphs. You should aim to organise each of your paragraphs around a specific idea or point. Each paragraph should be made up of a series of well-formed complete sentences. You can see then, that in a general way, the structure of a reflection has some similarities to essays and reports. However, in other ways, its structure is a little different.

Reflections are usually less clearly structured into distinguishable parts than, for example, an essay. In an essay, you should be able to easily identify an introduction, a body and a conclusion, but this is not always the case with a written reflection. This is because the purpose of a reflection differs from the purpose of other academic texts you may be asked to write. As we saw in Chapters 18 and 19, the purpose of an essay is to present a clear position to an audience of one or more lecturers and the purpose of a report is to examine a problem. The purpose of a reflection, however, is to demonstrate that your thinking and understanding has been changed, or transformed, by your learning.

This means that a reflection may not always be ordered in the way your other academic texts are. Rather, there are some other structural elements that should be kept in mind as you demonstrate to your marker how your learning is transforming your thinking. These elements include some explanation and thoughts around the topic of the reflection, as well as some writing that relates the topic both back to past experience and thoughts, and forward to how your new thinking can be used in the future.

Reflections can be divided into three stages. In the first stage of your reflection, you should introduce the topic and explain its significance. If you have been asked to do this, you might also relate your topic to a theory relevant to your current learning in the unit or to some experience you have had or can imagine having in a related area. The first stage of a reflection is a response to the topic or question and looks back. The second stage of your reflection is usually the longest. Here, you should focus on aspects of your topic, reasoning through it and relating it to your thoughts, reactions and perhaps relevant theories and/or experience. In the final stage, discuss what you have learnt and how this might change how you do things in the future. You can see examples of the three stages of a reflection marked out in Text 108 on the next page.

THINK ABOUT THIS

- If you have to write a reflective text, is it a reflection on:
  - ☐ something you have read
  - ☐ a placement or professional experience you have completed
  - ☐ both of these?
- Has the reflection enriched the experience or the reading? If so, how? If not, why do you think this is?

What sort of language is appropriate?

Let's start with how the language of reflections is similar to the language of other academic texts you may be asked to write. All academic texts, including reflections, are formal texts, intended to be read by your teacher/marker, which means that you should write in complete, well-structured sentences, using correct punctuation and spelling. Some teachers expect that a reflection will be a little less formal than an essay, using contractions and perhaps less formal expressions such as idioms. Other teachers will expect a more formal reflection, using more formal academic language and perhaps in-text referencing to support your claims. It is a good idea to check your assessment instructions and/or check with your teacher before you begin to write your reflection, so you know exactly what style you are expected to write. Text 108 is an example of a less formal style of reflection and Text 109 is an example of a more formal style. What sort of differences can you identify?

The purpose of a reflection is to demonstrate your thoughts, reactions and understandings, regardless of the degree of formality you need to adopt. This means that your language will be more subjective than the language you use in an essay or report. Unlike most other academic texts you will be asked to write at university, it is expected that your reflections will be written using first and second person pronouns (i.e., *I, my, you*). Reflections will use verbs of thinking, feeling, relating and understanding. You can see examples of these kinds of verbs, underlined with a solid line, in the reprinted Text 108 below and also in Text 109. Because you are relating current events to the past and to the future, your verb tenses will also move between present, past and future tense and the relationships between your ideas will be demonstrated through your choice of conjunctions (examples of these are shown with squiggly underlining) and time relators (see examples with double underlining). Finally, you will use evaluative language to appraise the topic of your reflection and indicate your reactions. Examples are shown in Text 108 with dashed underlining.

TEXT 108

I am writing this because I've been asked to reflect on my first tutorial at university and to think about the experience and how I can relate it to my ongoing approach to my studies. I guess the first week at university will set me up for the rest of my degree, so it's pretty important. Honestly, there were times through my last year at school when I wondered if I would even get into uni!

I was worried about turning up late so I made sure I downloaded a campus map and gave myself plenty of time. It was tricky finding the room (the university campus is like a maze with very strange building names! I wonder if all universities are like this?). I was about 10 minutes early and had to wait for the earlier class to finish. I wasn't alone – two students were already standing outside the door and I wondered if they were in my class.

The tutor arrived just after I sat down. She introduced herself and seemed nice. I feel she will be approachable and supportive so that should help me to do my best this coming semester. When I think back, a good relationship with my teacher has always been an important aspect of my learning process. When everyone had found a seat, the tutor called the class roll. That seemed funny to me at first – it was like being back at school. But now I can <u>understand</u> why she did this, <u>because</u> it helps the tutor get to know our names, and in this unit, you do get a small mark for participation, so I <u>guess</u> checking tutorial attendance helps the tutor to work out this mark <u>at the end of semester</u>.

The tutor <u>then</u> explained that the main activity we needed to cover in this tutorial was to introduce ourselves to the class. I <u>felt nervous</u> about this <u>because</u> I didn't <u>know</u> anyone <u>and</u> I was <u>concerned</u> I would say the wrong thing and make myself look <u>silly</u>. I've never <u>liked</u> public speaking! <u>But</u> then I <u>reminded</u> myself that most of the students would be in just the same position as me <u>and anyway</u>, if I want to improve speaking skills in front of a group <u>so</u> I can get better marks <u>later on</u>, <u>then</u> this would be <u>a good opportunity</u> to practice. The tutor gave us 10 minutes to prepare our short presenta-tions. I was <u>wondering</u> what I could tell the class, <u>so</u> I was <u>pleased</u> that she gave us a list of suggestions of points about ourselves that we might want to share. Actually, now I <u>think</u> about it, I <u>realise</u> that there was so much I could say about myself <u>and</u> the hard part was cutting it down to just 2 minutes! <u>When</u> it came to my turn, I was <u>nervous</u>. <u>But</u> everyone was <u>very supportive</u> and I <u>felt so good</u> <u>when</u> it was over. <u>In fact</u>, I <u>felt</u> like doing it again! <u>So</u> I'm going to <u>remember</u> that <u>for the future</u> when I have to do tute presentations etc. – <u>so long as</u> I'm well prepared, I <u>now realise</u> that public speaking can be <u>quite fun</u>!

The introduction process was <u>really successful</u> I <u>think</u>! <u>After</u> the tute, a few of us went for a coffee together <u>and now</u> I <u>feel</u> as if I've made not only new friends, <u>but</u> some potential new study buddies. <u>Even though</u> we didn't do much 'work' in the first tutorial, there were <u>some surprises and challenges</u>. <u>Thinking</u> and writing about these has made me see that I did <u>learn</u> quite a lot about others in my tute as well as about myself. I <u>feel</u> as if I've <u>learnt</u> about how to approach my public speaking (which I've always <u>dreaded</u>) <u>differently in the future</u> and I also <u>feel</u> I'm starting to build a peer support network in the tutorial. <u>Knowing</u> that I have others I <u>know</u> in the class to discuss the subject matter with is going to be <u>really useful</u> <u>over this coming semester</u>. I'm <u>sure</u> quite a few others in the class would feel the same way.

TEXT 109

I <u>feel</u> that the class discussion around different types of assessment in class this week can <u>be related</u> to my own <u>past</u> experience helping my children learn to read.	**Stage 1**: responding and looking back.

When my children were in primary school, I learnt that rewarding children only when they can successfully read their home reader book devalues the process of learning to read. I noticed that children are much more enthusiastic about the reading process if they are rewarded along the way, for the small achievements which will eventually lead to the big achievement of successfully reading an entire home reader aloud. For example, if a parent takes time to discuss with the child how the illustrations relate to the ideas expressed on a given page, the child learns the valuable lesson that the discussion and the process around the reading and learning is as important as the final outcome of that learning. I believe the process of learning is just as important as the product (or outcome) of learning, because it's important that children learn to enjoy learning, and also the process is the place where knowledge is transformed and the learner begins to participate more actively in their own learning process. I understand that viewing learning as a process as well as outcomes is an important aspect of Experiential Learning Theory, an approach that I like because it views learning as a result of enabling students to incorporate new ideas with older beliefs about the topic (Kolb & Kolb, 2005). Therefore I can understand why it will be important, when I am a qualified teacher, to introduce a good range of assessment types, some of which will reward the quality of the learning outcomes and some of which will reward students for their learning process and the effort they put into that learning. Kolb, Alice Y., and David A. Kolb. "Learning Styles and Learning Spaces: Enhancing Experiential Learning in Higher Education." *Academy of Management Learning & Education*, vol. 4, no. 2, 2005, pp. 193–212, doi:10.5465/ AMLE.2005.17268566.	**Stage 2**: reasoning and relating. **Stage 3**: looking forward

SUMMARY

1. A reflective text is one where you express in writing, or sometimes through video, your thoughts and reactions to some aspect of your learning.

2. A reflection is not just a descriptive text. Instead, it is personal examination how you engage actively or critically with the subject area

3. Reflections are similar to other academic texts because they are organised using paragraphs that focus on a specific point.

4. However, reflections are different from other types of academic writing because they have different stages than an essay, use language focussed around your thoughts and experience, and often refer to your past, present, and future experiences and actions.

5. Reflections use well-structured sentences. However, unlike other academic writing, they make use of the first and second person, verbs of thinking, feeling, and understanding, more frequent use of evaluative words and phrases, and sometimes incorporate nonstandard features such as contractions.

 SKILLS PRACTICE

Task 1

For Text 108, can you identify the three stages of responding and looking back (stage 1), reasoning and relating (stage 2) and looking forward (stage 3).

25 WRITING IN EXAMS

✳ **LEARNING OBJECTIVES**

When you have finished this chapter, you will be able to:

- identify different types of exam questions
- write an effective response to a short answer question
- develop a comprehensive plan for an exam essay
- understand the best way to manage voice in an exam essay.

Exams can be a particularly daunting experience for university students, especially for those who need to complete a written exam. However, given you are reading this book, you already have the skills to write a good exam! Remember that writing in your exams does not need to be an insurmountable task. This chapter will discuss how to plan for and write exams.

What's different about writing in exams?

Many students identify exams as one of the most stressful aspects of university study. This is because they are usually conducted in controlled environments that limit access to resources and materials. Exams are often handwritten rather than typed, which can add to the pressure students feel, particularly if they are more accustomed to typing than writing by hand. Students also face limits on the amount of time they have available to complete their exams. Time restrictions mean that students often feel that they do not have the space to produce an adequate response to the question. However, with careful analysis of the question, and a well-structured plan, you can produce a good response in the time you have available.

What do lecturers expect from you?

The most straightforward answer here is that your lecturers expect you to answer the question! We know this is easier said than done, but this can be achieved by carefully analysing the question and responding with an answer that has a clear and coherent structure. Another thing to remember is that unlike essays, reports, etc., exams are a chance to show your lecturers everything that you have learned while studying your unit.

What sort of language should I use in exam writing?

You should ensure that your responses flow so that your marker can follow your answers to short answer questions, and your arguments in longer essay responses. Another important thing to remember is that you should make the most of your writer's voice in exam essays. Yours is the most important voice in the essay, so you need to maximise your use of it. Remember also that your marker is looking for your interpretations, your thinking, your commentary and your analysis, all of which show how clearly you have understood the topics covered in your unit.

Types of exams

Exams can vary based on how they are delivered and the range of materials and information students can access while doing it. The most common type of exam is where students are expected to attend a specific location for a set amount of time, usually between one and four hours. These exams are supervised, typically by invigilators, who are responsible for ensuring that students do not breach any of the exam conditions. These usually include restrictions related to what, if any, materials and technology students are allowed to access during the exam. These sorts of exams are often described as invigilated exams. Invigilated exams that permit no access to any type of support material are also called closed-book exams.

In contrast to invigilated exams, some lecturers offer their students 'take-home' exams. Take-home exams are exams that are 'open' for a longer period than an invigilated exam, are not supervised, and as the name suggests, can be taken home to work on. Also known as open-book exams, students are allowed to access as many sources of information as they require to write the exam in the set time period. The type of exam that students are given depends on a range of factors, including the subject area and the requirements for professional accreditation.

Types of exam questions

Broadly speaking, you will be expected to know how to respond to three types of exam questions: multiple-choice, short answer and essay questions. Each of these requires a specific type of response. However, it is important to note that there are differences between disciplines, and it is your responsibility to ensure that you understand exactly what your lecturers expect from you. If you're not sure, ask!

The length and form of responses to each of these question types varies. Multiple-choice exam questions present you with a premise or question followed by a set of choices. Out of that set of choices, one question is likely to be completely wrong, one is the correct answer, and the rest are similar enough to distract you from identifying the correct answer. Consider the multiple-choice question below.

Q. Who described quantum entanglement as 'spooky action at a distance'?

A. Choose one answer from the set of four below:

    a) Erwin Schrödinger

    b) Albert Einstein

    c) Leonardo da Vinci

    d) John Stewart Bell

Of the four possible answers to the question above, option c, Leonardo da Vinci, who was alive around 500 years before the development of quantum entanglement theory, is completely wrong. Options a and d are distractors: both Erwin Schrödinger and John Stewart Bell were prominent physicists, and both were involved in developing our understanding of quantum entanglement. However, they were not responsible for this famous quotation. That leaves the correct answer as option b, Albert Einstein.

Be aware that multiple-choice exams are not easy exams that can be answered through random selection of options. You need to read carefully and analyse the potential answers to ensure you make the correct choice.

Short answer exam questions require a response that can range in length from a word to one or two paragraphs. What differentiates a short answer question from a multiple-choice question is that you are not given a set of possible responses to choose from. Instead, you must construct an answer that clearly responds to the question. That answer, and its length, are often determined by the complexity of the question and the amount of explanation you are required to provide.

Essay exam questions also require you to construct a response to a question. However, this sort of question requires a lengthier, and consequently more substantial, response. Exam essays take the standard three-stage essay structure: introduction, body and conclusion. However, exam essays tend to be shorter than standard essays, particularly in invigilated exams, usually in recognition of the limited time in which you have to write them.

THINK ABOUT THIS

Do you have access to past exam papers in your area of study? (If you don't know, ask your lecturer or look on your university's library website.)

- What sort of questions are in those past exams?
  - ☐ multiple-choice?
  - ☐ short answer?
  - ☐ essay type?
  - ☐ a mixture?
- If your answer is 'a mixture', how are marks allocated?
- Which type of question attracts the most marks?

Answering exam questions

Answering exam questions calls on the same skills you use to understand your assignment questions. You will be expected to provide both descriptive and analytical responses to the questions, just as you do for other assessment tasks. Descriptive responses are most likely to be required for short answer questions, and longer, more analytical responses are usually required for essay questions. However, some questions will require both an analytical and descriptive response. There is no fixed rule, and you will need to consider the question words within the questions to work out what type of response is required. Chapter 10 provides more information about how to analyse descriptive and analytical questions.

THINK ABOUT THIS

- Look at past examination papers in one of your modules. Do the questions focus mainly on descriptive answers, mainly on analytical answers or a mixture of each?
- If questions are a mixture of descriptive and analytical, how are marks allocated?

Planning effective short answer responses

Short answer questions are generally between a few words and a couple of paragraphs in length. The key to writing answers to these types of questions is to remember to make use of everything you have learned about good paragraph structure. Remember to begin your answers with a topic sentence that provides a generalised answer to the question. In a handwritten exam, it is very important to ensure your topic sentence is legible, since it will provide important context for what your marker can expect in the remainder of the paragraph. Once you have a general topic sentence, move to more specific detail in the remainder of the paragraph. Make sure you use language tools such as signposts and lexical chains to support your answers. See Chapter 17 for more detail.

Planning a successful exam essay

The key to a well-written exam essay is a good plan. Most students are surprised to realise that even in an invigilated exam, you need to plan a response to an essay question. One of the most effective ways to plan an exam essay is to construct an outline, which will act as a guide that you can refer to as you write the essay. As an example of the essay plan, let's work backwards from Text 40. Imagine you have sat down to a paper that asks you the following question:

> Question:
>
> *In recent months, the news media has focused on concerns within the international aid community about diminishing clean water supplies around the world. Write an essay evaluating the factors that contribute to this issue.*

Step 1: Analyse the question.

- What are the key words in the question? What are the question words? Remember that you want to identify what the question is asking you to do.

Step 2: Write down your central position or thesis statement.

- As you are writing an essay in response to an exam question, your position statement should be a succinct summation of your answer.

Step 3: Write a dot-point list of the topics you want to cover in the essay.

- This list serves two purposes: it will act as a list of key words to go into your topic sentences, and it can be developed into arguments in support of your position statement.

Step 4: Write your topic sentences.

- Use your topics and key words to formulate three to five topic sentences (the number will depend on the length of the essay required). When you set about writing your essay, make sure it is all legible, but especially your topic sentences, as these give your marker an outline of your response.

Step 5: Conclusion

- Construct a core sentence for your conclusion. This will usually be a re-framing of the position statement.

Text 110 provides an example of an essay plan for the question described above.

TEXT 110

Essay Plan

Question: *In recent months, the news media has focused on concerns within the international aid community about diminishing clean water supplies around the world. Write an essay evaluating the factors that contribute to this issue.*

- Key words: *water supply, diminishing,* and *factors contributing.*
- Question word: *evaluate*
- Position statement: Most causes of diminished water supply relate to human activity.
- Topics:
    - Mismanagement of water supplies
    - Waste of available water supplies
    - Pollution
    - Privatisation

Topic sentences:

Topic sentence 1: Overuse of water resources is a major problem all over the world.
Topic sentence 2: Water is used in ways that are wasteful and unproductive.
Topic sentence 3: Related problem is the wasteful model of agriculture that has turned food-growing into an industrial process which requires intensive irrigation.
Topic sentence 4: Pollution is another major problem.
Topic sentence 5: Privatisation favours the rich over the poor.

Conclusion: Water crisis being experienced around the globe is the result of poor water management.

How should I use evidence in exam essays?

In some exams, particularly in take-home exams, you will be given readings to be used as references for your essay as part of your exam paper. In these circumstances, you should use the evidence you have the same way you would in any other essayAvoid using direct voice because it drowns out the voice your marker is trying to hear – yours! In other words, use your own words to control the flow of ideas through your position statement and topic sentences, and use an indirect or an external voice to support the point you are making. Make sure you are very clear about why you are using each piece of evidence, and avoid simply dropping a citation into the text with no context. Most importantly, use the essay as a means of showing your marker that you can construct a logical and rational response to a question.

In an invigilated exam, you may find it difficult to remember the details of specific sources, but if you can memorise some key references, this will really improve your answers.

While the citation style will very according to your discipline, a basic author/date second-ary citation is something like this:

Herke (2014) indicated that student essays allowing the voices of others to dominate did not receive high marks.

 THINK ABOUT THIS

- Go through past examinations in your area of study and identify the question words of the essay questions.
- What does your area of study focus on?
- How can you prepare for these types of questions?

 SUMMARY

1. The most important thing about writing a response to an exam question is to answer the question.
2. There are three basic types of exam questions: multiple-choice, short answer and essay.
3. Short answer responses vary in length from a few words to one or two paragraphs.
4. When answering short answer questions, remember the key features of good para-graph structure, including topic sentences and the use of lexical chains.
5. Essay responses require a plan to ensure the question is clearly answered.
6. The steps for planning an examination essay are:
   - Analyse the question.
   - Write down your central position or thesis statement.
   - Write a short list of the topics you want to cover in the essay.
   - Write your topic sentences and make sure they are legible.
   - Insert evidence.
   - Construct a core sentence for your conclusion.

 SKILLS PRACTICE

a) Can you think of the types of words that appear in exam questions? A good way to help train yourself to decode exam questions quickly is to revise the types of words that are used in descriptive and analytical questions.
b) Create a table with two columns: fill one with descriptive question words and the other with analytical question words. (If you're not sure of the difference, re-read Chapter 9.)
c) Make sure you understand the type of answer each of the words demands.
d) Choose a lecture from one of your units and write one or more potential exam ques-tions about it.
e) Can you answer the question? If not, what might you do about it?

GLOSSARY

The glossary defines some of the most important terms used in this book. It does not present all forms or meanings of a particular word. Instead, it focuses on the forms and meanings that are used in the book. For example, 'academic' is used in two ways, as an adjective, in 'academic culture', and as a noun, meaning a person who teaches and/or carries out research in a university. Other meanings and forms are not presented.

academic	An academic is a teacher who teaches and/or carries out research in a university.
academic culture	See culture.
analysis	Analysis involves evaluating a statement, a claim or a theory. It involves critical thinking and includes some or all of the following activities: ■ identifying why something happens ■ identifying how important something is ■ comparing and contrasting different ideas or theories ■ identifying the implications of a statement ■ establishing the extent to which something is true ■ establishing whether an approach is useful or not.
analytical	If an argument is analytical, it uses analysis.
anime	Anime is a style of film or television animation that is usually created in Japan.
appendix (plural appendices; appendixes)	An appendix consists of supplementary material which is placed at the end of a report.
applied sciences	See sciences.
apprentice	An apprentice is someone who is learning new knowledge and skills through studying theory and through hands-on practical experience.
approach	In academic debate, an approach refers to a set of theories, concepts and ideas that are used to analyse an issue or a problem.
argument	An argument is another word for a position. In an essay, you present a position, which is the same as saying you present an argument.
deductive argument	In academic writing, deductive argument involves stating a position, then presenting evidence and reasons that support the position.

inductive argument	In academic writing, inductive argument involves presenting evidence, reasons and so on, then drawing a conclusion from them.
logical argument	In a logical argument, each step is clearly linked to the preceding step and rises out of it.
rational argument	A rational argument is one in which the evidence is collected in ways that can be checked.
article	An article is a piece of writing that is published in a journal, a magazine or a newspaper.
journal article	A journal article is a piece of writing published in a journal.
attitude marker	See marker.
audience	The audience for a text are the people who listen to it if it is spoken, or read it if it is written.
authoritative	If a source is authoritative, the information it contains is reliable because it has been collected and analysed according to accepted methods by researchers working in recognised institutions.
bibliography	A bibliography is a list of books, articles and other documents that you have used in writing your assignment.
blog	In the university context, a blog is a website or a web page that the student writer uses to discuss issues of academic interest. The language used in a blog is more informal and personal than that used in most other academic writing.
booster	Boosters are terms that allow you to express certainty and increase the authority of your voice.
brainstorming	You use brainstorming at the beginning of the writing process when you write down everything that you intend to include in an assignment in no particular order.
case study	See study.
categorical statement	See statement.
chancellor	The chancellor is the formal head of the university, but is not involved in its day-to-day running.
vice-chancellor	The vice-chancellor (VC) is the executive head of the university, or its CEO.
citation	When you use a direct voice from a source, it is called a citation.
citation system	A citation system is a set of rules for citing sources in academic texts and in their bibliographies and reference lists. There are many different citation systems.

cite	When you cite a source, you refer to it using a direct, an indirect or an external voice.
clause	A clause is a grammatical unit that contains at least a verb (often it contains other grammatical elements, too). A clause may form a complete sentence or it may be grouped with other clauses to form a longer sentence.
clause theme	A clause theme is the first grammatical element in a clause. It works as a signpost that tells the reader what the rest of the clause is about.
collection	A collection is a number of articles published in a book.
edited collection	An edited collection is a book that deals with a specialised academic topic, but each chapter is written by a different person.
concept	A concept is an idea or an abstract principle.
critical thinking	See thinking.
culture	Culture refers to the attitudes, values and ways of behaving shared by a group of people.
academic culture	Academic culture refers to ways of thinking and behaving that are shared by people who teach, work or study at university.
current	If information is current, it is up-to-date.
data (plural)	Data refers to a collection of facts from which you can draw conclusions.
database	A database is an index which tells you where to find journal articles, book chapters, conference papers and sometimes books. You use a database to locate readings for your essays, reports and so on. Some databases allow you to access the full text of an article. Others give an abstract only.
date of publication	See publication.
deductive argument	See argument.
department	A department is a part of the university that teaches and researches a specific discipline; for example, Department of Economics, Department of Information Technology.
description	Description, or descriptive writing, presents factual information. It focuses on defining, describing, summarising and exemplifying.
dialogue	A dialogue is a conversation or discussion between two or more people about a particular topic.
digital divide	The digital divide is the gap that exists between people who have access to technology (telephones, computers, internet access, etc.) and people who do not.

direct voice	See voice.
discipline	A discipline is an area of university study; for example, the discipline of economics; the scientific disciplines.
discussion	A discussion involves exchanging ideas about an issue in either talk or writing. In a written discussion, exchanging ideas involves commenting on other writers' ideas in an essay, report, blog or other text.
discussion forum	A discussion forum is a section of the Learning Management System that allows you to ask questions (in writing) and get responses from your fellow students.
doctorate	A doctorate is another name for a PhD (Doctor of Philosophy), the highest formal academic qualification.
drafting	After you have brainstormed and organised the things that you want to discuss in an assignment, drafting means that you write out the assignment focusing on getting your ideas clear. You do not worry about details such as correct grammar and spelling.
edited collection	See collection.
editing	Editing involves checking your drafted assignment to make sure that the ideas are clear and supported by evidence.
email	An email is a message sent to someone electronically using a device such as a computer, tablet or smart phone.
empirical study	See study.
end notes	End notes are a list of sources used in writing an article or book. They are placed at the end of the article or chapter, or at the end of the book. They may also be used to give the reader extra information.
essay	An essay is a text which presents an argument for a position. It may also argue against other positions.
executive summary	See summary.
explicit	If something is explicit, it is expressed openly and clearly.
external voice	See voice.
facilitator	A facilitator is someone who helps students to learn by discovering things for themselves.
faculty	A faculty is an administrative teaching and research division of a university; for example, Faculty of Business and Economics; Faculty of Social Science; Faculty of Arts.
family name	In English, a person's family name is the name they inherit from their father. It is placed last, and so is often referred to as the last name.
field	A field is a branch of knowledge; for example, the field of economics.

field study	See study.
finding(s)	Findings are the conclusions that a person reaches as a result of research.
focused	If something is focused, it has a clear purpose.
footnote/end note referencing	See referencing.
generalisation	A generalisation is a statement that is true in most cases and that is drawn from a number of examples.
general-specific	General-specific organisation refers to a way of organising information in which general statements are followed by specific examples.
general-specific text	See text.
given information	See information.
group work	Group work refers to assignments or tasks that are carried out by a number of people working together.
hedge	Hedges are terms used to modify positions and statements.
humanities	The humanities are subjects that are concerned with human ideas and behaviour, such as history, philosophy and literature.
hyponym	A hyponym refers to a specific member of a more general class. For example, the general class *vehicles* includes the hyponyms *car*, *bus*, *truck* and so on.
hypothesis	A hypothesis is a proposed explanation of a phenomenon.
identity	In academic writing, your identity refers to the way you present yourself to your reader. For example, the author of a research article presents himself or herself as an academic. As a student, you present yourself as an apprentice academic. Your identity determines the way you use language, especially pronouns, attitude markers and hedges.
implicit	If a concept or idea is implicit, it is expressed indirectly.
independent learning	See learning.
independent learning skills	See learning.
indirect voice	See voice.
individual	An individual is a single person. In cultures that value the individual very highly, each individual is seen as having their own unique interests and skills that need to be developed.
inductive argument	See argument.

infer	When you infer something, you establish it by logical deduction or draw a conclusion from something.
information	Information refers to facts, concepts and ideas that we know about a topic.
given information	In a clause, given information is information that the reader already knows. It is generally placed before the main verb in the clause.
information literate	A person is information literate if they have the skills needed to make effective use of information.
new information	In a clause, new information is information that the reader does not know. New information is usually placed at the end of the clause, after the main verb.
information technology	See technology.
journal	A journal is a magazine that is published regularly, usually once a week, once a month or once every three months. It deals with a specialised subject.
journal article	A journal article is a piece of writing published in a journal.
professional journal	A professional journal is a magazine which is published regularly and which deals with issues which are interesting to a particular profession.
key word	A key word is a word or phrase that refers to the main idea(s) in a talk, lecture or reading.
learning	Learning is the process of gaining knowledge and skills through study.
independent learning	Independent learning involves students deciding for themselves what they will learn, and when. It also involves deciding how and where they will learn.
independent learning skills	Independent learning skills are the skills that a student needs to learn independently.
Learning Management System	A Learning Management System (LMS) is a collection of websites that a university uses to present learning materials to its students. Each course has a separate site on the LMS that stores the leaning materials (lecture slides, readings, audio-recordings of lectures, discussion boards, etc.) for that course.
learning style	A person's learning style is the way that they prefer to learn new knowledge and skills.
lecture	A lecture is a talk on a subject given by an academic to an audience of students or of fellow academics.
lecturer	A lecturer is a person who teaches at a university.

literature	The literature on a particular subject is all the articles, books and so on that have been written on the subject.
literature review	A literature review is a summary and analysis of the research findings on a particular topic.
logical argument	See argument.
logical connector	A logical connector is a word or phrase that indicates the relationship between two clauses. Examples include 'and', 'but', 'so', 'as a result', 'because' and 'while'.
longitudinal study	See study.
marker	A marker is a sign.
attitude marker	Attitude markers allow you to indicate how you feel about a particular position or piece of information.
method	In academic writing, a method is the way that you go about investigating a problem or testing a hypothesis.
minutes	Minutes are a written record of a meeting.
natural sciences	See sciences.
new information	See information.
objective	If information is objective, it is not altered by personal bias or commercial considerations.
opinion	An opinion is something you believe to be true. In this book, an opinion is something that you believe to be true but may not have evidence for.
paper	A paper is an academic article, report or research.
peer-reviewed	If a paper is peer-reviewed it has been read by several academics before publication to ensure that the standard is high, the argument is clear and the evidence has been collected in ways that are acceptable and appropriate.
PhD	An abbreviation for Doctor of Philosophy. See doctorate.
plagiarism	Plagiarism involves using the concepts, ideas and information presented by other writers without indicating the source.
patchwork plagiarism	Patchwork plagiarism involves stringing together many short quotations from one or more writers in order to stitch together an argument.
statement of position	See statement.
proofreading	Once you have finished drafting and editing your assignment, proofreading involves checking the grammar and vocabulary of your writing for accuracy. You should also check that you have cited your sources correctly.

position	A position is an opinion that is supported by evidence.
post	A post is a written comment presented on a discussion board or in a blog.
PowerPoint presentation	See presentation.
professor	Professor is a title awarded to the most senior research and teaching staff in a university department.
presentation	A presentation is a talk in which you give information to an audience.
seminar presentation	A seminar presentation involves giving a talk on an academic topic at a seminar.
PowerPoint presentation	A PowerPoint presentation is a series of slides that accompany a lecture and that are created using a Microsoft computer program.
problem–solution text	See text.
process	When you say that the process is as important as the product, you mean what happens and how it happens is as important as the result.
product	The product is the end result of a process.
profession	A profession is a job that requires advanced education; for example, teaching, engineering, nursing, accounting.
professional journal	See journal.
publication	A publication is a text that is printed and distributed to the public on paper or electronically.
date of publication	The date of publication refers to the year a book was published, or to the month and year in which an article was published.
purpose	A purpose is a reason for doing something.
quotation	A quotation refers to the exact words of a source reproduced in an assignment. It can be either spoken or written.
quote	When you quote something, you repeat the exact words used by a source.
rational argument	See argument.
reading(s)	Readings are the books, articles and other documents that you read to supplement a lecture or to complete an assignment.
recommended reading(s)	Recommended readings are the books, articles and other documents that supplement the required readings.
required reading(s)	Required readings are the books, articles and other documents that you must read.

supplementary reading(s)	Supplementary readings are the books, articles and other documents which supplement the required readings.
recommendation	A recommendation is a course of action that is suggested as useful or helpful.
recommended readings	See readings.
recursive	A process is recursive if you go back over it more than once.
reference	i) A reference is a book, journal article, chapter and so on that you use in writing an academic paper. ii) Reference is also used to indicate the way in which one word refers to another; for example, *the book → it*.
referencing	Referencing involves referring to sources appropriately using a citation system.
footnote/end note referencing	When you use footnotes or end notes, you indicate the reference with a superscript number in the text, and place full details of the source (author's name, date and place of publication, book or article title and so on) at the bottom of the page or the end of the essay, report, chapter or book.
in-text referencing	In-text referencing involves placing the name of the author and the date of publication in the text.
reliable	A reliable source is one that can be trusted because it contains information that has been collected and analysed in appropriate ways.
report	A report is a text that examines aspects of a problem or a solution.
research report	A research report describes a piece of research. It presents a research question or hypothesis, describes the methods used to explore it, and presents and discusses the results.
reporting verbs	Reporting verbs are used to present the direct or indirect voices of other sources; for example, *state, argue, claim, suggest*.
required readings	See readings.
research	Research is an attempt to develop knowledge using logical and rational methods which can be checked by others.
research report	See report.
researcher	A researcher is somebody who carries out research.
scholar	A scholar is a person who specialises in a particular field of research.
school	In the university context, a school is an administrative division of a university. See *also* faculty.
science	Science is the study of the nature and behaviour of natural things.

sciences	The sciences are the different branches of science: physics, chemistry, biology, geology and so on.
applied sciences	The applied sciences are sciences that are concerned with the practical application of knowledge. They are closely concerned with the development of technology.
natural sciences	The natural sciences include physics, chemistry, biology, geology and other traditional areas of scientific study.
social sciences	The social sciences include economics, psychology, sociology, education and other subjects which are concerned with describing and analysing human behaviour.
seminar	A seminar involves the presentation of a paper on an academic topic followed by discussion under the leadership of a lecturer or researcher.
seminar presentation	A seminar presentation involves giving a talk on an academic topic at a seminar.
skill(s)	Skills refer to the knowledge and the abilities needed to do something well.
independent learning skills	See learning.
social sciences	See sciences.
source	A source is a book, article, research report or other text that you refer to in an academic argument.
spam filter	A spam filter is a program used to remove dangerous or malicious emails from an email account.
statement	A statement is a sentence that presents information.
categorical statement	A categorical statement expresses a concept in absolute terms; for example, 'All Australians think X'; 'Smoking causes cancer'.
statement of position	A statement of position is a sentence or sentences that tells the reader what the writer is going to argue in an essay.
study	A study is a piece of research on a particular topic.
case study	A case study is an in-depth study of a particular situation. It usually involves collecting data through observing, interviewing and collecting documents, then analysing the data to identify trends or suggest solutions to identified problems.
empirical study	An empirical study is based on experiment and observation, not on a theory.
field study	A field study is carried out in the community, the workplace, the school, or any other place outside a laboratory.

longitudinal study	A longitudinal study is one that is conducted over a period of time over months or even years.
subject	A subject is a course of study in a specialised academic area; for example, Introduction to Computing; International Management.
summary	A summary is a statement that presents the main points of an article in brief form.
executive summary	An executive summary presents the main points of a report and its recommendations (if any). It is placed at the beginning of a report.
supplement	If one thing supplements another, it adds to it.
supplementary readings	See readings.
supporting voice	See voice.
survey	A survey is a way of collecting data which involves interviews and/or the use of questionnaires.
synonym	A synonym is word that has the same or almost the same meaning as another word. For example, you might call a piece of furniture that two or three people can sit on a 'couch' or a 'sofa'.
technology	Technology is the practical application of scientific knowledge to develop new systems and devices.
information technology	Information technology refers to the mechanical and electronic devices that are involved in storing, retrieving, communicating and managing information.
technical language	Technical language is language that has a special meaning in a particular subject.
text	A text is a piece of writing or speech which has a meaning or a communicative purpose; for example, a stop sign, a journal article, a lecture, a telephone conversation.
general–specific text	A general–specific text organises information so that general information is followed by specific information that gives more information and examples about the same topic.
problem–solution text	Problem–solution texts are texts that discuss various aspects of a problem or discuss how to solve a problem. Most reports are problem–solution texts.
textbook	A textbook contains information about a particular area of study. It summarises the research and ideas of scholars in a particular field.
theory	A theory is an explanation of some aspect of the natural or social world that is based on evidence.

thinking	Thinking is the activity of using your brain to consider ideas, solve problems and so on.
critical thinking	See analysis for description.
timeline	A timeline is a detailed schedule of activities indicating each activity and the time at which it occurs.
topic sentence	A topic sentence is the sentence that indicates the topic of the paragraph. In academic writing it is often the first sentence in the paragraph.
transparent	An argument is transparent if you can see what evidence supports it, how the evidence was collected and so on.
tutorial	A tutorial involves the presentation of a paper on an academic topic followed by discussion under the leadership of a lecturer. It is similar to a seminar, but involves undergraduate students rather than postgraduates.
valid	If your argument is valid, it means that it is based on fact and the conclusion logically follows.
validity	If a source has validity, it is regarded as reliable.
variable	A variable is something that can change.
verbatim	If you repeat something verbatim, you use exactly the same words as the original.
verbs	See reporting verbs.
verifiable	If something is verifiable, it can be checked.
verify	If you verify something, you use different methods to check that it is accurate or true.
vice-chancellor	See chancellor.
voice	Voice refers to the source of information in a text. A writer can present information in his or her own voice, or indicate that the information comes from others by using the direct, indirect or external voices of others.
direct voice	You use a direct voice when you quote the exact words of a source.
external voice	You use an external voice when you summarise the ideas of a source and indicate the source in brackets at the end of the sentence; that is, outside the sentence structure.
indirect voice	You use an indirect voice when you summarise the ideas of a source.
supporting voice	A supporting voice is a voice that gives evidence that supports a particular position. Direct, indirect and external voices can all be used as supporting voices.

word chain	A word chain involves a number of related words that are repeated from one clause or sentence to another. Word chains assist in tying a text together.
writing process	The writing process refers to the steps that you undertake to write an assignment.

FURTHER READING

Ackles, N. M. (2003). *The Grammar Guide: Developing Language Skills for Academic Success*. Ann Arbor: University of Michigan Press.

Adel, A., & Erman, B. (2012). Recurrent Word Combinations in Academic Writing by Native and Non-native Speakers of English: A Lexical Bundle Approach. *English for Specific Purposes*, 31, 81–92.

Badger, R. (2018). From Input to Intake: Researching Learner Cognition. *TESOL Quarterly*.

Basturkmen, H., & Shakelford, N. (2015). How Content Lectures Help Students with Language. *English for Specific Purposes*, 37, 87–97.

Bhatia, V. K. (2004). *Worlds of Written Discourse: A Genre-Based View*. London: Continuum.

Caplan, N. (2012). *Grammar Choices for Graduate and Professional Writers*. Ann Arbor: University of Michigan Press.

Cottrell, S. (2017). *Critical Thinking Skills: Developing Effective Analysis and Argument* (3rd ed.). London: Red Globe Press.

Coxhead, A. (2000). A New Academic Word List. *TESOL Quarterly*, 34(2), 213–238.

Glendinning, E. H., & Holmström, B. (2004). *Study Reading* (2nd ed.). Cambridge: Cambridge University Press.

Godfrey, J. (2018). *How to Use Your Reading in Your Essays* (3rd ed.). London: Red Globe Press.

Greenbaum, S., & Quirk, R. (1990). *Student's Grammar of the English Language*. London: Longman.

Herke, M., Hoadley, S., & Wong, D. (forthcoming). Using Experiential Learning Theory as a Framework for Undergraduate Academic Communication Development. *Best Practice for Teaching and Learning in Languages, Literatures and Linguistics*.

Lynch, T., & Anderson, K. (2004). *Study Speaking* (2nd ed.). Cambridge: Cambridge University Press.

Swales, J. M., & Feak, C. B. (2009a). *Abstracts and the Writing of Abstracts*. Ann Arbor: University of Michigan Press.

Swales, J. M., & Feak, C. B. (2009b). *Telling a Research Story*. Ann Arbor: University of Michigan Press.

Swales, J. M., & Feak, C. B. (2011a). *Creating Contexts: Writing Introductions Across Genres*. Ann Arbor: University of Michigan Press.

Swales, J. M., & Feak, C. B. (2011b). *Navigating Academia: Writing Supporting Genre*. Ann Arbor: University of Michigan Press.

Swales, J. M., & Feak, C. B. (2012). *Academic Writing for Graduate Students: Essential Tasks and Skills* (3rd ed.). Ann Arbor: University of Michigan Press.

Weissberg, R., & Buker, S. (1990). *Writing Up Research: Experimental Research Report Writing for Students of English*. Englewood Cliffs: Prentice Hall.

Zwier, L. J. (2002). *Building Academic Vocabulary*. Ann Arbor: Michigan University Press.

INDEX